The Dragon is Easier to Draw Than the Snake

안 본 용은 그려도 본 뱀은 못 그리겠다

Cho Moo-Jung
(C. Bonaventure)

Book Lab Press
SEOUL, KOREA

The Dragon is Easier to Draw Than the Snake
(안 본 용은 그려도 본 뱀은 못 그리겠다)

발행일	2022년 3월 21일

지은이	Cho Moo-Jung		
펴낸이	손형국		
펴낸곳	(주)북랩		
편집인	선일영	편집	정두철, 배진용, 김현아, 박준, 장하영
디자인	이현수, 김민하, 허지혜, 안유경	제작	박기성, 황동현, 구성우, 권태련
마케팅	김회란, 박진관		
출판등록	2004. 12. 1(제2012-000051호)		
주소	서울특별시 금천구 가산디지털 1로 168, 우림라이온스밸리 B동 B113~114호, C동 B101호		
홈페이지	www.book.co.kr		
전화번호	(02)2026-5777	팩스	(02)2026-5747

ISBN   979-11-6836-227-7 04740 (종이책)   979-11-6836-228-4 05740 (전자책)
        979-11-6539-728-9 04740 (세트)

잘못된 책은 구입한 곳에서 교환해드립니다.
이 책은 저작권법에 따라 보호받는 저작물이므로 무단 전재와 복제를 금합니다.

(주)북랩 성공출판의 파트너
북랩 홈페이지와 패밀리 사이트에서 다양한 출판 솔루션을 만나 보세요!
홈페이지 book.co.kr • **블로그** blog.naver.com/essaybook • **출판문의** book@book.co.kr

작가 연락처 문의 ▶ ask.book.co.kr
작가 연락처는 개인정보이므로 북랩에서 알려드릴 수 없습니다.

To

June (주영)

And

Korean ancestors, who have continuously refined their proverbs over centuries

CONTENTS

FOREWARD ... 012
ACKNOWLEDGMENT ... 014
INTRODUCTION ... 015

301. A crying baby gets fed.
우는 아이 젖 준다.... 020

302. Nothing to eat at well-publicized feasts.
소문난 잔치에 먹을 것 없다.... 022

303. A one-year-old teardrop.
작년에 괸 눈물이 금년에 떨어진다.... 024

304. Take a pheasant along with her eggs.
꿩 먹고 알 먹는다.... 026

305. Could a fledgling dove fly over a hill?
햇비둘기 재 넘을까? 028

306. Every success to my credit, all failures to ancestors.
잘되면 제 탓, 안되면 조상 탓.... 030

307. Wild but pretty apricot.
빛 좋은 개살구.... 032

308. Surviving without teeth but with the gum.
이가 없으면 잇몸으로 산다.... 034

309. No help from too many helpers.
주인 많은 나그네 밥 굶는다.... 036

310. An unlucky hunter catches a bear without the gallbladder.
재수 없는 포수는 곰을 잡아도 웅담이 없다.... 038

311. Lose a pheasant while chasing a sparrow.
참새 잡으려다 꿩 놓친다.... 040

312. Wind for the flour vendor, rain for the salt salesman.
밀가루 장사하면 바람이 불고, 소금 장사하면 비가 온다.... 042

5

313. A fan in the fall.

추풍선 같다.... 044

314. Eating ooolod porridge.

식은 죽 먹기....046

315. An arrow in the air, water on the ground.

쏘아 놓은 살이요, 엎지른 물이라....048

316. Shallow water shows the pebbles underneath.

물이 얕으면 돌이 보인다....050

317. Beating the boulder with an egg.

달걀로 바위 치기다.... 052

318. A tiger out of woods, fish out of water.

산 밖에 난 범이요, 물 밖에 난 고기라.... 054

319. Knowing one thing only.

하나만 알고 둘은 모른다.... 056

320. Receiving a forced salute.

억지로 절 받기다.... 058

321. Count chickens in the fall that hatched in the spring.

봄에 깐 병아리 가을에 와서 세어 본다.... 060

322. When ready for shopping, the market is closed.

망건 쓰자 파장난다.... 062

323. The catacomb is just outside the front gate.

대문 밖이 저승이라.... 064

324. Even water, once frozen, can be broken into pieces.

물도 얼음이 되면 부러진다.... 066

325. My blood boils.

오장이 뒤집힌다.... 068

326. An immature *moo-dang* kills a person.

선무당이 사람 잡는다.... 070

327. Don't bother to look at trees you can't climb up.

오르지 못할 나무는 쳐다보지도 말라.... 072

328. Small streams produce dragons.

개천에서 용 난다.... 074

329. Slippery cobbles after pebbles.
   조약돌을 피하니까 수마석을 만난다.... 076

330. Fallen leaves asking pine needles to be quiet.
   가랑잎이 솔잎더러 바스락거린다고 한다.... 078

331. A cow's walk to a slaughterhouse.
   푸줏간으로 들어가는 소걸음.... 080

332. Must face the sky to pick a star.
   하늘을 봐야 별을 따지.... 082

333. *Jeong* lost over distance.
   멀리 있으면 정도 멀어진다.... 084

334. Even a ghost won't understand you if you are quiet.
   말 안 하면 귀신도 모른다.... 086

335. A man with a sword is felled with a sword.
   칼 든 놈은 칼로 망한다.... 088

336. Temptation to have red-bean gruel.
   팥죽 단지에 생쥐 들랑거리듯 한다.... 090

337. Mud of clay holds water.
   굳은 땅에 물 고인다.... 092

338. Tadpoles in a well.
   우물 안 개구리.... 094

339. A rabbit startled from his own flatus.
   토끼가 제 방귀에 놀란다.... 096

340. Nonsense from a well-fed man.
   익은 밥 먹고 선소리한다.... 098

341. Denuded pheasant.
   털 뜯은 꿩 모양이다.... 100

342. Your eyes are your glasses.
   자기 눈이 안경이다.... 102

343. The full moon also wanes.
   달도 차면 기운다.... 104

344. A village calf remains a calf, never a bull.
　　동네 송아지는 커도 송아지다.... 106

345. A drum in tho noighborhood.
　　동네북이다.... 108

346. Raising the floor lowers the ceiling.
　　마루가 높으면 천장이 낮다.... 110

347. A flaw in a gem.
　　옥에 티가 있다.... 112

348. The more you bang the drum, the more noise you create.
　　북은 칠수록 소리가 난다.... 114

349. Even a river dries up if used.
　　강물도 쓰면 줄어든다.... 116

350. Prairie after mountains.
　　태산을 넘으면 평지를 본다.... 118

351. Flowers from a dead tree.
　　죽은 나무에 꽃이 핀다.... 120

352. Slapping face follows enticing.
　　어르고 뺨친다.... 122

353. A big snake climbing over a wall.
　　구렁이 담 넘어 가듯 한다.... 124

354. A wealthy family at the expense of three villages.
　　부자 하나면 세 동네가 망한다.... 126

355. Placing persimmons and pears at a *jesa*.
　　남의 집 제사에 감 놓아라 배 놓아라 한다.... 128

356. Licking a watermelon.
　　수박 겉핥기.... 130

357. Three-inch togue ruins five-foot body.
　　세 치 혀가 다섯 자 몸 망친다.... 132

358. Time is the medicine.
　　세월이 약이다.... 134

359. Wearing a silk dress in the dark night.

비단옷 입고 밤길 간다.... 136
360. Sky seen through the eye of a needle.
바늘 구멍으로 하늘 보기.... 138
361. A ship with multiple captains climbs up a mountain.
사공이 많으면 배가 산으로 올라간다.... 140
362. Eat the liver of a flea.
벼룩의 간을 내어 먹는다.... 142
363. A sheet of paper is lighter when lifted together.
백지장도 맞들면 낫다.... 144
364. Cats cleansing their faces.
고양이 세수하듯 한다.... 146
365. Bad news travels faster.
나쁜 소문은 빨리 퍼진다.... 148
366. Chicken and cow glancing each other.
닭 소 보듯, 소 닭 보듯 한다.... 150
367. Even a flea has a face to carry around.
벼룩도 낯짝이 있다.... 152
368. Licorice to a medicine man.
약방에 감초.... 154
369. Jumping with a dagger between teeth.
칼 물고 뜀뛰기한다.... 156
370. Meet the lover, pick the mulberry as well.
임도 보고 뽕도 딴다.... 158
371. A thief finds his legs asleep.
도둑이 제 발 저리다.... 160
372. Old sayings are without flaws.
옛말 그른 데 없다.... 162
373. Fixing the barn after the cow escapes.
소 잃고 외양간 고친다.... 164
374. Deep water attracts fish.
물이 깊어야 고기가 모인다.... 166

375. The dragon is easier to draw than the snake.
    안 본 용은 그려도, 본 뱀은 못 그리겠다.... 168

376. Pull a sword out to fight a mosquito.
    모기 보고 칼 빼기 한다.... 170

377. Blood on the foot of a bird.
    새 발의 피다.... 172

378. Waiting for a morning moon early at dusk.
    새벽달 보자고 초저녁부터 기다린다.... 174

379. Catching a mouse without breaking a jar.
    독 깨질까 쥐를 못 잡는다.... 176

380. Close the eyes, lose the nose.
    눈 감으면 코 베어 가는 세상.... 178

381. A toddler playing around an open well.
    우물가에 애 보낸 것 같다.... 180

382. Can you spit on a smiling face?
    웃는 낯에 침 뱉으랴? ... 182

383. Without the tiger, rabbits are the master.
    범 없는 골에 토끼가 스승이다.... 184

384. A dull-witted horse pulls ten wagons.
    둔한 말이 열 수레를 끈다.... 186

385. Loss is part of business.
    한 푼 장사에 두 푼 밑져도 팔아야 장사.... 188

386. A cantankerous bullock with horns on the hip.
    못된 송아지 엉덩이에 뿔난다.... 190

387. A sage follows the aged custom.
    성인도 시속을 따른다.... 192

388. A bellybutton bigger than the belly.
    배보다 배꼽이 더 크다.... 194

389. Ill comes often on the back of worse.
    흉년에 윤달 온다.... 196

390. Neither push nor pull is an option.

빼도 박도 못 한다.... 198

391. Fanning a burning house.
불난 집에 부채질한다.... 200

392. See neither a bottom nor an end.
밑도 끝도 없다.... 202

393. Good times pass fast.
신선 놀음에 도낏자루 썩는 줄 모른다.... 204

394. Having wasabi in tears.
울며 겨자 먹기.... 206

395. Scold in private, praise in public.
책망은 몰래 하고 칭찬을 알게 하랬다.... 208

396. Get to blow a trumpet thanks to the boss.
원님 덕에 나팔 분다.... 210

397. A mute with troubled thoughts.
벙어리 냉가슴 앓듯 한다.... 212

398. No news is good news.
무소식이 희소식이다.... 214

399. A mayfly attacking fire.
하루살이 불 보고 덤비듯 한다.... 216

400. Vacillating between the gallbladder and the liver.
간에 붙고 쓸개에 붙는다.... 218

INDEX (in essay number) ... 220

한 권의 책을 쓴다는 일은 결코 쉬운 일이 아니다. 그것은 마치 화가가 백지 위에 그림을 그리는 일과 같다. 그러므로 책을 쓰는 사람은, 먼저 어떤 분야에 관한 책을, 어떤 언어를 사용하여 쓸 것인가를 먼저 정해야 할 것이다. 그런데 조무정 교수는 영어로 한국속담에 관한 책을 쓰기로 결심하고, 책 1 권에 한국속담 100 편씩 소개하며 해설하는 형식으로 책을 써서 출간했는데, 이미 발간된 책이 3 권에 이른다. 나이 80 에도 여전히 정열적인 조 교수는 이번에 "안 본 용은 그려도 본 뱀은 못 그리겠다" 시리즈의 제 4 권을 출간하게 된 것이다.

조 박사와 경기고등학교의 동기동창인 내가 이 책의 서문을 쓰게 된 것을, 나는 아주 뜻 깊은 일이라고 생각한다. 우선 조무정 교수가 고령에도 불구하고 왕성한 집필활동을 하고 있는 것에 대하여, 나는 아주 대단하다고 생각한다. 또 부럽고 존경스럽다. 조무정 박사는 한국에서 태어나서 경기고등학교와 서울대학교 약학 대학을 졸업하고 도미한 후 현재에 이르기까지 미국 대학과 연구소에서 교수 또는 연구학자로서 40 여년 이상을 봉직해 온 재미 한국인이다. 이와 같이 생애의 70%를 미국에서 살아 온 그가 2013 년에 은퇴한 이후에 평생의 전공인 약학 분야와는 전혀 다른 한국속담 해설 책을 벌써 3 권이나 출간하고, 이어서 이번에 4 번째의 책을 써서 출간하는 것이다.

또 이 책은 한국속담 100 편의 해설집이라는 형식을 취하고 있으나, 그 실질에 있어서는 조교수 개인의 인생관, 세계관 등이 지극히 생동감 있는 언어로 잘 표현되어 있다. 뿐만 아니라 그의 인생의 54 년을 살아온 미국의 문화, 미국에서의 삶으로부터 얻은 귀중한 경험 등도 유려한 문체로 쓰여져 있다. 따라서 나는 조무정 교수가 집필한 이 책을 아주 훌륭한 수필집이라고 말하고 싶다. 또한 이제는 나의 친구 조무정을 '약학 교수 조무정'이 아닌 '수필가 조무정'이라고 부르고 싶다.

그것도 아주 '훌륭한 수필가'라고. 그 까닭을 설명하자면, 그의 수필에는 억지로 꾸미거나 감추려고 하는 대목이 전혀 없다. 그의 삶이 그대로 묻어나는 문장을, 조 교수는 모국어인 한국어도 아닌 영어로 쓰고 있는 것이다. 다시 말하자면 솔직 담백함이 그의 문장의 최고 미덕이라고 나는 생각한다. 따라서 그는 밀도 높은 사유와 날카로운 현실 감각을 지닌 탁월한 수필가라고 나는 믿는다. 그래서 나는, 모쪼록 영어로 쓰인 이 책이 한국인은 물론 세계의 많은 외국인들에게 읽혀져서 한국의 오랜 역사 속에서 생성된 삶의 지혜가 세계인들에게 널리 알려졌으면 한다. 끝으로 나는 조 박사의 다음 역작이 기다려진다. 나는 조 박사가 더욱 건강하고, 계속해서 좋은 수필을 영어로 써서, 빛나는 한국의 문화를 세계에 알리기를 바란다. (2021 년 10 월)

주광일 법학박사
변호사 (한국 및 미국 워싱턴 DC)
시인 저서 "유형지로부터의 엽서"
전 한국국민 고충처리 위원장

FOREWORD

A painter facing a blank canvas must have a plan as to what to draw - landscape or portrait - and what medium to use - watercolor or pencil. Likewise, a writer should decide what to write about in what language. Professor Cho Moo-Jung had wanted to write essays on Korean proverbs in English, although the topic is far from his professional training and English is not his mother tongue. He has already published three books, each containing 100 essays. Each entry attempts to interpret a proverb and juxtapose its meaning with historic or contemporary events not only in Korea but also in the States. Now, he is publishing Volume IV, "Dragon is easier to draw than a snake," once again with 100 entries. It is a remarkable feat considering that he becomes 80 years old in a few years. I just envy and admire his passion.

Both of us went to Kyung-gi High School together, which led to this honor and privilege of writing FOREWORD. MJ was born in Korea and graduated from the College of Pharmacy, Seoul National University. With further post-graduate training in pharmaceutical chemistry, he worked for the industry as a research scientist as well as a university as a faculty member for a total of 40 years. After he retired in 2013, he embarked on the current.

Appearance-wise, this book interprets another 100 Korean proverbs. In truth, however, we hear his authentic voice on world affairs and life philosophy in vivid and unapologetic words. He has lived in the States for 54 years, almost 70% of his life thus far, which allows him to dig into American culture and history (albeit much shorter than ours). This book is again an outstanding collection of independent essays on a wide range of topics. For this achievement, I would rather call him an essayist rather than a scientist.

Why is he an outstanding writer? As far as I can tell, there aren't any far-fetched stories nor hidden agendas: MJ writes as he sees fit without much fanfare, all in English to boot. Those simple words he used in candid expression turn out to be the virtue of this book. Besides, he is an essayist equipped with not only a thoughtful cognitive ability but a sharp observation skill. I just wish this book finds a wide range of readership throughout the English-speaking world, disseminating the century-old Korean wisdom of life as well as her culture and history. I am looking forward to more books in the series while praying for his well-being. (October 2021)

Chu Kwang-Il, PhD in Law
Attorney at Law (Certified in Korea and Washing, DC)
Poet with a collection, *Postcards from the Land of Exile*
Former Chief Ombudsman of Korea

13

ACKNOWLEDGMENT

Dragon is Easier to Draw than a Snake is a sequel to the earlier three books, *The Tongue Can Break Bones* (written under a pen name, C. Bonaventure), *Easier to See* Jeong (*Love*) *Leaving than Arriving*, and *A Hole Gets Bigger Whenever You Work on It*. They were published in the spring of 2018, 2020, 2021, respectively, both in Korea and the United States. As before, this book also introduces 100 proverbs, starting with #301 and ends with #400. Unlike other storybooks, each entry is independent of the others, and has no formal beginning and end. Every two-page essay starts on the left side of the book so that one can open the book at any place for quick reading in a rush.

As I believe that the incidental interpretation of a proverb to be the best way to offer its underlying nuance, I have heavily quoted the Korean (hi)story as well as happenings in the United States. Although I had planned to use more time-tested old events, there has been much distraction from contemporary news, particularly from the political turmoil: my apology for this laziness on my part. Likewise, I have cited numerous novels and films that many readers may have read or seen them. Even with my long life, I realize there is only so much I can cite from my own experience.

In English, we do not have a gender-neutral third-person pronoun. Linguistics scholars suggest we use "they-their-them" instead of "he/she - his/her - him/her." Thanks to the LGBTQ movement, the use of "they-their-them" is gaining significant acceptance. Throughout this book, I will adopt their recommendation whenever gender appears irrelevant.

I would also like to acknowledge the fine job of my Editor, Paul Kim of San Diego. But for his help, the essays herein would still have shown rough edges: those are all mines, never his neglects. Since each essay is only two-page long, INDEX is in the entry number, not the page number. As before, whenever research of a given topic was warranted, I dug out the primary references cited by Wikipedia as well as NAVER and NamuWiki (나무위키).

INTRODUCTION

The beauty of proverbs lies in their simplicity. Spoken and written in plain language, any child can memorize them as soon as they learn to speak. However, the deep-rooted meaning of these old sayings evolves as we age. Most likely, children hear a given proverb for the first time from an older and thus wiser person who relates it to one occasion, and then, they hear the same proverb spoken later by others in a slightly different situation. Soon, these proverbs become children's own.

At least, that was how I acquired the essence of Korean proverbs. There was no class at school, neither at the elementary school nor at the university, where teachers taught us what Korean proverbs are all about. Now sitting here, several thousand miles away from Korea, without any reputable references or teachers to consult with, I am trying to present what I believe to be the true element of the Korean proverb. Even if there were books and articles written about the topic, I would probably not have read them lest they should affect my own understanding, thoughts, and feelings.

If there is one unique feature in Korean old sayings, it would be gentleness, often with humor derived from the everyday lives of average citizens. They are as if the sharp edges have been worn down through continuous use over many years. They are rolling hills under the blue sky peppered with lazy white clouds, never the Alps or the Himalayas under a windy snowstorm. They are small, gentle streams and the peaceful sound of a lullaby, never the deafening thunder of Niagara Falls. Many Korean proverbs end with a question mark. Instead of stating outright, "The first spoonful of food will never give you satiety," one asks, "Would the first spoonful of food bring about satiety?" You will come up with the same conclusion in the end, but it asks you with some level of subtlety. The gentleness and subtleness that I identify Korean proverbs with must be from the people's life as well as the geographic and terrestrial surroundings of Korea. Describing these two factors alone will take up a tome, and I will instead let these proverbs speak themselves.

And the wisdom therein! The oral history of Korea goes back for 5,000 years. The traceable history for the two millennia preceding the 15th century has been recorded in Chinese characters and our own alphabets since then. Although many idioms were thus written in Chinese, especially those four-letter phrases in Chinese characters, I suspect that they could not have been very popular among our ancestors, since most of them were simply illiterate in Chinese. The class division itself, between learned men, or 양반 (*yang-ban*), and the ordinary citizens, or 서민 (*seo-min*), has been a popular subject among the latter, sprinkled with their ridicule and wit. These ordinary people, who shared barely-won happiness as well as various adversities in their lives, invented and enjoyed their proverbs. They are the collective consciousness of Korean people, which defines who we are now.

Some 40 years ago, my sister who lived in Phoenix, Arizona, sent me *One-Thousand Korean Proverbs* in several loose pages. I do not know where they were originally from, but I knew that one day I would try to interpret them for English-speakers. I have kept them in a drawer for all these years. As I tried to translate a few of them in English just to gauge the scope of the job, I immediately encountered the difficulty of keeping alive those rhymes that are perfect in the Korean language, which has survived for decades, if not centuries. They are poetries. I do not know how to translate them into English. All I can say is that I did my best. In some fortunate cases, however, some English versions are almost mirror images of Korean proverbs. I hurriedly copied them in this book. If there is an English version that is similar in its implication to a Korean proverb, I introduce it in the text.

As to the implied meaning of a proverb, I take my prerogative: others may interpret it in different ways. The proverb may talk about an earthworm or spider, but I am more interested in learning about what their behaviors teach us about human interaction and interactions among institutions, communities, or even nations. I will be the first to admit that my thought in the interpretation process tends to drift widely and wildly. Japanese kamikaze pilots may appear in a story involving tiger cubs. The story about smoke from a chimney introduces those cheaters in contemporary sports world. Quite often, I find great pleasure in submitting my own opinion on various topics as I have not yet had opportunities to do so. Be it cynical or sounding ridiculous, the writing is, to the truest sense, my voice: good as well as bad that have been accumulated during my life close to 80 years.

Language is a culture, which leads to the next problem of how to take care of the stark differences between the two cultures. I naively thought that I should be in a good position to address this issue since I have, after all, lived more than two-thirds of my life in the United States. It was once again my guesswork to determine to what extent I ought to cover cultural background in these essays. I apologize in advance if I have too many superfluous words or too little on the Korean culture.

Then, there are many words with different nuances and meanings: krill and shrimp are completely different from each other, but we Koreans call them both 새우, or *saewoo*. Tangerine and orange are both 귤, or *gule*. Since the topic of proverbs varies widely and since there is no framework for sorting them in some rational manner, I list them completely at random. As far as I can tell, the *One-Thousand Korean Proverbs* that I received many years ago do not appear to have any discernable order either. I simply present them in chronological order with the date of write-up at the end of each entry. I have tried to avoid discussing ongoing events as much as I could. I wanted to cite time-tested, well-established historical accounts. However, I could not let the episodes involving the current political turmoil just pass by unnoticed. Many stories from Washington DC, often ridiculous and beyond my comprehension, provided an immeasurable amount of priceless examples of how one should not govern the nation and its citizens. I am thus thankful for the contribution of those politicians.

The most impressionable and formative period of my life in Korea was just after the Korean War (1950-1953). There was a large contingent of American soldiers in the country. Whether we liked it or not, their presence offered us a great deal of exposure to the American culture. We read Hemingway and Steinbeck, followed the fights of Cassius Clay (Mohammad Ali since then), admired Mickey Mantle's career at Yankees, hummed along with Beatles, watched American films like *From Here to Eternity*, and even monitored closely what was happening in the political arena of the United States. At night, my ears were glued to the AFKN (American Forces Korea Network) radio station, which carried songs requested by the loved ones back at home for the American soldiers in Korea, largely what I later realized was country music. My poor English did not allow me to fully understand what the lady announcer was saying, but I figured it was all about boosting troop morale. I still vividly remember the alluring voice she spoke in. As I look back now, I understood America far better than they did Korea.

Imbalance in cultural understanding between nations has undoubtedly added fuel to ongoing animosity, often igniting a full-blown war. Even at that tender age, I found myself wondering how many Americans knew anything about Korea, the exception being the Korean War and our cold winter. Years later, I discovered that the Peace Corps campaign by the Kennedy administration was to help Americans understand the culture of developing countries. In token of a similar spirit, I hope that this book could contribute to the understanding of Korean culture among English-speakers. It is one tiny grain of sand on the vast oceanic beach but is better than nothing.

Having been a scientist, it has become a habit to always reveal the source of a given piece of information in my writing. Here, I am greatly indebted to Google, Wikipedia, NAVER, and NamuWiki. Even with these online encyclopedias, whenever warranted, I went back to the primary literature to confirm that what I was writing is indeed correct. My Korean is no longer what it used to be when I was a college kid in Korea. Inevitably, I had to consult Korean-English as well as English-Korean dictionaries, both by Dong-A Publishing and Printing Company. To my delight, they sometimes introduce an English version of a Korean proverb. These occasions were like finding a few coins between the cushions on a sofa.

I used a pseudonym, C. Bonaventure, as the author of the first volume, *The Tongue Can Break Bones*. It was published in the U.S. in June 2018. As writing essays has never been my profession, my real name would not mean anything. Bonaventure was the Christian name given to me when I was baptized as Catholic. There is neither more nor less significance associated with the pseudonym. Just accept it as is. Now that all of the first three books have come out in Korea, there is no reason not to use the name given to me when I was born. Some of my old Korean friends may still recognize the name.

I immensely enjoyed writing these essays. I hope that readers find this collection somehow meritorious and enjoy reading as much as I did with my writing. (adopted from *The Tongue Can Break Bones:* (11/15/2021)

The Dragon is Easier to Draw Than the Snake

Cho Moo-jung
(C. Bonaventure)

Book Lab Press
SEOUL, KOREA

301. A crying baby gets fed.

우는 아이 젖 준다.

"A mother feeds milk to a crying infant" would be the closest translation, but I re-wrote in a passive form such that a baby is fed and added the word "mother" although the original does not have the Korean word for mother. There is a strong nuance that only crying infants get fed and that one has to be vocal to attract attention.

A facial expression or body language can convey one's emotion to some extent but it is only to nearby people who can see the person. The next level of attracting attention would be through sound; for instance, crying or laughing out loud. We can communicate better with sound than sight, as the sound travels a bit farther. This is particularly true in dark surroundings. In a crowded party, one must overcome the noisy background. The master of the ceremony may bang the side of a wineglass to gather attention.

When all fails, one could take another step. The master of the ceremony may fire a pistol. In the deafening silence that follows, the person may have forgotten what to say. "Now, I forgot what I was going to announce," and just sit down with a silly grin. Noise along with laughter will come alive in no time.

This proverb seems to contradict the aphorism that silence is more desirable than eloquent speech, as in Entry #10, "An empty wheelbarrow makes more noise." In fairness, however, we must acknowledge that people cannot understand us unless we express our thoughts and emotions. A tongue-tied teenager does not express his longing for a particular girl, not because he believes in the merit of silence but because he may simply not be able to muster the courage. At home all by himself in his room, he kicks himself for the lack of courage, devising other means of relaying to the girl his feeling.

A student may not ask the teacher to repeat an explanation on a certain topic lest the whole class consider the question ludicrous and the student stupid. The school semester will be over soon without the student acquiring that particular piece of new knowledge. Likewise, if I do not vote, I essentially fail to represent my opinion and thus I cannot and should not complain later. All said, the key point of the present discussion is when and what to speak.

An infant who is yet to acquire speaking skills may not be able to tell their mother that they are hungry or feel pain. The only way to make the mother feel their discomfort would be crying loud so that she grabs the baby for an immediate remedial action. Before a situation reaches this point, the only other way for a baby transmits their distress is through their gesture to their mother. My wife is a professor in pediatrics. As part of her research, she analyzes the mother-infant interaction recorded in a videotape. In particular, she measures the frequency of touching, looking, caressing, kissing, smiling, etc. This effort is for collecting any tell-tale sign of the wellbeing of a prematurely born infant as well as the stress of their mothers.

If an adult complains rather frequently, as in "a crying wolf," people tend to ignore their appeal or request for help. Thus, in between those two extreme ends of dead silence and motormouth, there must be some happy medium: speak only when warranted. This generalized advice itself is of little use. For instance, if a person has a low pain threshold, they will complain more often than, say, Viking warriors. In a broader perspective, our subjective perception of risks such as injury and even death varies significantly from one person to another person.

Unless we know very well the person who is complaining now, there is no simple way to tell how serious and severe their complaint is. Here, to us, they are the same as an infant who cannot communicate verbally. Friend *A* might be a typical crybaby while friend *B* may a model of "no brain, no pain." We accordingly respond to their complaints. Close friends mean just that.

The first thing a mother of a crying baby usually does is breastfeeding. This intuitive response makes sense since hunger is perhaps the only complaint a baby may have at that stage of life development. They would not have any pressure or stress that an adult is exposed to. If the infant refuses to accept the mother's milk to continue tantrum, the mother becomes more seriously concerned. When none of her responses seems to be of any help, she may start to consult other young mothers, her own mother, and later a pediatrician. But she would be glad that her baby cried in the first place to let her know about their problem. We must maintain such responsive and sensitive interactions with others throughout our lives. Maybe my wife is right: we can indeed learn a lot about ourselves from the mother-infant interaction. (11/24/20)

21

302. Nothing to eat at well-publicized feasts.

소문난 잔치에 먹을 것 없다.

At the well-publicized party that you were invited to, you are looking forward to having a great time with delicious foods and abundant drinks, not to mention an agreeable crowd and entertainment. Then you find nothing but irritations. Publicity precedes reality, so to speak. Or perhaps you have been expecting too much. As it turned out, the party was like mediocre cosmetics wrapped in a fancy box. From the start, the night did not go very well. Here is the conversation you had with your buddy as soon as you entered the hall:

"Wow, who is that woman over there?"
Your friend told you, "Married, for God's sake!"
"She is? Really? Too bad."
"No, you're," was his reply.

Nice parties I now remember were all small gatherings of sit-down dinner with a good conversation flowing all night. When I was a graduate student, I did not have any place to go for the Thanksgiving or X-Mas celebration. My mentors knew the situation and I was always invited to their homes along with a few other international students. Professors Modest Pernarowski and Alan Mitchell had me at their places while I was their student at the University of British Columbia. Professors Takeru Higuchi and Ian Pitman did the same at the University of Kansas at Lawrence.

From 1990 to 2013, I was a professor myself at the University of North Carolina at Chapel Hill. Every year since I married, I had my students come over to our place for the Thanksgiving dinner. On average we had about a dozen attendees. Meals consisted of some Chines dishes we had ordered in advance, ham from a store, and honey-baked turkey from our oven, and Korean desserts. Drinks were more important: beer, wine, scotch, and sake, plus whatever our guests brought along. Their combination would guarantee a serious hangover the next day.

I cannot remember exactly how we, especially my wife, were able to manage such a feast every year. We were certainly young and must have been full of energy. Since using disposable utensils was never permitted by my wife, washing dishes was even more than one may assume. And what about cleaning the whole house the next day? But, all said, it was the only way I know how I pay back what I received from my mentors when I was young.

In my experience, research conferences are the same way. Most of the well-publicized national conferences are usually held at a big hotel often in a resort town. There is nothing wrong to hold a gathering in Hawaii or Las Vegas, but intimate interactions among the attendees are rather limited. As soon as one's presentation is over, they tend to disappear for the rest of the conference since their spouses are usually with them. For them, it could well be a paid vacation. For a purist like me, they are generally disappointing, like a well-publicized party that offers little to enjoy.

My favorite conference was Higuchi Conference, which was an annual event held in Four Seasons in Lake Ozark, Missouri. Dr. Higuchi would rent at a discount rate a significant portion of the hotel for several days just prior to the hotel opening for the summer season. Attendees are Higuchi's students and his colleagues who were invited. Since everybody knew everybody, most discussions were full jest. It was pure joy and fun to be with them, just like homecoming day.

Gordon Research Conference was another one I used to attend. It was held at the peak of every summer in a small town in New Hampshire. Attendees slept in a college dormitory and we did not have any formal session in the afternoon. Instead, we would go to a nearby lake in the afternoon. The particular lake we used to go to for swimming and sunbath was the one where the 1981 movie *On Golden Pond* was filmed, featuring Henry Fonda, Katharine Hepburn, and Jane Fonda. We all took pictures standing beside the gas station for boats. There was a small board announcing the history of the famous spot. Since there was little to do in the college town without any students, we were more or less stuck to evening sessions, where some were quite drunk but still sharp in arguments.

The Chinese idiom, 虛則實, means that emptiness is fullness. As usual, the phrase is as enigmatic as one can be. The expression is exactly opposite to the above proverb and yet conveys the same meaning. One can apply its hidden wisdom to many situations, ranging from "playing a dead possum" to defeating an almighty enemy: see Entry #124, "Burning a house down to rid of bedbugs." (11/25/20)

23

303, A one-year-old teardrop.

작년에 괸 눈물이 금년에 떨어진다.

A teardrop has just fallen, which began to form this time last year. It has taken a whole one year for the single drop to materialize, an exaggeration, for sure. Here, the teardrop may signify something good that you have been looking forward to for a while or something you have been avoiding as long as you could. If it is the former, say, inheritance from one of your relatives, the crux of the proverb appears to be: "Being late is better than never." It has been slow in coming but it has finally arrived. If that something delivered at your doorstep is bad news, like death or overdue tax, it says that your time is up.

Either way, it isn't a matter of "if" but "when." So, the proverb simply says that some things will happen albeit slowly, if they are meant to happen. I cannot tell you why the proverb chose, of all things, a single teardrop for the passage of time, but it implicitly highlights its smallness relative to the duration of its production.

I introduce the following story today, November 21, replacing what I wrote almost a year ago. Last week, the Manhattan district attorney asked a judge to toss out the convictions of two persons in the murder of Malcolm X. The news seems to perfectly illustrate a case where a good thing, justice in this case, has finally arrived, albeit grudgingly: it has taken more than five decades.

Malcolm X rose to fame in the early 1960s as the national spokesperson for the Nation of Islam, a Black Muslim group. Though he was considered a radical by many, he was quite a persuasive speaker with charisma who decried how racism affected the lives of Black Americans. In February 1965, he was gunned down in New York City. He was only 40 years old. This happened less than a year after he broke with the Nation of Islam and its leader, Elijah Muhammad. The latter obviously was resentful of Malcolm X's departure, which might have prompted several death threats to him prior to the murder.

It has never been clear for the past several decades if the assassination was carried out or aided by the Nation of Islam or how much law enforcement agencies such as the FBI were involved in the killing. Immediately after the shooting, they arrested three suspects and convicted them. Muhammad Aziz had spent 20 years in prison but was released on parole in 1985. Another innocently convicted was Khalil Islam, who was granted parole in 1987 but died in 2009. The third one, who confessed to the killing, was released in 2010. It is noteworthy that this man had always maintained that the other two were innocent. This is what Aziz said just after his conviction was overturned: "I do not need this court, these prosecutors or a piece of paper to tell me I am innocent," said Muhammad Aziz last week. He knows he has been innocent and that was sufficient enough for him.

The second approach to interpreting the above proverb is that one has been avoiding that "something" as long as they could, like tax and death. It is human nature that we try to put off what we do not want to face right now for some dubious excuses. In many instances, they are simply inconvenient or unnecessary as we are running around following the busy schedule in modern living.

In some instances such as death, we certainly know of the certainty. Here, we live more or less in resignation. In other instances such as man-made disasters, we can predict it coming if we are vigilant and diligent in monitoring, as in "A stitch in time saves nine later." Some examples along this line of reasoning were offered in Entries #5, "Would a pagoda of labor crumble soon?" and #179, "Save a penny, or pun (푼), to lose a fortune?"

In 1995, a luxurious Sampoong Department Store (삼풍백화점) collapsed due to its own weight right in the busy district of commerce in Seoul. The collapse took mere 20 seconds, killing over 500 and injuring 1,000 people. The building had four floors underground and five stories above the grand. It was completed in 1989 but later expanded bits and pieces without much scrutiny and tests for safety. Several hours prior to the collapse, the employees of the store noticed some significant cracks on the wall but the management apparently decided to fix it while the store was open. That was the time they should have vacated the building.

War is one of the worst man-made disasters. History tells us that nations always knew a given war would come soon. That was the time the parties involved should have devised some sort of peace treaty, but every effort was to no avail. Is war then as inevitable as a death in humanity? As much as I want to answer negatively, the way many conflicts I have heard of or gone through myself tell me otherwise. (11/28/20)

304. Take a pheasant along with her eggs.
꿩 먹고 알 먹는다.

A man captures a pheasant and notices that the bird has several eggs in the nest also. The lucky man takes both, effectively killing "several" birds with one stone. So, this proverb describes such an instance where one act leads to a multitude of favorable outcomes.

Two mediocre sports teams, say, two NBA (National Basketball Association) teams, after trading players, win the pennant race in their respective division during the playoff season. The trade must have been an excellent move for both teams. Building a bridge over a river that has separated two towns not only facilitates the commerce between them for prosperity but also offers an opportunity for mutual understanding for respective local customs. In June 2018, the Korean national soccer team defeated the almighty 2014 World Cup Champion Germany in a score of 2-0. This major upset ensured Mexico their next knockout stage despite having been thrashed by Sweden earlier. Suddenly, Koreans became Mexican's long-lost brothers. We were happy for the win over Germany as well as having acquired a new brother.

In a Korean fable, "*Hung-bu and Nol-bu* (흥부와 놀부)," a peasant *Hung-bu* repairs an injured foot of a swallow out of kindness. The bird then comes back with a pumpkin seed, which *Hung-bu* plants. In the fall, he harvests a big pumpkin, the biggest one he has ever seen. When he opens it with a saw, there are all sorts of treasures inside: see Entry #17, "When it rains, it pours."

In general, any charity works entail many happy outcomes. Donors and volunteers for food banks come to my mind. First, the benefactors feel good and are proud of their good Samaritan act. This is the result of empathy. People who receive the aid appreciate their kindness and likely become as such when they can. This is the outcome of an honest give-and-take between both sides. For third-party bystanders, what they observe serves as a good model to follow. This is quintessential to humanity. Such acts reject any cynicism and potential Scrooge of *Christmas Carol*. All of these constitute the essence of the above proverb.

The way the old saying was written implies that pheasant eggs were something unexpected. It just so happened that there were several eggs as a bonus so to speak or after-thought. On the other hand, if someone tries to exploit others deliberately for both "pheasant" and "eggs," the whole scheme can become a disgusting spectacle. The global imperialism and colonialism of the 18th and the 19th century would be a good case of the point. Most of the aggressive international tugs of war were based on national greed and interests, be it economic or religious. Such tradition remains intact as we speak.

Modern India began with the arrival of the British East India Company in 1599. The so-called Indian Rebellion took place about 250 years later in 1857, which dissolved the Company, but direct administration of India was merely transferred to the imperial British government. The fighting spirit for fairness and justice underlying the Rebellion had all but disappeared for another century till India became independent in 1947. In effect, the cunning and manipulating British ruled the land for almost 350 years.

The economic gain by Britain from exploiting India during such a prolonged subjugation is one thing, but how it has affected the national psyche of present India is another matter that historians must continuously address in many years to come. We can also raise a similar question in the relationship between the British government and China at the dawn of modern China.

Excessive import of Chinese silk and tea resulted in a trade imbalance between China and Britain during the early 19th Century. The same British East India Company had the native grow opium in Bengal and allowed private British merchants to export opium to Chinese smugglers: read *Sea of Poppies* by Amitav Ghosh, for a more nuanced background.

Opium addiction had become a serious social issue in the Qing Dynasty and Chinese officials banned the opium trade in Canton while the British government insisted on free trade. In the end, the technologically superior British navy defeated the Chinese. In 1842, the Qing dynasty was forced to sign the Treaty of Nanking. Once again, we do not know how such a humiliating international event has shaped the general attitude of the Chinese toward the Western World. Britain captured a "pheasant" as well as her "eggs," but history will never be kind to what Britain, "an empire on which the sun never sets," did to others. (12/01/20)

27

305. Could a fledgling dove fly over a hill?
햇비둘기 재 넘을까?

The master bedroom on the second floor of our North Carolina home had a small three-sided balcony, about two by five feet. The three-foot vertical rails surrounded it every five inches or so. The bottom was made the same way. They were all made of cast iron with curved support and painted black. If I may say so, it looked very nice and elegant against the beige stucco surface of the house.

Every spring, we would place two baskets of Boston fern on the floor of the balcony. We bought them in a green plastic pot from Home Depot and just put them out there. Late in the fall I simply threw them away. Along the top of the rail, we used to place two identical three-foot-long rectangular pots end to end. These were once again from Home Depot, reasonably priced green plastic affairs, made in China. Here, we planted various annuals like petunia or vinca. They were held with bottom supports that hooked on the vertical rails.

On one early spring day, a mourning dove laid four eggs right on the rectangular pot. A finch did the same but on the floor of the balcony, just beside the pot holding Boston fern. In both cases, their nests were not what I would expect for raising chicks: just piles of sprigs and pine needles were thrown in haphazardly. There was no engineering to speak of or aesthetics to praise about. Every Saturday morning when I had to water the plants, I would open the door to the balcony very slowly lest they startle. The dove, ever nervous, would cry out a short burst of noise and take off to a nearby tree leaving the eggs behind. It always made me feel sorry and guilty.

The following year, no finch showed up. Instead, a dove built a nest beside the fern on the floor and laid two eggs. Since the bottom was just an extension of the side rail, there was no way for a pile of pine needles to stop the cold air underneath. It was too late to place cardboard below the nest with two eggs already inside. The only thing I could do to keep the eggs continuously warm was watering the plants without having the dove leave the nest. I would open the balcony door as slowly as I could and start to water the annuals first, furthest away from the dove family. In a few weeks, the dove did not fly away even when I watered the fern, right beside her. She kept on resting over the eggs. My own Pavlov experiment of conditioning was successful and we were all happy.

As the weather warmed up nicely with the month of May coming along, I noticed the mother dove taking a break more often. She just sat on a tree less than 10 feet away, watching closely what I was up to. In due time, the eggs hatched and the two babies were growing very fast. On one particular Saturday morning, the mother was away leaving her two babies in the nest when I watered the plants. They did not seem to mind my watering activity.

The following Saturday morning, when I opened the door, the mother wasn't there, but one baby dove jumped, flipping vigorously its wing. Thanks to this effort, she or he landed on the soft grass instead of on the brick pathway in the front of the house. I saw the mother immediately landing on the ground within a foot of her baby. I did not know where she had been but I was more concerned about the fledgling baby, who was now moving about a bit, more importantly, all in one piece.

I hurriedly came downstairs and went out to the lawn. I caught the baby dove using a baseball hat. The baby was surprisingly docile and calm. The darkness inside the hat did the trick. I ran upstairs and gently placed the bird back on the nest beside its sibling. This baby appeared to be in shock with both legs all spread out outwardly. Later on that evening, however, the dove family all got together in an easy grace and appealing peace.

The next morning, on May 12th of 2013, Sunday, I found only one baby dozing off in the nest. A quick glance to the outside failed to locate either the sibling or mother dove. I assumed that the baby took the first flight with the mother's approval and encouragement. When I came home from the church, I found a dead baby dove right in the front yard, several feet from where one would expect from the virgin flight out of the balcony. The first thing I discovered was scattered feathers, then a bloody body with exposed internal organs. I buried him in a shallow grave just under the bluebird house. On the balcony upstairs, I found an empty nest. Everyone had left.

The above proverb asks if a fledgling pigeon could fly over the small hill yonder. If they do, however, they may encounter a red fox or a hawk. This is the same as asking young people if can handle their first assignment in their first job. They should be able, so long as they can identify and avoid adversary. (12/02/20)

306. Every success to my credit, all failures to ancestors.
잘되면 제 탓, 안되면 조상 탓.

This household has just two inhabitants, my wife and me. If something has happened it was by either me or my wife. It is as clear as the blue sky of Nevada in the Fall. Even if she denies that she did not leave the living room lights on last night, I know she did because I did not. I am sure that she knows that I know it was her but we usually let things as they are. Why do we usually let it pass in peace despite she is lying? Because that's what I usually do myself. Likewise, say, I drop a glassful of water from the table to the hard floor by accident, my immediate reaction is "Why in the world did she leave the glass there?" If she is around, I'd yell at her with these words. Blaming her is my first reaction. The second thought arrives later: was it me who dropped the glass causing a big mess on the floor?

I've just removed a whole bunch of her old shoes from a drawer so that I can put some precious stuff of mine. She has not worn those shoes for years and won't miss them for many years to come. If I don't say a word on this, peace prevails. It is a sneaky way of doing domestic businesses, but I have to survive myself also. Besides, not saying what I've done is not exactly lying. My point is that she does the same all the time.

A few days ago, I was looking for a small bamboo thing that I use to pull out ear wax whenever my ears are itchy. It usually stays in a pencil holder cup along with a small ruler, a pair of scissors, screwdrivers, a pencil-type rubber eraser, etc. It's gone from my desk in my room. Since it was such an esoteric item and since I've never seen her using it, it never occurred to me that she could have stolen it. But I asked her. What can I lose just asking? She handed it back to me in a nonchalant way as if I begged to borrow it from her. No words of explanation or apology. I was about to express something outrageous but I left her room with my mouth still open and the bamboo earwax extractor in my hand: the mission accomplished as President G.W. Bush used to say. Why was I so docile? Because that's what I usually do also. One could say that blaming each other is the backbone of this family of two.

I used to have some mysterious headache out of nowhere at any time of the day. Usually, one 200-mg ibuprofen (Advil®) tablet along with some light neck exercise takes care of it. Still not knowing the cause bothered me. My wife had enough with my repeated complaints and bought a fancy blood pressure (BP) monitor, believing that the headache was something to with BP. Earlier my physician had been mumbling about the same possibility but he said my high BP was marginal. For the whole month of March this year, I started to record BP three times a day: in the morning around 7 AM, afternoon at 3 PM, and at night around 9 PM. The average systolic BP was 135, 151, and 141, respectively. In April, I began to take 2.5 mg amlodipine (Norvasc®) every morning. The corresponding BP dropped to 117, 136, and 126.

The mysterious headache has disappeared and I have not taken any Advil® in the past several months. It was all due to the "nagging" from my wife. Whenever a situation warrants, she asks me when I have taken an Advil® last time, obviously reminding me where the credit for my recent physical well-being should go. I don't dwell on the question long, just long enough to say, "you."

Why do I play down my wife's warranted credit? Because she does the same: what about her successful research grant applications, my cooking for dinners not to mention cleaning dishes afterward, long-distance driving, preparing a playlist for her cellphone, wiring money to her mother, occasional back message? In short, in this household, we do not have any proper way to sort credits for any successful outcome of an event, but much blame is going around all the time. This is in good agreement with the above proverb.

My claiming credit for what I have achieved is fair and square. But claiming credit for what another person has accomplished is a fraud. This is as bad as the infamous 1916 Cumberland versus Georgia Tech football game. The latter won the game with the final score of 222 – 0. How could Georgia Tech claim glory when the other team was so helpless? They can claim all credits, but I think they are plainly mean and cruel. Why do we tend to blame our fault or failure on others is not easy to explain. Is it because my failure or mistake would make me look silly and inferior to other people? Is it that important when my honesty and integrity are on the line? Or is it a matter of responsibility? All said, blaming ancestors makes sense though as they cannot protest from six feet under. (12/03/20)

31

307. Wild but pretty apricot.
빛 좋은 개살구.

A wild apricot is a tall vine that has large flesh-colored flowers, known as passionflowers. It can also simply refer to its smooth, somewhat reddish-yellow fruits in egg shape. One can eat those wild fruits but there isn't much to eat. It also tastes bitter especially immature ones. One can induce saliva inside a mouth just by imagining an apricot: 상매소갈 (想每消渴). It was a trick that ancient Chinese soldiers used to practice during a long trek on hot and dry land. The raw apricot and dried apricot we buy in the market are all from commercial apricot orchards. Once again, however appealing a wild apricot may look, there is very little to eat. Besides, its seed contains as much as 5% of amygdalin and 0.3 % of deadly poisonous cyanide. Taken together, this introduction leads to an unequivocal interpretation of the above proverb: looks are deceiving.

A beautifully wrapped package may contain a not-so-great gift. A beautiful woman may be a character of rotten personality. A well-built, great-looking man in Amani suits turns out to be a rather boring person with an empty space between ears. A smooth talker can be a con man, a book with a beautiful cover can be a lousy book, what you eat at a restaurant may not taste as good as you have anticipated from the pictures on the menu, a fancy sports car may be too temperamental, and many other absurd events we witness daily all support the notion derived from the above proverb.

A friend of mine explained how he had broken his pair of glasses. He meant to kick what appeared to be a small pebble during his walk just for fun but at the last minute, he discovered it was dog poop. It was too late to stop his kick and stumbled to the ground losing the glasses. However, he proudly told me that no part of his body touched the dog's poop. Speaking of a silver lining, this is it.

Korean President Moon's current approach to North Korea appears to be based on pacification and appeasement, akin to the British Prime Minister Chamberlain's diplomacy towards Italy and Germany in the late 1930s. It followed the so-called "Sunshine Policy" adopted by one of the earlier presidents, Kim Dae-Jung, for which he was awarded the Nobel Peace Prize in 2000. Note that World War II started on Chamberlain's watch whereas the political and military tension between the two Koreas remains as high as ever. The temporary successes in foreign policy in both cases were short-lived. Indeed, an appearance is often too superficial to be of any use.

Conversely, as pointed out in Entry #302, "Nothing to eat at well-known feasts." what we perceive to be empty or shabby may not be so. There, I introduced a Chinese aphorism that emptiness is fullness. Way back a few decades ago, a friend of mine, different from the guy who successfully avoided dog poop, damaged the car he was driving in a self-inflicted accident. He thought a cardboard box on the street he was driving was just an empty box and because he was in a playful mood, he drove right to the box to flatten it. Alas, inside the box there was a heavy auto engine or some such thing. Flatten was the front fender of his car. As inscrutable they are, Korean proverbs seem to prefer this line of reverse psychology in conveying an identical message: Entry #50, "The smaller pepper is hotter;" #77, "Hot tea doesn't show steam;" #83, "A drizzle still can wet your clothes;" #138, "Startled by a turtle and now by a caldron lid;" and the above #302, "Nothing to eat at well-known feasts."

What appears to be a trivial event could become a significant matter later. See, for example, Entry #4, "You steal a needle now, then soon a cow," and #234, "A hole gets bigger whenever you work on it." Many disasters we have gone through could have been avoided had we detected its potential harm at an early stage. Just to name a few, we can perhaps prevent wars, collapsing buildings and bridges, car accidents, divorce, serious diseases, and failures in various ventures such as business and sports.

In the case of cancer, by the time we discover a palpable matter in, say, the breast, it might be too late for a simple intervention such as surgery. The classifies methods of early detection into three categories. The first is imaging. It includes: methods based on radiology, computed tomography (CT) scans, mammograms, magnetic resonance imaging (MRI), and ultrasound. The second category includes various endoscopies, which put a camera in a tube into the body to look inside. The last one is biopsy and cytology. They help classify cancer. Each method is for a specific purpose but has its own limitation in utility. Suffice it to say that all for one, one for all: early detection is more desirable than chemotherapy in eradicating cancer. (12/07/20)

308. Surviving without teeth but with the gum.

이가 없으면 잇몸으로 산다.

Without teeth, we cannot grind solid foods in the mouth and thus cannot enjoy them, let alone eat and digest them. But the above proverb says that we can yet survive because we still have gum tissues. However miserable it may be, we can wet and soften meals for gentle grinding with the gum. In due time, the gum may become accustomed to such an inevitable responsibility. The more I read the old saying aloud in Koreans, the more I became to realize that it tries to define the minimum requirement in living. In corollary, it implicitly addresses what the upper limit might be in a very luxurious life.

Another Korean proverb similar to the above is: "Would a spider build a web in one's throat?" (산 입에 거미줄 치랴?) The answer is, of course, no, meaning that so long as you are alive there will be always food going through your throat and that you would somehow survive regardless of who or what you are. What is missing in both proverbs is the quality of life, which would lead to a subjective question as to the true meaning of life, etc. Instead of going through such a solemn topic, we will treat the topic rather lightly.

Nelson Mandela (1918 – 2013), a South African anti-apartheid revolutionary, spent 27 years in jail before released to become the President of South Africa from 1994 to 1999. He was imprisoned in 1962 for conspiring to overthrow the state. During the first 18 years in the prison, he slept on a straw mat in a damp concrete cell measuring 8 ft (2.4 m) x 7 ft (2.1 m) and was harassed by several white prison wardens. Along with other prisoners, he spent his days breaking rocks and the glare from the lime rock permanently damaged his eyesight.

At night, he was studying for an LL.B. from the University of London through a correspondence course. The Bachelor of Laws (abbreviated as LL.B.) is an undergraduate degree in law prior to applying for a Juris Doctor (J.D.) degree to formally become a lawyer. He devoted his spare time to gardening and reading. Twenty-seven years of his 95-year life were without any meaningful human interactions and freedom. Only in 1980s, Mandela started to gain international fame of "the world's most famous prisoner." How he survived during the first 20 years in the prison is up to our imagination.

Certainly, but for his faith in South Africa and its people, he might not have survived to inspire the whole world with his vision of a new world. His faith in humanity was the gum without teeth.

All my Korean contemporaries went through the Korean War as well as the accompanying adversity and hardship. I was seven years old when the War broke, too young to fully understand what was really happening. The only bridge over the Han River was destroyed intentionally by the fleeing South Korean soldiers to stop the rapidly advancing North armies. While we were trapped in Seoul, the War was going ablaze in other parts of the Korean Peninsula.

Even to a seven-year-old boy, the atmosphere was spooky and leery during the occupation by the North Koreans. It was commonplace to hear so-and-so in our neighborhood or a family acquaintance was killed or heavily injured, our mother prohibited older sisters from venturing outside, we had steamed rice only occasionally, meals were with little of our favorite dishes, there was no school to attend, North Korean soldiers with a rifle was everywhere, strangers with red armband were scrutinizing our neighbors, and my parents would speak in a whisper without a smile. To avoid the conscription by the North Korean military, my oldest brother was in virtual hiding. Then, how did we, my parents to be exact, survive?

The South Korean army and the UN forces were able to push the battlefront to the North and re-capture Seoul. But it did not last long as China sent some 600,000-strong army to help North Korea. This time, our family was able to flee from Seoul to the southernmost city of Busan. My education in elementary school resumed, first in an open field and later under a tent. By 1952, humanitarian aid poured into the nation mainly from the US. It included not only foodstuff but also clothes and school supplies for children. I even received a harmonica, which I learned to play for the rest of my life. What is remarkable was that our family survived the War intact: the eight siblings and parents. As it turns out, the (hi)story of our family is the crux of the above proverb. My parents might not have had the "teeth," but must have maintained healthy "gum tissue" along with a strong will to persist and survive.

I have never lived a luxurious life and do not foresee any different life in the remaining days. That is to say that I am least qualified to address what the upper limit could be in a life of luxury. It would be limitless by definition. (12/08/20)

309. No help from too many helpers.

주인 많은 나그네 밥 굶는다.

A lonely traveler has just arrived in a small village and knocked on the door of a huge residential home of a wealthy *yangban* family for a meal and possibly a place to sleep overnight. Since he does not receive any response and since the big front wooden door, really a gate, was left open slightly, he ventures into the foyer. From there, he could see people hurriedly running around for whatever errand they are carrying on. No doubt, they are all servants. Apparently, some sort of fest is about to take place in the evening.

He finally grabs a man asking for a quick meal but the man says he will discuss his plea with his boss and hurriedly disappears. With his stomach still empty, he couldn't wait any further and this time asks a woman servant for the same. She says essentially the same though: she would relay his request to her supervisor. Everyone seems to be very busy but the traveler is still standing hungry with his tattered hat in his hands. This is what the above proverb is describing: a lone traveler goes hungry in the midst of feast preparation with so many potential helpers busying themselves.

One day this summer my laptop just quit. It died of the so-called Blue Screen of Death in Window 10. Being an honest student, I went to Microsoft (MS) Community and YouTube that offer hundreds of possible causes and repairing procedures for the problem. A few hours later, I eventually went to the MS help site. The problem was the infamous Blue Screen Loops. After another few frustrating hours of going around the same steps repeatedly, I just gave up. There were just too many instructions or helpers. It was like two outfielders in a baseball game losing an easy fly ball, either believing that the other guy would catch the ball or losing the ball upon a spectacular collision. One player too many, I'd say.

Another irritating situation is when I have to repeat an identical request for help for a given problem to numerous people in the same organization such as banks, merchant suppliers, US post office, Amazon Books, wiring service providers, TV streaming services, Homeowners Association, etc. They listen carefully and ask me for all relevant credentials to make sure I am a legitimate customer before transferring my inquiry to another person in another department. After explaining the same story, the listener may say, "Oh, you've got a wrong helpdesk. I will connect you to the person who can help you." Then I have to repeat the same story all over again.

Another interpretation, an alternative to the one with a lonely traveler, could be from a manservant in a traveling family, say, on horses and wagons. Imagine a vagabond migrating on a few thousand miles of trail to the West during the frontier movement of the 1840s, essentially a scene from cowboy movies. After helping the group settle after supper during overnight camping, the young manservant might have been left unfed. On discovering this mistake, the head of the family profusely apologizes to the young man by saying that he thought the young man's supper was taken care of by another man. Too many bosses could result in such a mistake. This may be a better direct translation of the above proverb.

Once again, the proverb says that a request for a simple favor like a meal or an overnight stay could fall through the cracks if there are too many helpers. Now, we can also ask what could happen if one asks for excessive help or assurance, as a person suffering from obsessive-compulsive disorder or lack of self-confidence might do.

Imagine a young woman who is constantly worrying about getting a sexually transmitted disease from public places, like a lady's room in a library. Out of anxiety, she may wash her hands over and over, literally every few minutes. She may also seek assurance from close friends or siblings that their hands are equally germ-free. Even when they tell her everything to be okay, she may keep saying "what-if." Responding kindly with assuring words to her may appear supportive, but scholars in the field seem to believe that such casual assurance may in fact make the behavior continue to be worse. Besides, her friends and family members may not want to do anything with her anymore.

Regardless of which perspective one chooses in interpreting the above proverb, one message is clear: anything excessive should be avoided. See also Entry #96, "Drinking can be medicinal with proper consumption, but …." Why would anyone avoid excessive wealth? What could be possibly wrong with indulging in power? Why do some wise men shun the limelight? How do we relate these questions with our own happiness? In the end, are these sorts of questions only the "losers" raise? (12/11/20)

310. An unlucky hunter catches a bear without the gallbladder.
재수 없는 포수는 곰을 잡아도 웅담이 없다.

Korean folk medicine is largely derived from traditional Chinese medicine, which has enjoyed remarkable popularity for several millennia. Although modern medical science has discredited numerous claims by traditional Chinese medicine, global demands have not significantly diminished. In the 1970s, traditional Chinese medicine attracted much attention in the United States along with Oriental health practices in general such as *taichi*, acupuncture, and even mindfulness. In Japan, Korea, and Vietnam, its popularity has steadily increased. This is even though many ingredients are parts of endangered species and thus its questionable use for medical purposes has been frowned upon.

Plants are the most common source of folk medicine. However, also used are many animal parts as well as minerals. Examples are tiger bones, antelope, buffalo or rhino horns, deer antlers, testicles and penis of the dog, tissues, and organs from bear or snake. The more esoteric and rarer, the higher demand and value seem warranted: gelatin derived from the hide of donkeys, deer penis, feces of the flying squirrel, toad secretions, leech, scorpion, etc.

The scale of pangolins is boiled, dried, roasted, then sold on various claims including stimulation of lactation. Only a few days ago, the pangolin received national news coverage because the species has maintained a remarkable immune system that allows for survival for several tens of million years. Scientists believe we can learn their immune system in warding off COVID -19. However, the medical research community is now complaining about its paucity of research because of the rampant poaching in Africa for Chinese consumers.

One of the items in high demand and thus quite expensive is the bear's gallbladder. Located just below the liver, the organ stores bile and release it into the small intestine for facilitating the digestion of fats. It is a class of endogenous surfactants. Bile gives the awful taste you experience upon vigorous vomit following a terrible hangover. In this context, the gallbladder is known in Korea as a "bitter sack," or 쓸개, 웅담 in Korean Chinese.

So, this unlucky hunter, after all his troubles and efforts, shoots and kills a bear but discovers that the beast does not have the gallbladder, the most precious organ there is! This hunter is just an unfortunate loser, not by his own making but by chance. What would be the probability to capture a bear without a gallbladder? We have already come across such a person in Entry #36, "An unlucky man breaks his nose even when falling backward." There, we went over the Gaussian distribution of luck or probability of finding a bear without a gallbladder as applied here.

"Loser" is eponymous to a person whom the current, but soon-to-be-replaced, President Donald John Trump doesn't care much about or outright dislike. To him, everybody who is not "obeying" his "marching order" is a loser. Just yesterday, the Supreme Court of the United State summarily rejected the argument that the Attorney General of Texas can invalidate the final votes of four other states where Trump lost. This is what Republicans received after all their hurried but successful effort to appoint a new conservative justice in the court, Amy Coney Barrett. The verdict effectively killed all legal challenges of Trump and his cronies. This is the end of their quixotic attempts to reverse the outcome of the general election. Speaking of a loser, Trump is now the very word he resents most. Unlike the case of the unlucky hunter, Trump has become a loser in his own game.

I do not have any ready-made answers to the question as to why our ancestors so heavily relied on luck or misfortune as part of fate, un-myung (운명), in their lives. See Entry #2, "Sunny spots and shade change places." One possible explanation may well be their repeated "defeats" or disappointing outcomes of their sincere efforts to succeed. After generations of struggles for betterment in their lives gone to the south, many might have reached a point of absolute resignation and abandonment.

They might have said in a deep sigh, over a bowl of *mag-geol-li* or a glass of soju, "what's the point?" A lack of opportunity or a social caste system that created a hidden ceiling in pursuing a happier and more fulfilling life might have caused such attitude of resignation. Given take-it-or-leave-it, ambitious young people may decide to go for a land of better opportunities. Here, I am speaking of myself and all Korean expatriates in this and other foreign lands. It has been the driving force of all diasporas of humanity in the past, very little to do with the gallbladder of a bear. (12/12/20)

39

311. Lose a pheasant while chasing a sparrow.

참새 잡으려다 꿩 놓친다.

It is straightforward to explain this proverb. A man has already caught a pheasant but not securely fastened the bird. Then, he sees a sparrow right in front of him and tries to catch it. During this sneaky maneuver, unknown to him, the big bird successfully escapes quietly. We often do not see what is more significant at the spur of the moment and go for 15-minute fame rather than a life-long interest. What makes us blind to our long-term goal? Why do we react the way we have when an event of a temptation appears? How much thought or rationale do we go through before (re)acting? How much do moral and ethical principles influence the decision?

Instinct (본능) and various reflexes are not really based on learning from experience or require brain activity. Dodging just before a head-on car accident is an innate behavior. So is covering the head when a rock is falling on you. Intuition (직감) carries a slightly different nuance: it is a body of unconscious knowledge. The "gut feeling" of a businessman or a detective is an acquired ability. The third behavioral category in the present context is what I would call "scheming (음모)." It is this and the second category that the above proverb is addressing. The guy who lost the pheasant acted upon his intuition in terms of greed. The "scheme" category is usually associated with plenty of time for analysis of a given situation before drawing on a course of action. As such, it is the most interesting case, at least to me.

December 11, 2020 will be remembered, albeit in infamy, as a significant day in the history of American democracy. The U.S. Supreme Court unanimously rejected a lawsuit filed by the Texas State attorney general, Ken Paxton. The litigation was asking the Court to overturn the results of the presidential election in four other states where Joe Biden won. For most U.S. citizens, this baseless lawsuit was so utterly ridiculous that it was beyond laughable.

The filing was supported not only by other 17 states where they have a Republican attorney general but also, more noticeably, more than half of House Republicans. The minority leader, Kevin McCarthy, later said that his name was inadvertently omitted from the original list. After the litigation was rejected, this vocal group of Republicans has suddenly become very quiet. The only noise we have heard was a Tweet from President Trump himself yesterday: "It is a legal disgrace, an embarrassment to the USA!!!"

The herd mentality we have witnessed from the above episode lucidly reflects the crux of the proverb. Republicans now behave as if there is no tomorrow in their Party. To be fair, I would like to point out that there are many Republicans, especially at the state and local level, who stood tall and proud against the worst "scheming" of Trump and his cronies. Just for a record, important people associated with the State of Georgia's general election were all exemplary: Attorney General, Christopher M. Carr; Lieutenant Governor, Geoff Duncan; and Secretary of State, Brad Raffensperger.

Power, money, sex, and fame are the major driving force of a wrong decision that one may regret later. It is often made for an immediate glorification rather than a long-term interest. See more in Entry #45, "Could sparrows skip a grain millhouse?" What had gone through the mind of those 126 Republican House Representatives when they decided to support the useless lawsuit from Texas? Preservation of power at all costs is probably what they were thinking shamelessly with the skin of stainless steel. Or are they simply afraid of Donald Trump? After all, he also received over 70 million votes and those spineless politicians tried to avoid any backlash from Trump supporters when their election time comes around.

Ken Paxton, who had been under indictment for securities fraud, might have decided to file the lawsuit hoping that he will receive a presidential pardon from Trump before he steps down in January. This would let Paxton exempted from any federal crime. His immediate cause of the lawsuit was most likely to divert the public attention from his indictment to some fresh topic on a national stage. As far as I can tell, Paxton and those Republican Congressmen who had endorsed the lawsuit went after a "sparrow" while losing a "pheasant," the sparrow being an immediate reversal of the election while the pheasant being the trust of their constituents for a long run. This logical, but rather metaphorical, the comparison is valid only if the constituents are fully aware of what is really happening behind these unprincipled politicians. It is a lot to ask of ill-advised people and is a great deal of faith we will have to assume in the final analysis of the above proverb. (12/15/20)

312. Wind for the flour vendor, rain for the salt salesman.

밀가루 장사하면 바람이 불고, 소금 장사하면 비가 온다.

A man tries his luck in the flour business in an open market. Then a gust of wind is blowing just after he opens his shop for the first time, losing most of the fine flour to the thin air along with his investment, not to mention his efforts. Much disappointed but resilient he is, he now takes a different tack with renewed determination: this time it is for selling table salt. Unfortunately, the grand opening coincides with the beginning of monsoon season and the salt he displays in front of his shop is being washed away with torrential rain. However you look, he has nothing but a streak of bad luck.

First, here are some background materials. When this proverb was spoken, markets for ordinary rural residents did not open all day like a typical supermarket of modern days, but only on a local market day known as *jangnal*, usually every five to ten days or so. There was no building for the market. It took place on an open field. The place on *jangnal* would be bustling with people from nearby villages, engaged in barter trade or selling and buying everything under the sun. See more in Entry #17, "When it rains, it pours."

Vendors of grains such as flour and rice and vendors of salt would typically set up the business on a simple straw mat spread on the ground. On the mat, the proprietors would place various grains in open burlaps along with a sample in a measuring cup. Depending on the origin, some rice or flour must have been more expensive than other variants. If one could afford it, a makeshift roof was hung over the burlaps with poles at four corners.

In all transactions, the seller would use a square wooden cup for measuring grains. He would scoop excess of rice, for instance, with this measuring cup and edges off the top with a rectangular wooden boom for a quantity known as *doe*, or 되. This quantity is equivalent to about 1.8 L, or a half-gallon.

For regular customers or when the seller was in good mood, the seller would not slide the boom all the way to top it off. Instead, he could stop a bit earlier so that there might be slightly more than exactly one *doe*. This was one way for the vendor to keep the customer happy. That much flexibility, with good-humored bantering, was practiced by the seller and expected by the buyer.

As it so happened, the opening day for the new venture of this man was quite windy. The gust of wind not only blew away the clumsy makeshift roof but also flour from the displayed samples in the measuring cups as well as from the open burlaps. Flour was now flying all over the place, like a small-scale tornado. What a sorry state of affairs he encountered! His ambitious new business did not start as he had hoped. He hurriedly tried to close all burlaps and salvage the flour in the wooden cups. In the end, he was crying over the "spilled milk." So much of the grand opening.

Much disheartened and dejected, the man comes home, lamenting his bad luck. A few days later, he ventures into a new business, with a renewed vigor. This time, he is selling salt. After all, salt is as essential in any household as rice. Besides, salt is heavier and thus will not be blown away easily by wind. That much confidence has brought him some level of assurance in his luck.

There are a variety of salts: in sea salt alone, there are different shades of white and grey from different places of the country, all with varying prices. Likewise, there is a variety of salts from various salt mines at different locations. Some are expensive for their unique purported medical benefits. The opening day on a local *jangnal* was somewhat windy but his salts are not going anywhere. However, his confident smile does not last long as dark clouds are gathering and rain starts to pour down heavily. It washes away much of his salts. This young man fails once again, none to his faults.

Most people do not particularly enjoy sad stories per se unless the stories have a happy ending. We all seem to have a limited capacity of sympathy to share. Likewise, those stories do not make headline news unless they are part of fundraising. In this regard, the above proverb is unique: it neither has a happy ending nor asks for sympathy. The young man in the above story must have put his best foot forward to become a successful businessman. And yet, none to his fault, he fails in the venture, twice already in short succession. Is pretending that we have not heard of this man's misfortune and misery because it is an isolated incident that does not bear anything to do with us? What the proverb says is that there are indeed people who are born to lead a very unfortunate life. Most of our ancestors would just shrug off mumbling, "It's all his fate." (01/14/21)

313. A fan in the fall,

추풍선 같다.

In cool autumn weather, there is no deed for a fan. The above phrase is describing something unwanted now, which was once an essential item. An ice delivery man must have been very popular during the summer, but probably not in dead winter. A sudden drop of value may be reversible as in the case of ice, which will recover its value as summer approaches. Belonging to this group may include; seasonal dresses, summer sandals or flip-flops, corporate stocks, resilient politicians, the hair on a shaved head, perennial flowers, a bicycle with a flattened tire, leftover pizza, writers with a mental block, old ice skates, dull knife, divorced young people, and air conditioner and portable heater, etc.

In the 55th Super Bowl that will play tomorrow, 43-year-old quarterback Tom Brady of Tampa Bay Buccaneers is pitted against up-and-running, electrifying 25-year-old Patrick Mahomes of Kansas City Chiefs. Brady, at the age considered a "fossil" in the world of professional football, was not offered a new contract last year from his previous team of many years, New England Patriots. The team owner and management decided not to renew the contract presumably because his value to the team would soon "irreversibly" diminish to very little in the near future. This was a cold reality of time passing in spite of the unprecedented record of six wins out of nine appearances in the Super Bowl with the Patriots.

I do not like any team hogging that many Super Bowl trophies, but my dislike of Brady began in earnest in 2004 when the Patriots beat my team Carolina Panthers in the 38th Super Bowl. That particular match has been considered one of the "Greatest Super Bowls" of all time. We lost by three points from a field goal with four seconds left in the game. Yes, it was the game where Janet Jackson's wardrobe malfunctioned so that millions of viewers had a chance to see her nipples at the half-time show. No, to my much regret, I missed the scene but heard about it a lot later.

When, the arrogant but brilliant, Patriots coach Bill Belichick let Brady go after the 2020 season, many sports fans started to wonder how much credit would go to the coach and how much to Brady for their spectacular runs together in the past two decades. Many pundits claimed it was Belichick who should receive the bulk of the credit by pointing out that it was, after all, Belichick who had "discovered" and picked Brady in the sixth round in the 2000 draft. Admittedly, Brady was nobody then. I did not like either of them; however, Brady a bit more than the coach and thus I joined the general sentiment that Brady's career is now effectively over without Belichick.

To the shocking surprise of many observers, it was Brady's new team, Tampa Bay Buccaneers, who are playing tomorrow while the Patriots couldn't even make the playoff. For a record, Buccaneers had not made the playoffs in the past 14 years and thus we can safely attribute their successful 2020 season to Brady. More important, now that Brady is appearing at the Super Bowl in 10th time, this time without Belichick, I begin to see the whole situation with a new perspective, now much favorable inclination to Brady. All of a sudden, I feel that I might have spoken ill of Brady without water-proof arguments and that the victory tomorrow would shame all naysayers, including myself, once and for all. In short, I wish his team wins tomorrow. It would be a sweet vindication on his part.

I have introduced Tom Brady's story just to illustrate that we should not prematurely discard old stuff just because they are old. Brady may not last long but I applaud wholeheartedly his return to Super Bowl. Old matters and stuff can come back with a roaring vengeance. Just give some time, the bell-bottom pants and long sideburn on men's faces will come back in fashion.

Truth be told, however, more cases are irreversibly gone astray with no foreseeable return. They become obsolete with time or broken beyond repair, resulting in a sudden drop in value. Some items belonging to this category - besides myself, that is - may include; one shoe with a missing pair, typewriters of the gone era, slide rule for engineers, Wang calculator, free-standing radios with alarm clock, land-line phones, banknotes from bankrupt firms, yesterday's weather forecast, and lovers of the past.

Rudy Giuliani, the former New York City mayor and Trump's one-time lawyer, is an interesting case. Having been loyal to a wrong boss and hung around with bad crowds, "America's Mayor" won't be able to come back to anyplace anytime soon. His public noise just served as chaos before the collective recovery of calmness and from hysteria. He is "a fan in the autumn" right now. (02/07/2021)

314. Eating cooled porridge.

식은 죽 먹기.

When I was a child, my mother used to feed me rice porridge whenever I had an upset stomach. It is easily prepared by boiling already-prepared steamed rice with additional water and occasional stirring. The meal, if you can call it a meal, is almost digested already with prolonged boiling and bears no burden on the troubled stomach. As one may expect, the final product, called *jook* (죽), is a thick paste absolutely without any taste, neither terrible nor tasteful, but just bland. To add some taste, she would add a few drops of soy sauce over the porridge and would bring a spoonful to my mouth, but only after blowing it over to cool it. After a few demonstrations, it would be left to me to eat it myself. After all, she had other urgent matters to tend to besides taking care of this sickly infant.

So, the trick of eating *jook* is not so much about overcoming its tastelessness but handling its high temperature. In my memory, *jook* is always associated with hotness, and blowing over the spoonful of *jook* was an essential part of the ritual. The heat capacity of *jook* is high as its matrix lacks channels inside the sticky mass that would allow the passage of air. That is, it holds the heat quite well for a while. The preparation has nothing to chew, much less than grits; all you do is just swallow the paste as if you eat ice cream or yogurt. Accordingly, the above proverb implies that eating warm, neither hot nor cold, *jook* is one of the easiest jobs one can imagine. We can thus use the expression in describing an easy job, as in "Yes, you can do it. It's like eating cooled *jook!*"

The difficulty of a given task would depend on the circumstance and the people involved. The question would be subjective and defy generalization. Instead, it would be much easier to find some commonality in defining a difficult job. They used to say that coaching and maintaining a successful football program year after year at Norte Dame University is as difficult a job as the president of the United States. The Fighting Irish has won as many as 22 times the national NCAA (National Collegiate Athletic Association) championships and seven Notre Dame players have won the Heisman Trophy. The team again made the Final Four last year.

46

It was Knute Rockne who, beginning in 1918 as head coach, firmly established the Norte Dame football as a team you will have to reckon with. They posted 105 wins with only 12 losses, which was an astonishing winning rate of 90%! During his 13-year tenure, they won three national championships including Rose Bowl in 1925, and also produced players like George Gipp. When the 25-year-old Gibb was dying of a simple infection, he was said to utter the famous line, "Win one for Gipper" to Rockne. In the 1940 film *Knute Rockne, All American*, the 40th President of the United States, Ronald Reagan, then a Hollywood actor, played the title role.

Fans' anticipation from such a storied football program would weigh upon the shoulder of the head coach as much as the expectation of citizens from their president. Some people excel under pressure, thriving for more achievements than expected by colleagues. To them, adversities seem to render the foundation of challenges and dangers are the very source of opportunities. At the other end of the spectrum, some people would flee or excuse themselves at the first glimpse of difficulty ahead. They will avoid the seemingly tough job until they realize that the alternative to evading is not an option. When your army is outnumbered and facing a ferocious enemy with your back abutted to a precipice, the only choice you will have is fighting back with your lives on the line.

Dedicating one's life to public service would be one of the noblest, and often most difficult, sacrifices throughout the history of humanity. Mother Teresa of Calcutta (1910 - 1979) comes to my mind. Another form of public service is politicians. And yet we seldom place them both on the same page, unless the politician happens to be King Se-Jeong (1397 - 1450) of the Joseon Dynasty or "Honest Abe," Abraham Lincoln (1809 - 1865).

Compared with these great leaders in the past, the current Korean President Moon Jae-In's popularity has been rather dismal for a while except for a short period of time at the early stage of the COVID-19 pandemic in Korea. Since I live several thousand miles away from Korea and since I have not closely monitored their political landscape, I am not well qualified to make any intelligent comments: however, I do understand and appreciate how difficult his job would be in guiding the nation among many threats lurking from powerful nations like the United States, China, and North Korea. We can safely say that his job is far from eating cooled *jook*. (02/23/2021)

47

315. An arrow in the air, water on the ground,

쏘아 놓은 살이요, 엎지른 물이라.

In spite of Zeno's paradoxes, a flying arrow will son hit its target and stop its journey. There is no way one can stop once it is in the air. Likewise, no one can recover the water spilled on the ground. This proverb is the same as "The dice is cast." Once done, many things and phenomena in this world cannot be undone. Of these, death is perhaps the weightiest topic. It is a journey of not only no-return but also singular occurrence. The only recorded event to the contrary is in the New Testament inclusive of the Resurrection of Jesus Christ.

Lazarus who lived in a Palestinian town Bethany, with his sisters Martha and Mary, had been dead and in fact in a tomb for four days before Jesus arrived. According to the Gospel of John [11:1-44], it was his sisters who sent words to Jesus; "Master, the one you love is ill." He did not come right away: Two days after the message arrived, Jesus started the journey to Bethany, claiming that Lazarus was simply asleep. Upon arrival, Jesus heard from Martha "Lord, if you had been here, my brother would not have died. But even now I know that whatever you ask of God, God will give you."

When they took away the stone entrance to a cave where Lazarus was laid, Jesus cried out in a loud voice, "Lazarus, come out!" The dead man came out, tied hand and foot with burial bands, and his face wrapped in a cloth. As the miracle was conveyed to Jews, their chief priests were afraid that "Romans will come and take away both our land and our nation." Thus, Jesus was condemned to die because he revived Lazarus. The justification was "national security," an irony at its best. It was Jesus' last miracle before the Crucifixion.

In the early 1980s, a group of research scientists at the pharmaceutical company I used to work for had been working on a potential pharmacological intervention of subarachnoid hemorrhage (SAH) resulting from, say, a severe head injury from a car accident, came up with a class of steroidal compounds termed "lazaroids." I thought it was a very proper name because most SAH patients face a dire prognosis. Efficacy studies with lazaroids in animal models of spinal cord injuries were very promising. After I left the company, they entered human studies but apparently, results were not as good as expected from animal experiments.

The reversibility of a chemical reaction introduces the concept of equilibrium. Acetic acid, the main component in vinegar, in water produces hydronium ion (H_3O^+) and acetate ion (CH_3COO^-). Under a given condition, only so much of the total acetic acid produces both ions, resulting in a pH of about 3. Thus, by definition, it is a weak acid and its dissociation to ions is a reversible reaction.

$$CH_3COOH + H_2O \leftrightarrow CH_3COO^- + H_3O^+$$

If we add extra acetate ions from, say, sodium acetate, then the equilibrium is shifted to the left: that is, we will have less hydronium ion, or pH would increase. This phenomenon is said to follow the so-called Le Chatelier's principle. An easy way to illustrate the principle could be as follows. Imagine two opposing armies in a stalemate. Neither side makes any moves lest the "dynamic equilibrium" becomes disturbed to their disadvantage. Once, however, one side gets reinforced with additional supporting soldiers, the battle line may move as the other party starts to retreat. A new equilibrium will be established when the fleeing army stops after losing some ground and licking their wounds.

Examples of irreversible change such as death are abundant in our lives. One simple case is given here though. In contrast to the above case with acetic acid, hydrochloric acid (HCl) in water does not leave any trace of intact HCl molecules. All of them completely dissociate into chloride ion and hydronium ion. This is the definition of a strong acid and its dissociation is irreversible for all practical purposes. Note that I am using an arrow for one direction in contrast to the double arrow used above.

$$HCl + H_2O \rightarrow Cl^- + H_3O^+$$

The current oppression of the Islamic Uyghur population by the Chinese government seems irreversible, leaving absolutely no recourses for the oppressed to appeal to. We must stop such systematic religious, racial, and political oppression by the Chinese at all costs. Once occurred, there is no way to recover them as they are akin to a flying arrow and water spilled on the ground. (02/25/2021)

316, Shallow water shows the pebbles underneath,

물이 얕으면 돌이 보인다.

The above proverb implies that the true intention behind an act becomes apparent when the behavior of a person is based on superficial pretensions. A motive of an honorable deed is usually not well-publicized until accidentally discovered. Remaining anonymous is often the sincere wish of the person who did the good deed.

A serious condemnation of hypocrites by Jesus is amply illustrated by the Gospel according to Matthew [6:1-4]: "[But] take care not to perform righteous deeds in order that people may see them.... When you give alms, do not blow a trumpet before you, as the hypocrites do in the synagogues and in the streets to win the praise of others.... But when you give alms, do not let your left hand know what your right is doing, so that your almsgiving may be secret."

Rafael Edward (Ted) Cruz is a Republican Senator from Texas and has been serving for the past eight years. His political career began after graduating from Princeton University and Harvard Law School, an impeccable pedigree if I may add. His conservative stand in many economic and social issues has been the source of enthusiastic support from right-wing Republicans and an eyesore among the progressive liberals. People seem to either like him or hate him, none in between.

In the 2016 Republican primary, Cruz ran for President of the United States and ended up at second place behind Donald Trump among more than a dozen of candidates. The acrimony between these two candidates during the primary remained as such for a while as demonstrated by numerous public personal attacks and Cruz's refusal of endorsing Trump's candidacy. Once Trump became elected, however, Cruz became a staunch Trump supporter. Just two months ago, following baseless conspiracy theory, Cruz objected to the certification of Joe Biden's victory over Trump along with another Senator from Missouri. Cruz even delivered an encouraging speech for the rioters who stormed the United States Capitol on January 6.

Another controversy erupted just a few weeks ago when Cruz took a family vacation in Cancun while millions in his state went without heat or water after severe winter weather crippled supplies of electricity. The storm pummeled Texas and other parts of the U.S. and has resulted in about 70 deaths, including more than a dozen who died in their homes after losing heat.

After facing a public backlash, he cut his trip short and apologized for the trip. His explanation was that he just wanted to drop off their daughter who had planned the trip with her friends. This story differed from what his wife said in one of her text messages to her chat room friends: "Is everyone warm? That's a must! ... Anyone can or want to leave for the week? We may go to Cancun, there is a direct flight at 4:45 pm and hotels with capacity. Seriously."

Last summer, California experienced wildfires and extreme heat waves that strained the state's power infrastructure and caused many outages. Governor and local officials urged Californians to turn off unneeded lights and limit their use of appliances, especially air conditioners. Cruz did not waste any time in mocking the failed energy policies in California: on August 19, he tweeted, "California is unable to perform even basic functions of civilization, like having reliable electricity." Now, Texas' power grid has failed; the state's infrastructure is largely unequipped to handle ice, snow, and freezing temperatures. No California State officials reminded Cruz of his earlier tweet.

Just last Friday, February 26, Cruz was speaking at the Conservative Political Action Conference (CPAC) in Orlando, Florida. The first words coming out of his mouth mocked the public criticism of his trip to Mexico. "Orlando is awesome. It's not as nice as Cancun, but it's nice." The comments were met with laughter from the audience. A few weeks earlier, he was all in remorse and offered a seemingly sincere apology. Now, he is a different person. These people – the Cruzes and the folks at CPAC – are those pebbles under shallow water that anybody can see.

Many people seem to think the political career of Ted Cruz is now numbered, but I am not so sure. First, people have a very short memory. Perhaps I am one of the few who remember for a long time a grave mistake of others, especially intentional ploys of politicians and celebrities. I seldom forgive and accept them as professionals. How can I still admire Lance Armstrong who won the Tour de France seven consecutive times, while under the regimen of performance-enhancing drugs? I have recently added Ted Cruz to that list, which is already pretty long. (03/01/2021)

51

317. Beating the boulder with an egg,

달걀로 바위 치기다.

Emulsions are formally defined as a dispersion system in which two immiscible liquids co-exist as in oil droplets suspended in water or water droplets in oil. An emulsion is prepared with vigorous agitation of the liquid mixture. The size of droplets follows a normal distribution, some are big and others very small. If one monitors the change in size, one can readily observe that the system continuously changes, with more large droplets at the expense of smaller ones. This phenomenon is referred to as Ostwald Ripening. In the end, of course, a complete separation of the two phases could occur.

In my lifetime alone, I have observed many mom-and-dad stores ranging from bodegas to bookstores disappearing to become part of a corporate run by financial wizards. Similarly, we no longer find any independent physician's office. The change has come about mainly due to paperwork involved in dealing with insurance companies and liability litigation from malpractices. No matter what the true reason might have been, the trend is quite similar to what was observed and described by Wilhelm Ostwald in 1896. In essence, molecules of oil and water "feel safer" with themselves rather than facing other foreign molecules at the interface. They simply want to maintain a smaller ratio of interfacial area to inner volume.

The dominance of American corporates in national commerce and finance in the society of economic inequality is an inconvenient truth that we often overlook or consciously ignore (as in my case). It is a good thing that we do not think about it all the time because, even if we do, there seems to be very little we can do individually. It is like "David facing Goliath," or trying to beat a huge boulder with a single egg as the above proverb expresses. There is no way you can win the war, and the resulting frustration from the feeling of impotence may well suffocate us before anything else. We just abandon the hope of righting the wrong. Hear no evil and see no evil, uh?

That the remnant from a broken egg on the boulder may leave an ugly scar for a long time and that David eventually beat Goliath are certainly an element of consolation but real life can be harsher than that. In September 2011, the so-called Occupy Wall Street movement began in New York City's Wall Street financial district in a protest against the undue impact of financial establishment upon the political and economic world and ultimately our daily life. Now, a decade later, I ask myself what has been achieved from the movement.

June Cho was a successful pediatric professor who had shown an excellent track record in research grants from the National Institutes of Health (NIH). Just after she received another grant at her then-employer, the University of Alabama at Birmingham (UNLV), she wanted to come "home" to Chapel Hill, North Carolina, where her husband had been a university professor. With the funding record, she did not have any problem landing a position at Duke University in May 2015. With a renewed enthusiasm and full support from her husband at home, she embarked on the research in full steam.

After a brief honeymoon period, she began to notice that her research grant - her sweat, blood, and tears - was generously siphoned off by her school administrators to support the causes she couldn't recognize. She did not like what these "parasites" were doing with her grant without any prior discussions, and expressed her displeasure in no uncertain terms. This was the beginning of a bad relationship she had with her Associate Dean of Research (ADR). Her research suffered a screeching halt by a University audit and Institutional Review Board invited by the ADR. It took almost a year for June to receive a complete vindication from all charges.

When June informed her ADR and Dean that she planned to submit a formal complaint to Duke University Grievance Committee about unwarranted interference in her research by the ADR, their retaliation came furiously and swiftly. First, they tried to fire June, which they cannot as a faculty hearing is pending. Then, they worked with the University to deprive June of the Principal Investigator status, without which June cannot run any research. Finally, they successfully requested the NIH to terminate her grant with three years still to go.

With ample evidence that their accusation is all based on concocted reports or lies, she hired an attorney to bring Duke to the U.S. District Court in Greensboro, NC (Case No. 1:18cv00288f). She was convinced that the truth and justice were on her side, although her attorney Nancy kept saying otherwise. Moving fast forward, late in 2018, a federal court summarily dismissed her case. June and her husband didn't know what they were facing. In short, June fought Duke as if she were fighting a huge boulder with an egg. (03/06/2021)

318. A tiger out of woods, fish out of water.

산 밖에 난 범이요, 물 밖에 난 고기라.

Out of their habitat, any animals, and for that matter any plants, would be vulnerable to a new surrounding regardless of how powerful they used to be. Just imagine how long a shark or a killer whale could survive out of water. This is true because the habitat is a fundamental part of any living creature, helps define the evolution of a given species. So says the above proverb: you are at your wit's end so to speak when you are deprived of your own comfortable environment.

Likewise, a change in career could entail a lag time to get acclimated to a new field. But, once in the orbit, some people can be quite successful as their plan is based on a strong will and desire for the new field they embark on. For them, the change may be part of their new branching from what they have been pursuing, but to a casual bystander, it may appear a completely unrelated field. Why would anyone venture into uncharted territory when their own career has been firmly established and well flourished?

Schrödinger (1887-1961) was awarded a Nobel Prize in physics in 1933 for his contribution to quantum mechanics, particularly for the Schrodinger Equation. The so-called Schrodinger's Cat, illustrating an apparent paradox of quantum superposition, is still debated today and remains his most enduring legacy in popular science. However, what amazes or amuses me most is his keen insight into human genetics.

In 1944, he wrote *What Is Life?* The book was based on a series of public lectures he presented at Trinity College, Dublin. Some 400 audiences were warned in advance "that the subject matter was a difficult one and that the lectures could not be termed popular, even though the physicist's most dreaded weapon, mathematical deduction, would hardly be utilized." Instead, he focused on one fundamental question as to the genetic code for living organisms. Note that this was approximately a decade prior to the structural elucidation of DNA by Watson and Crick in 1953. They, together with Maurice Wilkins, but not Rosalind Franklin whose X-ray crystallography data were extensively used in their quest, won Nobel Prize in 1962 for the discovery of the double-helical structure of DNA.

According to James Watson's memoir, *DNA, the Secret of Life*, Schrodinger's book gave him the inspiration to search for the origin of life. Similarly, Francis Crick, in his book *What Mad Pursuit*, described how he was influenced by Schrodinger's speculations about how genetic information might be stored in molecules. The great physicist had seeded a hypothesis in biology that has challenged molecular biologists since then, resulting in modern medical science, in particular molecular genetics. Years later Crick held a research professorship at the Salk Institute. His research centered on theoretical neurobiology and attempts to advance the scientific study of human consciousness. He remained in this post until his death in 2004. Once again, he provides another example of a scientist who changed the research direction significantly after a big breakthrough.

In 1954, Linus Pauling (1901-1994) was awarded the Nobel Prize in Chemistry for his contributions to the theory of the chemical bond and the electronegativity of elements. Pauling also worked on the structures of biologically relevant macromolecules such as proteins employing various modern approaches such as X-ray crystallography, molecular model building, and quantum chemistry. His works directly led to the work of James Watson, Francis Crick, Maurice Wilkins, and Rosalind Franklin on the structure of DNA mentioned above.

In his later years, he promoted nuclear disarmament, not so much as a chemist but as a peace-promoting world citizen. This was in part influenced by his wife, an ardent human rights activist. In 1946, he joined the Emergency Committee of Atomic Scientists, chaired by Albert Einstein. Its mission was to warn the public of the dangers associated with the development of nuclear weapons. Because of his political activism, the US denied him a passport in 1952. It was not granted until 1962, just prior to the ceremony in Stockholm where he received his second Nobel Prize, this time in peace.

In the above examples with Schrodinger, Crick, and Pauling, we witness some brave scientists who decided to embark on basic research in a field rather unfamiliar to them with a great deal of zeal. They are not exactly like fish out of water, but I cannot stop admiring their courage and mental fortitude for "starting over." An interesting thought was if the change would be also equally feasible in the reverse direction: would a wizard in Wall Street with a PhD in math go back to graduate studies in physics? (03/12/2021)

319. Knowing one thing only,

하나만 알고 둘은 모른다.

The ancient Chinese philosopher Confucius (552-479 BC) mentioned that intelligent people tend to love water, 지자요수 (知者樂水), while patient and resilient people seem to appreciate mountains more, 인자요산 (仁者樂山). Water is, of course, moving constantly and accommodating itself to its surroundings even when contained. Flexibility is thus part of water. Mountains are, on the other hand, sit immobile for all practical purposes. In short, wise men are flexible to enjoy moments, while patient men are of compassion for longevity.

In Entry #76, "Learn one thing, understand 10 things," I tried to categorize college students into three groups. In the first group, students learn one topic but the new knowledge is quickly abandoned just after an exam. The second group includes those who learn one thing and hang onto it dearly throughout their lives. There is no room for updating or applying the new knowledge to practical matters in daily life. The last group is made up of students who learn one thing, but they can extrapolate their knowledge to other matters. The above proverb refers to the second group of people who stubbornly refuse to compromise their opinion with the prevailing consensus. Once convinced, their mind is set on a boilerplate, period.

In Entry #200, "Flexibility over rigidity," the current political standoff between Korea and Japan was attributed to the lack of flexibility in diplomacy. The rioters, who attacked the U.S. Capitol on January 6 this year, firmly believed (and still believe in jail, I am afraid) that the result of the 2020 Presidential election was stolen. No one can change their ill-informed opinion. A mass hysteria based on false accusations or conviction is not as rare as we may assume.

Although trials of witchcraft had disappeared pretty much in Europe by the mid-17th century, one such occasion took place in Salem, Massachusetts of colonial America between February 1692 and May 1693. At that time and in that somewhat isolated region, it was the prevailing Puritan belief that women were inherently sinful and more susceptible to damnation. They believed that men and women were equal in the eyes of God, but not in the eyes of the Devil.

Women, especially those who had not married yet were vulnerable to Devil, more likely to surrender to witchcraft.

The incident began with several young girls who without any obvious provocation started to scream, throw things about the room, uttered strange sounds, crawled under furniture, and contorted themselves into peculiar positions. They were" "beyond the power of epileptic fits." Parents of these cantankerous children blamed their neighbors, whom they had not gotten along well, for practicing witchcraft. Such accusations were rampant among feuding neighbors during that particular period of time and region. Some admitted that they might have been temporarily overtaken by the Devil. With whatever law they had back then, people did their best to proceed with the protracted trials. In the end, more than 200 people were accused, 30 were found guilty, and 19 (14 women and five men) were hanged. As one can imagine now, it must have been literally a hell, all caused by mass hysteria regardless of fact and truth.

In the mind of many amateur historians, Hitler's hypnotic power over Germans allowed the nation to unite with common enemies and to eventually start World War II: see Entry #61, "I can't find my sword in somebody else's scabbard." More than 900 followers of deranged Reverend Jim Jones committed mass suicide in 1978: see Entry #142, "A mad dog can kill a tiger." In 2017, the dully elected Korean President Park Geun-Hye was impeached unanimously by the overjealous eight members of the Korean Constitutional Court. Surely, they were under heavy pressure from mass movement on the street, but the jury should not bend their legal principles no matter what. It has been my perception that the Korean citizens at that time were in mass hysteria: see Entry #96, "Shaking the tree when one is up on it."

People with one track of mind, as alluded by the above proverb, are dangerous not only to themselves but also to others around them: see Entry #78, "Three shoemakers can outsmart Einstein." Likewise, as shown by a few examples given above, a population convinced by false information can create a historic disaster. What is most alarming is the consequence of the hatred derived from the "them-against-us" mentality of those narrow-minded people. Isn't it why we begin to call ourselves nowadays "The Divided States of America?" How can we prevent such herd mentality from dictating the course of humanity or abolish them once and for all? (03/15/2021)

320. Receiving a forced salute.

억지로 절 받기다.

Although saluting is a voluntary act that one offers to another person in expressing respect, the situation may be quite different in a highly hierarchical organization such as the military or even some private firms. It is a big deal for the person at the receiving end as it is supposed to be a sincere form of compliments. It also provokes a good feeling to the person who extends their admiration because they know they can be truly humble before another person. Thus, when properly executed, salutes satisfy everyone involved. Just like anything else in this world, however, there exist people who just cannot leave good things alone as they are: these tyrannic people force others to salute regardless of whether they deserve it or not.

Not long after he was elected as the President in 2017, Trump asked his cabinet members to swear their loyalty, which everybody did like good lapdogs. The occasion is a perfect illustration of the above proverb. I do not know which side was worse but before we leave the episode, I also want to point out that not all of them obeyed the ridiculous demand. When the President told then FBI Director James Comey at a private dinner in January: "I need loyalty. I expect loyalty," Comey did not positively respond and subsequently got fired.

All dictators in the past demanded a blind submission with loyalty from their cronies and probably received satisfactory responses. It was of course because those subordinates were afraid of revenge in case they resisted the marching order. Here, I cannot stop wondering how and what the dictator felt at private moments all by themselves. If Trump truly felt good about the sworn loyalties of his staff, he did not or could not distinguish honesty from pretense. In effect, he is a blind man. If he felt some uneasiness because he had forced them to do so, then he is a deceitful person as he maintained two different faces, one in private and the other in public.

I might have been too sensitive, but truth is that I have always felt uncomfortable throughout my life whenever someone expresses words of compliments with a bowed head. The heavier their praises were, the more uncomfortable I would become, to a point I found myself wondering if they might want something from me. As I see now,

I have never been a graceful recipient of praise. Call it paranoid. Or I might have witnessed too many false loyalties in my lifetime.

Hung-bu and Nol-bu (흥부와 놀부) is undoubtedly one of the most famous and beloved children's fables in Korea: see also Entry #17, "When it rains, it pours." In the story, Hung-bu's older brother Nol-bu intentionally breaks a leg of a swallow before releasing the bird. Earlier Hung-bu rescues a swallow with a broken leg who later brings him a seed of pumpkin. The pumpkin that Hung-bu harvests from the seed produces a boxful of treasures. Nol-bu's bird also brought him a pumpkin seed and grows into a huge pumpkin. Guess what was inside. It suffices to say, the reward Nol-bu receives from disguised kindness is quite different from what his younger brother receives.

The foreign policy of any nation reflects the status of the nation in terms of economy, culture, military, education, justice, etc. They can adopt an approach based on the "hard" power of military and coercion or "soft" persuasion with cultural exchange and economic development. In recent years, Chinese President Xi Jinping has appeared to emphasize economic globalization via "soft" power, arguing that all nations should commit to developing global free trade and investment. This is in contrast to the American protectionism of Trump. In addition, their proclaimed goal of lifting over 700 million people out of poverty was well received by the international economic community. These guiding principles of China's foreign policy catapult them as a major player in the global order, reflecting their popularity in Africa, for instance. Let us see how long such a honeymoon lasts.

Just yesterday, several garment factories financed by the Chinese were vandalized and set on fire in an industrial suburb of Yangon, Myanmar (previously Burma), during violent anti-government protests. Many Chinese employees were trapped inside and injured as the factories burned. At least 22 people were killed. It was the first time foreign businesses have been directly caught up in the violence in Myanmar. Apparently, the protesters viewed China as supportive of Myanmar's military government and have criticized Beijing for refusing to condemn the military takeover and violence against protesters.

Is China, with a soft-power approach to Myanmar, a wolf disguised as a sheep? Were Burmese angry enough to condemn Chinese business investments on their own land when they were "forced" to express gratitude in the form of salute? In the context of the above proverb, these are timely questions. (03/16/2021)

321. Count chickens in the fall that hatched in the spring.

봄에 깐 병아리 가을에 와서 세어 본다.

The following story by Sasha von Oldershausen is from today's *New York Times*. My excerpt is repeating verbatim the original article.

A vintage children's hardback turned up recently in the mailroom of the Queens Public Library. The book was "Ol' Paul, the Mighty Logger," by Glen Rounds, a collection of Paul Bunyan tall tales. Betty Diamond, of Madison, Wisconsin, had sent it back after more than 63 years, along with a $500 donation to the Library, which more than covered the late fees. As a girl, Betty had been "too ashamed to go to the library with an overdue book," she recalled. So, "Ol' Paul" ended up staying with her as she grew up, establishing a career in academia and settling in the Midwest.

As a young girl, she read just about anything she could get her hands on. Books offered her a secret life apart from her parents, immigrants from a small town in what was then called Czechoslovakia who were less familiar with American culture. "That was actually great for me because that meant I could read whatever I wanted," Ms. Diamond said, adding that her parents had their own secrets. They spoke to each other in Hungarian, their mother tongue, while addressing Betty and her older brother only in English or Yiddish. For Betty, going to the library as a child was like "being in a candy store." This was the backdrop of her grade-school interest in "Ol' Paul."

As years went by, the book simply got lost in the shuffle of her young life. On the odd occasion that she came across it, she said, she couldn't bring herself to deal with the issue. Throwing it out was out of the question. "I have a great fondness for books and I really regard them with honor," said Ms. Diamond, who, in case readers need further proof, ultimately received her Ph.D. in English from the University of Wisconsin-Madison, and would later go on to teach literature at the University of Wisconsin-Whitewater.

As an adult, she kept the book tucked among the many others she's collected in her home, occasionally coming across its red spine while searching for something else. But recently, she decided to "make amends." Ms. Diamond, now 74, called her old library to let officials know of her plan and to ask that the book be preserved. Then she put "Ol' Paul" — along with a note and check — in the mail.

Nick Buron, the chief librarian of the Queens Public Library, said it was not uncommon for patrons, in the middle of an attic purge or a big move, to return books they've held onto for a few decades. "People have a really hard time throwing books in the garbage," Mr. Buron said. "I think that says a great deal about how much we as a society value the written word." Still, he continued, this situation was unique: "Most librarians would go through many careers before they would find a book that is 63 years overdue and actually get it back by that same person."

More common is the universal shame of realizing a borrowed book is way, way overdue. Mr. Buron said that the Queens Library stops recording late books after seven years, and of the nearly 80 million items currently in circulation, 11,000 are more than seven years overdue. Customers with ridiculously overdue books should not worry too much about the late fees, Mr. Buron said. "Our goal is not to make money off our customers," he said. Since the pandemic started, all of the city's library systems have waived late fees. Mr. Buron said there have also been discussions about eliminating late fees altogether.

This month, the Queens Public Library celebrates its 125th anniversary. Like many institutions, the city's public libraries have suffered financially during the coronavirus outbreak. Much of the Queens Public Library's budget for 2020 had to be reallocated to purchase PPE (personal protective equipment). Mr. Buron anticipates another tough year ahead, though he doesn't see the public library system going anywhere soon. "The library is one of the last places that allows everyone to come in for free," he said. For Ms. Diamond, it's bigger than that. "It just seems to me like such a statement of faith in humanity," she said, "just giving people books and believing they will return them." She said she's continued borrowing books from her public library in Madison. "And they're not overdue," she said. "You can check the records."

The above proverb says that chicks hatched in the spring but the farmer waits till the fall to count chickens. The farmer might have been too busy, forgetful, or plainly lazy. His delayed action is like the above story. (03/17/2021)

322. When ready for shopping, the market is closed.
망건 쓰자 파장난다.

Mang-gun (망건) is a headband made of woven horsehair. It is thin but quite durable. Men wear it inside their *gaat*, a formal hat also made of horsehair: see Entry #268, "Standing on his hands with a hat on." So, this man is ready for a marketplace with a *mang-gun* on his head and about to put his *gaat*, but he is too late: the market is already closed for the day. If one procrastinates too long, he cannot achieve anything. That is the lesson that the above proverb tries to convey.

If there is one thing we should not wait too long in our lives, it would be taking care of parents while they are still alive. When I was ready for looking after my parents, financially if not timewise, both of them had already passed away. See Entry #140, "Parents can take care of their ten children, but not vice versa." The regret that I could and should have done much more for my parents earlier became more exacerbated because I had known it all along from listening to friends and elders who had gone through the same agony.

In the same vein, young parents should not put off the time they could share with their children as they are growing rapidly. We all strive for professional success, which simply means many hours of hard work every day. By the time you come home late at night, your children must be in bed sleeping soundly. The hectic morning hours are not the best time to have some quality time.

A few years ago, Paul Ryan from Wisconsin retired at the age of 48 from the 54th Speaker of the US House of Representatives, the position he had held since 2015. This was what he said for the early retirement: "If I am here for one more term, my kids will only ever have known me as a weekend dad. I can't let that happen." As a politician, I did not agree with much of what he and his Republican colleagues were up to, but I couldn't stop admiring his sense of priority. See also Entry #151, "No son is good enough for the long-term care of parents."

I don't know if it reflects the rapidly advancing age, but lately, I find myself procrastinating quite often before making any decisions. It is not taking time for analyzing all facts in making a right decision: it appears that I simply drag my feet or avoid the task while wishing somebody – most likely my wife – to decide for me instead.

I could have saved a molar, had I seen my dentist a bit earlier and visited a specialist in time. Now, I had them put an implant, a time-consuming and expensive procedure. Another time, I missed the plane leaving Washington, D.C. for Raleigh, NC, as I took my sweet time to finish some stupid article in a morning newspaper at a friend's house. Instead of a trip of fewer than two hours, it took a whole day to get home. It was worse than waiting for another plane for a canceled flight because it was all because of my carelessness.

We own some shares of Real Estate Investment Trusts, which are income-generating commercial real estate investments. This particular one deals with office space, which had been working nicely for many years providing a steady income. I knew I had to dump them as soon as the COVID-19 pandemic began. As more people work at home, why would there be any new demands for more office space? By the time I was seriously thinking about selling off the shares, it was already too late. Now, I will have to wait it out.

The Capitol riot on January 6th this year was one of the biggest national security breaches since the 9·11 attacks in 2001. There have been numerous reviews, including Congressional hearings, on why various governmental security forces were not prepared to control the violence. One specific question raised ad nausea has been why the National Guard appeared at the scene so late after Capitol Police desperately asked for their assistance, as rioters breached the Capitol. Condensed below is what I learned from an article by P. Sonne et al. in the 03/16/2021 issue of *The Washington Post*.

Unlike in the 50 states where governors control the National Guard, the DC Guard answers only to the president, who delegates authority to the defense secretary and Army secretary. The Army leadership felt strongly that the military should not be used unless a federal agency was designated to lead the activities. As such, the Justice Department was in charge of coordination for the various agencies including the FBI but not Capitol Police.

Amidst these confusing bureaucracies involved, journalists and Democrats seem to make sure there have not been any political incentives involved in the Army's initial reluctance. There have been many political appointments in the Department of Defense as well as top generals in the Pentagon who had been quite supportive of Trump, creating more suspicion on top of confusion. Oh, what a mess! (03/18/2021)

323. The catacomb is just outside the front door.

대문 밖이 저승이라.

As in Christian, Buddhist, and Islamic Muslim, the Confucianists in the East also believes in an afterlife, usually consisting of heaven and hell. Collectively these worlds are referred to as *jeo-seung* (저승) meaning the afterlife in the proverb and *yi-seung* (이승) of the present world we now live in. The proverb says, "The world of the dead, *jeo-seung* (저승), which I metaphorically call catacomb, is just outside your home." It appears to lament that death is lurking over our shoulders all the time. "Death keeps no calendar," or "At every hour death is near."

Death plays a key role in the tradition and the custom of every culture, ranging from such practical issues as how to dispose of the corpses to intangible imagination of the afterlife. What is fascinating most in the belief of the everlasting consciousness is that it cannot be proven without having to actually die. However, this proverb is more concerned about philosophical aspects of daily life stemming from the "resignation" that we all die sooner or later. Here, one could just say that "All is vanity in life," or "Life is but an empty dream."

Indeed, facing death, we - billionaires or homeless men alike - are all equal. This is an egalitarian thought at its best: see Entry #110, "No one can go to the bathroom or heaven's gate on your behalf." Then, what is the point of arguing who is right or wrong, or fighting over, say, the financial gain? These are all too trivial and meaningless. Even the Bible offers a similar sentiment: "You have no idea what your life will be like tomorrow. You are a puff of smoke that appears briefly and then disappears (James [4:14]).

Aside from the monastic lives of various religious orders, a nihilistic view of our existence and its corresponding practice of a simple and honest life may be best illustrated by numerous Chinese and Korean poets of a gone era. Li Bai (701–762) or *Yi Baik* (이백) of China's Tang dynasty, was introduced earlier: see Entry #195, "True stories from a drunken man." The life of the poet Kim Saat-Gat, (김삿갓) (1807-1867) during the *Joseon Dynasty* consisted of an open-end journey, mainly on foot from one village to another, was accompanied by poems that often tried to define a life. His eccentricity likened to

Don Quixote and his simple life represented the best of a minimalist. See Entry #218, "A needle beats an ax."

Christopher McCandless died all by himself in 1992 in a bus, known as "Bus 142," long-abandoned since 1961 on the Stampede Trail near Denali National Park, Alaska. Initially, people assumed that he died of starvation, however, a new theory is that he died of a neurotoxin in seeds that he ingested unknowingly. He was only 24 years old. After the 1966 national bestseller *Into the Wild* by Jon Krakauer immortalized his solitary odyssey and the movie of the same title, directed by Sean Penn, came out in 2007, the rusty green-and-white bus had exerted a dangerous and almost mystic power over hikers for nearly a quarter-century. It was removed only last summer by the Alaska Army National Guard helicopter.

Chris McCandless was from a well-off East Coast family. He had given away virtually all the money in his bank account and his college fund to various charity organizations such as Oxfam and had driven west before abandoning his car and burning the cash he had. In Alaska, he survived for four months alone. A question was why he had taken such a life of the hermit with hardship. Was he renouncing material goods on a spiritual journey into nature? Was McCandless then the Henry David Thoreau (1817-1862) of our time?

I cannot stop wondering how much of their disappointment of humanity, rather than the allure of nature and simple life, led them to such an isolated life. It is only natural for anyone to try to avoid what we do not wish to witness, like when many American citizens wanted to flee to Canada soon after Donald Trump was elected president. If I recall, the website of the Canadian immigration office was temporarily shut down as too many Americans rushed to explore the possible move to Canada.

We, the humanity on this planet Earth, are collectively ignorant, deceitful, disloyal, cunning belligerent, greedy, intolerable, pseudo-religious, quarrelsome, selfish and self-centered, xenophobic, hateful of others, dishonest, vengeful, unlawful, narrow-minded, lying, etc. I believe that disappointing humanity must have driven them off to the life of a hermit, not so much the magnetic power of nature. I wouldn't blame them. Indeed I often wish I could be as courageous as they were. The above proverb unequivocally, albeit indirectly, reminds us that only one life is given to all of us and that how we live is completely up to us. (03/21/2021)

324. Even water, once frozen, can be broken into pieces.

물도 얼음이 되면 부러진다.

Water shows numerous peculiar properties: for instance, it is the only liquid that expands upon freezing. Earlier, we attributed such uniqueness to the extensive hydrogen bonding between water molecules: see Entry # 125, "Blood is thicker than water." As a liquid, it assumes the shape of its surrounding, showing flexibility at its maximum. Cutting or breaking is an irrelevant concept associated with water. However, once frozen solid, one can create any form out of ice. It can be broken into pieces, the proverb says.

A standard interpretation of the above proverb is that a person with a rigid mind, although appeared very strong, can be easily defeated. How a personality or character is developed in a person is beyond the scope of this essay: it suffices to say that it would evolve from both biological and environmental factors, or nature versus nurture. In lieu of such analytical approaches prevailing in the Western world, Korean ancestors tended to accept the topic in a passive manner as dictated by "fate," or 운명. Here, I would like to assess specifically the influence of divination and horoscope on the character development in Korean culture.

The zodiac of the Western horoscope consists of 12 astrological signs: Aries, Taurus, Gemini, Cancer, Leo, Virgo, Libra, Scorpio, Sagittarius, Capricorn, Aquarius, and Pisces. Likewise, the Chinese zodiac is also based on a 12-year cycle, possibly representing zodiac constellations: Rat, Ox, Tiger, Rabbit, Dragon, Snake, Horse, Sheep, Monkey, Rooster, Dog, and Pig. Among Koreans, it is often said, if not generally believed, that the year of your birth can significantly affect your personality.

For instance, a woman born in the year of Horse, 말띠 (*mal-dee*), would enjoy a bright future, be somewhat noisy and outgoing, humorous, and attracted to people with ease. They "dig one well" once the goal is established and hence enjoy a high chance of success. Her family and immediate surrounding are the centers of her attention. A downside is that they have a tremendous impetus at the beginning but their initial enthusiasm tends to wane off easily.

Because they can be impulsive, they can "lose everything" in a spur-of-the-moment. They ought to be careful in spending. Finally, they can change their mind quite readily.

My wife was born in a year of Horse and the above description is quite accurate except for the part, "noisy and outgoing." She can be as such only when she is relaxed among friends. That she has a very strong personality is an understatement. She can indeed "raise a hell" when something upsets her. Fortunately, it does not happen often. We do not dwell upon or regurgitate those episodes caused by her impulse. I know she regrets those incidents and reminding her of them would not be necessary.

Now, my turn: I was born in a year of Sheep. We are a peace-loving people with bottomless compassion and thoughtfulness. Because of the kindness and generosity, we are generally bestowed upon good fortune. Time and money are not the sources of anxiety: even we are born poor we inherit from our parents something more valuable than wealth. Under duress, we are like children: not really courageous and often prone to the pessimistic prognosis of an event. We are seldom a decision-maker but followers in earnest. One downside from the passivity may well be that we whine easily.

Except for the last sentence, I like what see in the above paragraph as it describes my character in a flattering manner. There is a deep chasm between a man born in a Sheep year and a woman in Horse year. What do they say about a married couple with such a different background? The compatibility involved in a marriage is known as *goong-hap*, 궁합. It would be desirable for young couples who are about to get engaged for marriage to assure of agreeable *goon-hap* beforehand. Indeed, one of the major incomes of fortune-tellers is from assessing the *goong-hap* of young people in love.

Speaking of our marriage, it has turned out to be a blessing to have a partner with quite a different personality, for it offers fresh and different perspectives of the matters surrounding us. More importantly, the very effort to accommodate the difference has served as cement in this family. If what the above proverb tries to convey is that we ought to avoid any rigid stand on any subject matters just for sake of consistency or some ill-defined principles, then I think my wife and I have been doing alright. We think it wise to behave like soldering wire that can be bent easily rather than a piece of hard iron that can be broken like ice. (03/27/2021)

325. My blood boils.
오장이 뒤집힌다.

In a classical treatment of human anatomy in old Korea, there are five major organs, *oh-jang* (오장): heart, lungs, intestine, liver, and kidneys. Extreme irritation from frustration, impotence, and hopelessness can upset the whole body, inclusive of these five organs. It is an expression of despair and fury, perhaps equivalent to "blood boils" in English. When could our Korean ancestors experience such fiery anger with a wrenching gut?

During the 7th century, Korean Peninsula was occupied by three small nations: see Entry #45, "Could sparrows skip a grain millhouse?" One of them, perhaps weakest and thus peace-loving one, was *baeg-je* (백제). In 660, the nation was invaded by the army of the Tang Dynasty of China (618-907). Legend has it that, just before the palace near the present-day *Boo-yeo* (부여) in Southern Province of Choong-chung fell in the hand of invading armies, as many as 3,000 court ladies jumped down to a river from a high cliff to certain death rather than suffering physical assaults by the barbarians.

The boulder, which has been known since then as 낙화암 (*nak-hwa-ahm*), was where the court ladies plunged to the river like "falling flowers." From a distance, these falling ladies in white *han-bok* dress, must have resembled falling flowers. The river is equally famous: 백마강 (*Baek-ma* River), or a river of a "white horse." Taken together, the site was designated as a national treasure #110. The cliff isn't very imposing like El Capitan in Yosemite National Park, but has reminded Koreans of the tragic event for centuries. The incident reminds me of "Give me liberty, or give me death!" declared by Patrick Henry in 1775 at a political rally in Virginia. Both are good examples of the expression presented by the above proverb.

After its birth, the Joseon Dynasty (1392-1910) remarkably enjoyed a peaceful period of a few centuries. Then, it suffered from two major foreign invasions when they were most vulnerable with internal strives among political factions: one by the Japanese in 1592 and the other by Qing Dynasty army of China in 1632. From a historical perspective, these events marked the beginning of the downfall of Korea as a truly independent nation. Presiding kings had to flee from the palace and people were disheartened. While the world expanded outwardly, Joseon became more isolated.

This period coincides with aggressive missionary works by Roman Catholics, notably by Jesuits. Their "invasion" to Fareast Asia and China began in earnest during the 16th century without much success initially. It was not until 1845 that we had a first missionary arriving in Korea and had a first Korean priest, Dae-Gun Kim (1822-1846). On the other hand, the modus operandi of the ruling class, yang-ban, was two-fold: they wanted to maintain the status quo of serving China as their master while instilling average citizens, seo-min, the notion that they exist as "servants" with somewhat convoluted Confucianism. Why would they "rock the boat?" which had been serving them well. In retrospect, the Jesuits could have spread the true egalitarian ideals but they did not or could not.

The birth of the Industrial Revolution, which began with the discovery of steam engines in Great Britain during the 18th century, reached different nations at different speeds. Those nations that had adopted the transition early from hand-to-machine production became powerful nations on global affairs not only in commerce but also in political gesturing. The Commonwealth nations centered around Great Britain "with no-sunsets" were possible only through the power generated by the Industrial Revolution. Joseon Dynasty had not opened its door to foreign powers like Russia, Japan, the United States, France, and of course Japan, while the country was suffering from mass corruption and peasant rebellions from poverty.

In the mid-19th century, Joseon was forced to sign unequal treaties with foreign powers, much like Qing Dynasty via the Opium War. After the Donghak Peasant Revolution in 1894 and the assassination of Empress Myeongseong in 1895, the Korean Empire (1897–1910) came into existence, heralding a brief period of rapid social reform and modernization. In the end, however, Japan's domineering influence on Korea was solidified by their victories in the Sino-Japanese War (1894–95) and the Russo-Japanese War (1904). Finally, the Japan–Korea Annexation Treaty was signed in 1910, and Joseon Dynasty ceased to exist. This was the first time in the 5,000-year history we lost our country. To every citizen of Joseon nation, this must have been the experience that can be described only by the above proverb. (04/03/2021)

326. An immature *moo-dang* kills a person.
선무당이 사람 잡는다.

Earlier, in Entry #36, "An unlucky man breaks his nose even when falling backward," I introduced *moo-dang* as a practitioner of spirit medium in a kind of shamanism. They are at the boundary of religion and superstition and offer a service called *good* (굿). The ritual, similar to Catholic exorcism, consists of wild dancing of a middle-aged, spellbound lady in a colorful dress and deep trance with closed eyes, following music not only frightening but also noisy. She would wield swords or some such accessories wildly. It was outright scary to the weak-minded folks and can be dangerous to bystanders if executed wrongly. This is exactly what the proverb is describing, implying that an ill-prepared or ill-qualified person can bring about a disaster. If a *moo-dang* is fully aware of her own weakness as a practitioner and is willing to listen to an experienced *moo-dang* and learn the trade for a fruitful completion, we do not worry about anything. It would be simply a matter of time for the disciple to become a master. After all, that's what training is all about. Or, as shown below, if one admits an error and tries to correct the wrong, all will be alright also.

The course I taught in a PharmD program at a university was a team-taught class. Since I was the course coordinator, I constantly monitored the progress of the course and made sure that other participating professors followed the course syllabus diligently. One day, I learned from some students that a junior faculty had misled the class with a wrong piece of knowledge. When I sat down with him to explain the topic correctly, he readily admitted his mistake and encouraged me to announce the correct interpretation of the subject. If I were to publicly correct the topic, his reputation as a teacher could be somewhat compromised. If I were to pretend that all were well, then students would learn something incorrectly.

In the end, I chose not to do anything. First and foremost, the misinformation will not harm patients when these students start to practice as a pharmacist. Besides, I realized that this particular professor, who had just joined our faculty, will never disseminate the same wrong information in the future and that he would become better prepared as a teacher from thereon.

Although a young *moo-dang* is still in training and thus not quite ready for practice, she could convince herself that she is well qualified. This could happen owing to her overambition. If the occasion of *good* (굿) deals with some serious matters like life-saving medical practice, premature practice can be fatal to everyone involved. In a reverse situation, say, a young novice hypnotist kept on failing in his early venture in spite of his master's assurance that he is more than ready. One day, the teacher sent him to a new patient whom they have not met before and asked the trainee to assume his well-known name. *Voilà*, he was able to induce hypnotism without any difficulty. As in the case of *moo-dang*, if a young hypnotist fails to mesmerize their client, he will fail.

Even when a young *moo-dang* understands she is not ready, she could jump into the profession prematurely on the encouragement from people around her. Here, everyone involved will be in trouble. This is like a pimp who is luring a young girl into prostitution. Most of the rioters at the U.S. Capitol on January 6th this year knew, or by now have fully realized, that they were committing a grave crime when they forcefully entered the building. They might have felt that their act was justified because of assuring words from Donald John Trump.

Speaking of Trump, I have had a hard time figuring him out. Is he a genius-turned-con man, as some pundits claim? The other extreme question would be if he is an idiot not knowing anything but himself? Either way, one thing is very clear to me: There are a lot of "active ignorant" people who worship him rather blindly. According to an article in *the New York Times* just the other day, a 63-year-old, battling cancer and living on less than $1,000 per month, contributed $500 to Trump's election campaign last September, assuming it was a one-time deal. This was in response to an appeal from a conservative radio show host Rush Limbaugh on whom Trump bestowed the Presidential Medal of Freedom just before he passed away.

The poor man soon discovered that $3,000 had been withdrawn in less than 30 days. He called his bank to report a fraud. He should have waded through a fine-print disclaimer and manually unchecked a box to opt-out. Many Trump loyalists were ripped off in a similar manner, but do I feel sorry for them? Oh, well, you figure out the answer for me. I am glad though they were not *moo-dang*. (04/06/2021)

71

327. Don't bother to look at trees you can't climb up.

오르지 못할 나무는 쳐다보지도 말라.

I would like to introduce the following story to illustrate what could happen to those who defy the lesson offered by the above proverb. It happened during the 1980s and 90s. In this particular instance, an old man with tons of money and time fell in love with a dancing girl in a sleazy strip joint and died only a year after they married. The sexual prowess that the old man assumed was a false reality based on his longing in vain. Likewise, the girl should not have pursued the affairs to her premature demise.

Anna Nicole Smith (1967- 2007) dropped out of high school at age 14 and married in 1985 a cook at a fast-food joint where she was working also. Their son, Daniel Smith, was born a year later but they divorced in 1993. In 1991, while performing at a Houston strip club, she met 86-year-old petroleum tycoon, Howard Marshall. In 1993, Smith became the Playmate of the Year by *Playboy* magazine. Her popularity was at its peak when she married in 1994 Marshall after a two-year affair with his lavish affection and expensive gifts on her. She was 27 years old, at the pinnacle of her life in every sense. The marriage sparked an outpouring of speculation that she married him for his money. She maintained that she loved Marshall and that age did not matter to her. Just a year after, Marshall died at the age of 90.

Smith immediately began a lengthy legal battle over a share of his estate. Although she was not in Marshall's will, she claimed half of his estate, then worth $1.6 billion, while the Marshalls disputed the claim. Her cases reached the US Supreme Court twice, 2006 and 2011. She lost in 2014 from the initial award of $450 million in 2000. While this legal battle was going on, Smith had a daughter in 2006. Only three days after the birth, her son Daniel, by now 20 years old, died while visiting her of an overdose of methadone. This all happened in Bahama where they had been residing.

Since a large sum of money could come to her directly from the pending lawsuit, many men stepped forward insisting they are the father of the newborn baby. Her longtime personal attorney said that he and Smith had been in a relationship for a very long time and that due to the timing of the pregnancy, he was confident that he was the father of the baby. A photographer Larry Birkhead maintained that he was the baby's father and filed a lawsuit to establish paternity. So did Zsa Zsa Gabor's husband and her former bodyguard. Her half-sister said that Smith had used Marshall's frozen sperm. In the end, a DNA test established Birkhead as the father. In 2007, Smith died at the age of 40 in a hotel room in Hollywood, Florida, as a result of an overdose of prescription drugs. Both the vivacious young woman with a huge set of breasts and red lipstick and a shriveled old billionaire not only looked up a tree that they cannot climb but also attempted the climb leaving the above story behind.

There is no reason to envy something that you know for sure you will never be able to afford because of, say, a dire financial situation or simply because you are not physically up to a given challenge. What is the point of longing for a luxurious yacht, a private jet, a white Rolls Royce as well as the newest model of Porsche, your own football team, beautiful women in tow, and some other similar possessions and perks that only billionaires can afford? All can be a matter of vanity originated from a daydream of longing. Wake up and smell the stench of the sewer over there. That is the reality you are in. Just walk away if a tree is too tall for you to climb is what the above proverb is saying.

We have already come across a few similar sayings: Entry #6, "A sparrow tears legs racing against a stork," and #281, "The penniless man goes after a bigger cake." The advice from these proverbs is that we must live our lives within our means. It boils down to "Know thyself." If you pretend to be somebody else, then you are cheating yourself. If it doesn't bother you, there is no need for a further discussion. Let's save everybody's time.

What would be the source of envy and longing for something they cannot afford? One explanation may well be a more comfortable life one may expect. It would simply reflect the difficult life one is facing at the moment. Would the life of excess and hedonism be what they could enjoy every day for the rest of their lives? I believe that most people will be lost without any goal or purpose in their lives. Even a billionaire or the greatest philosopher must have something to live for. I doubt that one could just stop at someplace saying, "Enough is enough." A logical conclusion must be that we will never be satisfied with what we have at a given time and that we will be in perpetual pursuit of something more appealing. (04/09/2021)

328. Small streams produce dragons.

개천에서 용 난다.

In Korean and Chinese legends, a dragon is usually depicted as a kind of hybrid between a giant lizard-like Komodo dragon and a big snake, with a scale-covered body and four legs equipped with sharp talons. Their nostrils and mouth are capable to shoot out fire. According to some old Chinese literature, a dragon carries parts resembling those of nine different animals, ranging from camel to rabbit. They can fly although they do not have any discernable wings. They are followed by a cloud: see Entry #207, "The dragon runs with a cloud, the tiger with the wind." According to a Korean myth, a snake becomes a giant python after 500 years, which then becomes a dragon after another 500 years of survival in water.

Unlike in Western culture where a dragon often appears in bad connotations to be slain by a knight rescuing a princess, in old Korea and China, a dragon symbolizes a man of greatness in almighty power, courage, and fierceness. It is a God of water, and thus God of agriculture. They are born and live in water. In short, people believe that a dragon is a protector of the nation. As such, in ancient Korea, a dragon was worshiped and always associated with its emperor.

Although a dragon is endowed with almighty power and demands an absolute reverence from people, the above proverb says that it comes from a very humble origin like a small creek, like "a black hen laying white eggs." Its implication is that anyone, regardless of their familial background, can become somebody that people will look up to with awe, equivalent to sort of "rags-to-riches." The proverb was popular in our family when I was a child, serving as part of encouragement for a big dream for each of us. It might have been because my parents saw their limit in resources for the future of their many children. We all turned out to be alright to become, not exactly dragons, but living a happy life. In the end, the above proverb has never harmed us, for sure.

A rigid caste system had been in place throughout Korean history, especially during Joseon Dynasty (1392-1897). It began to slowly fade away only after a democratic republic was born after the Second World War. Under such a circumstance, a little opportunity existed for an average young man to get ahead in society. There was a national exam system, known as 과거 (*gwa-go*), for getting a position as a civil servant in the government. It was available only to the youths from *yang-ban* (양반) families, the upper echelon of Korean society. See Entry #37, "No need to envy others: you take care of yourself. "It thus appears puzzling what the above proverb suggested in the real world. Becoming a dragon, or "용이 된다," especially from a small stream must have been almost impossible. That was exactly what the proverb tries to emphasize: "It may look impossible but it can be achieved."

Admiral Yi Soon-Sin (1545-1598) has been one of the most celebrated heroes in Korean history. *Gwang-hwa-moon* plaza in Seoul proudly displays his bronze statue. Yi's fame is from the victories against the invading Japanese during *imjin-oeran* (1592-1598). He and his navy fought over 20 battles, always outnumbered and without necessary supplies. In one battle, his navy was outnumbered by 333 to 13 and yet he was able to destroy 31 Japanese warships without losing a single boat of his own. As the name implies, his so-called "turtle ship," or 거북선, was covered with planks and spikes to stop incoming arrows as well as enemies from boarding. The ship was equipped with 11 cannons on each side with two at the stern and the bow. The figurehead, resembling that of a dragon, emitted a smokescreen and offered a fierce appearance, just perfect for psychological warfare. A replica can be found in his Memorial in Yeo-soo, Southern Province of Jeolla. He died in 1598 from a gunshot wound at the height of a battle with the last words, "Beat my war drums. Do not announce my death."

Yi's father, a *yangban* himself, was disillusioned with politics early in his life and never entered government service as expected of a *yangban* family. Yi Son-Sin grew up primarily in Asan, Chung-cheong-nam-do, where his shrine stands now. It was his mother who had the most significant influence on his adulthood: she raised her son in the most disciplined fashion one could imagine. As a young boy, Yi apparently excelled in war games with other friends, displayed outstanding leadership, and was inventive enough to make his own weapons like bow arrows. When he was 28 years old, he applied for admission to a special training session for soldiers but failed. After four years of painstaking training, he was finally able to serve in a military position for the first time.

Although Yi Soon-Sin was from a *yang-ban* family, he self-made, after various adversaries in his youth, to the most prominent place in the history of Korea. If a kid on a street in Korea does not know who Yi Soon-Sin was, the kid is certainly not a Korean. One could now say that Yi was a dragon from a small stream. (04/14/2021)

329, Slippery cobbles after pebbles,

조약돌을 피하니까 수마석을 만난다.

As one walks shallow shores of inland waters like a river or a lake, perhaps with rolled-up trousers and a pair of shoes in hand, they often come across the beach of pebbles. It is a pleasant walk during hot summer, especially if a cool breeze comes along. However, it is seldom like walking on a paved road: they cannot run easily, for instance. As one begins to feel it no longer fun but awkward, they encounter ashore full of moss-covered cobbles. They are also slippery, and bigger than a foot so that one can stand on them but small enough that it shifts when stepped on. Avoiding sprained ankle becomes a chore. This proverb describes such a situation: after an eventful walk, come to a road more difficult to walk on.

To our ancestors, life was full of difficulties or bad lucks. Many old sayings imply that life has never been fair and will be the same in the future. Such a pessimistic view of life is well presented in my essays. A cursory review identifies the following entries in a similar vein. They are: #14, #17 ("When it rains, it pours"), #36 ("A lucky man break his nose even when falling backward"), #59, #101,#106 ("The mountain and river get deeper as you enter"), #138, #165, #186, #189 ("Lend the money and lose a friend"), #234 ("A hole gets bigger whenever you work on it"), #255, and #283 ("Get hurt from a fall on even ground"). Are we paranoid people? Why were they so pessimistic? It looks like a "lucky break" seldom happens to Koreans. I can find only one, out of 300 thus far, with a fortunate outcome: Entry #229, "A lucky family harvests watermelons from eggplant seeds."

On March 28 this year, the US Men's National Soccer Team lost a game against Honduras, a small nation in Central America, approximately 43,000 sq mi (112,500 km^2) in size and a population of mere nine million. The 2:1 loss in the CONCACAF (Confederation of North, Central America and Caribbean Association Football) semifinal, effectively eliminating the US team from competing at the Tokyo Olympics Game this summer. The team has played in four Olympics in the past but has never won a medal. The team last competed in the Olympics in 2008 in Beijing.

The devastating loss was immediately followed by a series of public discussions on unequal pay between men and women soccer players, causing further humiliation of the men's team. If you recall, the US Women's National Soccer Team has won four Women's World Cup titles, four Olympic gold medals, and eight CONCACAF Gold Cups. It is an understatement that the team has been the most dominating team in the world in recent decades, lately outstripping the men's team in TV ratings. Their star player Megan Rapinoe even testified at a congressional hearing and had an opportunity to appeal with the issue personally to President Biden. The following historic events from Korea also epitomize a case for the proverb.

China had remained the most influential nation throughout Korean history for several millennia. It effectively ended when China lost big in the Sino-Japanese War (1894–95). In layman's terms, Japan ordered China to stay away from Korea, which was then under their firm control. The message was clear to other nations also including Russia, Britain, the US, and France, who had been drooling with a ceaseless appetite for Korean Peninsula.

In 1910, Korea was forced to sign the Japan–Korea Annexation Treaty. For the first time in more than 5,000 years of Korean history, we lost the nation. During the Japanese occupation of 35 years, the national identity was at the brink of permanent disappearance: our own language was suppressed, we were to have Japanese surnames (to this day, I still remember my Japanese name), Korean traditions were ridiculed, and valuable artifacts of Korean heritage were siphoned off to Japan, etc. We were the secondary citizen in our own land.

As if these were not enough, the liberation from Japanese occupation in 1945 was immediately followed by utter social, economic, and political chaos. Then in 1950, the Korean War broke with the Soviet-backed North Korean army invading without any warning. During the War, which ended with an Armistice Agreement in 1953, more than 1.2 million died and cities were destroyed. Many families, certainly including my parents, were uprooted from home during this eight-year period of helter-skelter from 1945 till 1953. I don't even know who our relatives are and if any of them are still alive in the North. Nothing seemed to break in our favor. How can we be not pessimistic in all things including humanity? We have sure walked on pebbles as well as slippery cobbles. (04/16/2021)

330. Fallen leaves asking pine needles to be quiet.

가랑잎이 솔잎더러 바스락거린다고 한다.

In late autumn, if we listen carefully, we can hear the rustling sound that dead leaves on a street make while rolling in the wind. It is the melancholic sign of the season, along with crisp dry air and blue sky. Dried pine needles do not make such noises unless one stamps on them in the dead silence of the forest. And yet, the pine needle complains about the rustling sound from dried leaves and asks them to be quiet. A standard interpretation of the proverb is that we tend to see other people's faults with ease but not our own, including blaming others for our own faults. We have seen similar ones in Entry #115, "The pot calls the kettle black," and #206, "The winter complains about the spring chill." In both cases, I liberally used the behaviors of numerous hypocritic politicians as examples.

Just like people, nations are bickering each other all the time, some are on trivial matters and others with serious businesses. Blaming other nations often serves well in unifying its own people while avoiding public condemnation of policy failures. See, for instance, Entry #290, "Charcoal briquettes burn better together." Sometimes, it is well justified and sometimes it is just a ploy by the powers that be. Most citizens are bought into the scheme.

The Korean Peninsula, especially Seoul, has been constantly suffering from smog and air pollution from fine dust. I do not know if the problem is all due to westerly wind that carries the polluted air from ill-regulated, coal-burning industrial developments in China. It is, however, well established that fine sandy dust, known as "yellow sand (황사)," is from the Gobi Desert. It is another reason for Koreans to dislike China and by extrapolation to the Chinese. Shame.

At the peak of the COVID-19 pandemic last year, Americans, headed by none other than then President Trump, began an implicit campaign against anything from China. This is quite understandable as the first infection by the virus was discovered in Wuhan, China. Besides, the Trump administration had been waiting for any scapegoats to blame for the already tense America-China relationship. To be fair, the Chinese government appeared to deserve a bulk of blame also. Beginning in April 2020, China imposed restrictions on publishing academic research on the novel coronavirus. Investigations into the origin of the virus would receive extra scrutiny and must be approved by Central Government officials.

Unlike HIV infection that was well traced to its origin with sound scientific evidence, we still do not know how the coronavirus was first transmitted to humans. Some conspiracy theorists believe that the virus was from the Wuhan Institute of Virology, although a WHO report prepared by a joint WHO-China study and issued just last month stated that it would be "extremely unlikely." The public hysteria seemed to spill over to recent anti-Asian hate crimes. What a shame. Not surprisingly, on numerous Chinese social media, there are many postings that claim reverse blame: they believed that the virus was deliberately constructed as a bioweapon by the US government (from the 02/01/2021 issue of *Fast Company* by K. Chen, a professor at the University of Wisconsin-Madison). This is yet another example of how science can be distorted by national sentiments. Another shame. The bottom line is still the same: dry leaves complaining about the noise from pine needles.

Michael Cloise Stocking of Richland, Michigan is a good friend of mine until we play golf one-to-one, that is. Everyone calls him Mike, but I always call him Cloise on the golf course just to get under his skin. He is a better player than I was, but he very often misses a less-than-three-foot putting. His fury would be my pleasure, although I express some level of sympathy. I know he knows that my sympathy was false kindness. It thus serves as fuel for his further rage, which used to be exactly my intention all along.

One time, Cloise banged his putter on a big tree trunk in such a force that it was bent for good. Realizing that it was gone, he tossed it far into the adjacent pond. I was watching in stealth the whole action in some distance with a sly smile. I knew he was going to borrow my putter on the next green. He, out of what is left in his pride, never asked me for my putter and I did not have a chance to say, "No, Cloise." I believe he used a three-wood or something for putting for the rest of the day. I won the game on that outing, him complaining about his discarded putter on the 19th hole over a glass of beer. This was not the way to play the gentleman's game but I couldn't stop enjoying the pleasure of beating that man. My golf career was over after I moved down to North Carolina. I blame Cloise. He was not there. (04/18/2021)

331. A cow's walk to a slaughterhouse.
푸줏간으로 들어가는 소걸음.

They watched as hog after hog was upended and whisked screaming down the cable into the butcher in chamber below, where men with blood-caked knives expertly cut their throats. The hogs, some still alive, were dipped next in a vat of boiling water, then scaped clean of bristle – the bristle saved in bins below the scraping tables. Each steaming hog then passed from station to station, where knifemen drenched in blood made the same few incisions time after time until, as the hog advanced, slabs of meat began thudding wetly onto the tables (from *The Devil in the White City* by Erik Larson).

This is the scene of a slaughterhouse in the Union Stock Yards of Chicago in 1893, the year they had the World's Columbian Exposition. A slaughterhouse our ancestors used, if they had one, could not have been on an industrial scale with assembly lines as depicted above. Instead, they must have processed a few hogs and cows on an as-needed basis.

The proverb describes cows being forced to take a walk they do not want to. It is like a rebelled crew on a pirate ship pushed to the end of a gangplank by the tip of the captain's sword. The proverb tries to capture the mood of a cow walking to its sure demise. Would the animals be aware of what is about to happen to them? In the absence of any evidence indicating otherwise, we would assume that they should know – let's call it instinct. Then, we may wonder what would go through their mind – call it emotion. We will never know.

Last year I received an email from an old colleague with whom I worked in Michigan. It announced an imminent passing of another colleague, currently on a death bed in a local hospital. I called him to say goodbye but I had hoped he would voluntarily share his utmost inner thoughts. But it never happened. As he does not have a family, we just talked about who is going to inherit his old vinyl record album collections, one of the most extensive ones in the country.

Citizen Kane, a 1941 film, produced, directed, and acted by Orson Welles, has been considered by many critics and filmmakers to be the greatest film ever made. In an opening scene, one of the richest men in the world, Charles Foster Kane, is on his deathbed in his palatial mansion. While holding a snow glove, Kane was mumbling a word, "Rosebud" just before he dies. This remains a great mystery to his biographer throughout the movie till the end. People who have watched the film instinctively realize that Kane's last thought was with the snow globe and the word, "Rosebud."

When Kane was a child growing up in Colorado, his mother discovers gold on their land. In the movie, it is in the 1871 wintertime. She hired a professional financial advisor to establish a trust that would provide for Kane's education and to assume guardianship of him. While they discuss arrangements inside their house, the young Kane plays happily with a sled on the snow outside. By the time he is 25 years old, the mining business and other investments are so successful, Kane has already become an extremely wealthy man. In due time he established a newspaper empire and runs for Governor of New York.

His marriage to a niece of the U.S. president disintegrates and starts an affair with an amateur singer. This was discovered by both his wife and political opponents to become a public scandal, which ends his political ambition. After his death, his belongings are cataloged and much of them discarded by the staff. In the last scene, we see the sled he played with on the day he was taken from his home for the boarding school. They throw the sled with other junk into an incinerator. As it burns, we see its trade name, not noticed by anyone else, "Rosebud."

I have heard that, when young unmarried men die, say, in a battle filed, they usually leave last words to their mother, whereas married men send regards to their children. This seems in agreement with the first and last scenes of *Citizen Kane*. Then, what about the old colleague of mine in Michigan that I talked about earlier, who has never married, or an old man like me who does not have any children?

What I will think about on my own death bed would not make any headline in the world that I am departing, but I am already curious about the happening in the not-too-far future. Such a thought is all about death itself and the afterlife. Would "nothingness" will follow as it was discussed before in Entry 97, "How long could deer's tail be?" A corollary is of course, "What is meant by nothingness?" (05/01/2021)

332. Must face the sky to pick a star,

하늘을 봐야 별을 따지.

The common phrase, "picking a star" out of the night sky epitomizes an insurmountable task in the Korean expression. However impossible the job may sound, we must look up the starry sky. This would be an absolutely necessary step. Likewise, embarking on a new venture requires some basic preparations. To make money, you may need seed money. To acquire new knowledge, you need some level of education. To graduate, you would need to pass all exams. To marry a girl, you will have to court the girl for a while; etcetera, etcetera.

Last night my wife and I had dinner with two other Korean couples. It was the first time for us to eat out after the COVID-19 pandemic began more than a year ago. We had so much ground to cover that everybody was talking rather than listening. Since the other couples have lived in this area for a longer time, my wife and I - the new kids in the block, so to speak - were on the listening end. However, when our chat drifted to the poor quality of health care service in southern Nevada, I offered the following story.

Las Vegas is the 28th-most populous city in the United States, well known for its gambling and entertainment industries and with two major sports teams, Golden Nights of the National Hockey League and Raiders of the National Football League. And yet, we do not have a university-affiliated medical center in the city. This contrasts to the University of Nevada at Reno, which opened a medical school in 1969 and has produced more than 1,500 physicians so far. Note that Reno is about 450 miles north of Las Vegas and is further than Los Angeles or Phoenix. The University of Nevada at Las Vegas opened a medical school only in 2017, currently with less than 100 students. Funds from various foundations and an anonymous donation of $25 million a matching $25 million from the Nevada Legislature were the seed money for the school.

I argued that the sorry state of the medical field, not only in practice but also in research, needs more upfront investment from the State. It should attract more prominent faculty as well as biomedical researchers from all over the world. Better students and practice would then follow. The State of Nevada does not collect any income tax from its residents. I asked my friends if this could be the reason why the State does not have sufficient funding for medical professions. They did not think it to be the case and explained that the State just has a different priority in spending the State revenue. The Clark County where Las Vegas belongs is still less populated than other major metropolitan areas like New York City or Los Angeles. According to my friends, this may be the reason why we do not a full-blown medical center. To contradict their view, I presented the case of Duke Medical Center and the University of North Carolina Health Care System in Research Triangle Park, NC. Note that none of Durham, Chapel Hill, and Raleigh is considered major metropolitan city.

As the 65th Governor of North Carolina during 1961-1965, James Terry Sanford advocated public education and introduced a number of reforms and new programs for higher education in the State. With his vision and lobbying skills, Sanford and the State officials were able to recruit innovators in the 1960s and the Research Triangle Park has now become one of the most prominent high-tech research and development centers. Having witnessed such a success in North Carolina, the lack of visionary leadership in Nevada has been painful to notice. As I understand that a new kid on the block should not unduly criticize what has been well established for many years in the past here in Nevada, I maintained silence as much as I could.

Towards the end of our conversation, we all sensed that the topic essentially boils down to "Which is first, hen or egg." Does a demand have to precede the supply? Or do people come if we build new houses in a new city with new roads and parks? Why are Californians moving to Texas rather than coming to Nevada? Would they come if we offer an excellent health care system and education? Do they think Las Vegas is still a "sin city" to avoid?

I could have gone further to raise the old question as to the role of a government. What happened to Ronald Reagan's declaration in 1980, "Government isn't the solution to the problem, the government is the problem!" Then, why is the Biden administration now trying to spend as much as six trillion dollars in rejuvenating the economy? An ideal approach to social wellbeing must accommodate both demands and supplies in a timely manner, but I would prefer a significant one-time investment to incremental tweaking here and there. We have to look at the night sky to pick a star. (05/01/2021)

333. *Jeong* lost over distance.

멀리 있으면 정도 멀어진다.

There was a young couple who tried very hard to maintain a long-distance relationship as successful and intimate as can be. The young man involved really longed for his fiancé and wrote a love letter every day. She wrote him back as much, but her letter slowly dwindled down to only a few a month. As it turned out, she developed more affection for the mail delivery man whom she saw every day and eventually married him. You might have heard this story already, but it fits perfectly with the above proverb.

In any human interaction, the distance of separation seems to dictate how often they meet. If we do not get together, we simply cannot share any common activities. In this spirit, just after I left Korea in the late 1960s, I began to play the game, go, with a dear friend through mail correspondences. But it did not last long. I do not believe we had ever completed the game. With time, what we have had in common becomes just the memories of our time together in the past without any replenishing new memories. The old memories themselves do not remain the same either as our brain function deteriorates with the advancing age.

Earlier, I tried to explain the meaning of the Korean word, *jeong*: see Entry # 153, "Easier to see *jeong* (love) leaving than arriving." The closest English word is love. In the above proverb, a better word may well be affection or friendship. It essentially tells us that, if you are far away from a loved one, the affection you had once would eventually fade away unless you invest a tremendous amount of effort.

This old saying should resonate well with many of us, Korean expatriates in this country, as it was exactly what we have found during many years of life in this country, several thousand miles away. And the time elapsed, more than a half-century in my case. Admittedly, Zoom, Skype, Facetime, Kakao-Talk, and other such video technologies of communication have diminished the size of the planet. And yet, it is still not as good as a face-to-face meeting. The main complaint I hear is that we cannot touch the other party, not to mention the big time difference.

Last year I joined a Kakao-Talk chatroom of over 150 high school classmates, most of whom I have not had any communications for more than 60 years. What I noticed immediately was that everyone speaks politely in respectful tones. Perhaps we are entitled to such a treat, now that we are all approaching 80 years of age and have presumably become men of respect. This was rather pretentious to my taste, considering what kind of foul language we used to exchange. Gone was the very fun part of being buddies. What we seem to have now is self-imposed respectability.

After re-introducing myself rather timidly, I began to inquire about many friends. Some have already departed this world, but there are still many whose whereabouts are unknown. One guy directed me to a guy I used to hang around all the time after both of us failed to pass the entrance exam for a college in 1961. Now he lives in Cambodia of all places. I sent him a long email with the subject line, "Hello from Ancient Time," regurgitating old memories. There was no reply. There have been a few other instances where my tardy but sincere regards were met with silence. I thought that we were once very close but apparently, their memory must be otherwise. The silence from these friends was disappointing and sad, but having been far away for so long will bring about such an experience.

There is one particular friend with whom I have failed to re-connect for the past several years in spite of my diligent efforts. He had a stroke in, I believe, 2010, losing mobility of one side of his body and speech ability. The last time I saw him was in 2013 in Seoul. His wife brought him in a wheelchair to a restaurant where we had lunch. Then he literally disappeared: a rumor has it that he might be living on the East Coast of the United States.

Then there is a cohort of friends who do not bother to keep any contact with anyone. In an instance, a guy has fallen out of a friendship because of a hotly contested business deal with another classmate. In other cases, some plain old grudges still separate them. In one particular case, a friend remarried a young widow when he was 65 after his wife had passed away. A rumor started that the woman married him because of his wealth. That was the end of his social interactions with others. They say that his new wife stopped him from seeing his friends. However, in most instances, friends appear to stay away simply because others seem to enjoy a more successful career and a prosperous and happier life than them. (05/04/2021)

334. Even a ghost won't understand you if you are quiet.
말 안하면 귀신도 모른다.

The very first step in learning a set of new knowledge is learning how to pronounce a new terminology, or jargon if you will, which is then followed by the understanding of its meaning as related to the relevant concept. This is such an obvious statement that people do not consciously think about it. If you cannot express yourself simply because you cannot properly pronounce a word that is essential to your thoughts, you are effectively nobody with nothing to offer to others: nothing, nil, zilch, nada! Unless, of course, if you wish to keep the knowledge all to yourself and carry it along to your afterlife.

The crux of the above proverb is just that: if you keep quiet all the time, even the almighty ghost or demon, 귀신 (pronounced *gui-shin*), cannot know you. As I introduced in Entry #191, "The very ghost at your home will carry you away," *gui-shin* is like a spirit of a bad person becoming after death. They are capable of doing anything and everything including reading the inner thought of anyone. Even with this ability, they may not understand you.

I used to have my PharmD class of about 150 students repeat five times in unison how I pronounce a new jargon. Typical examples may be: accelerating stability testing, pseudo-first-order kinetics, rate-determining step, crenation, liposome, unstirred diffusion layer, hydrophilic, solvolysis, etc. A type of white blood cell known as polymorphonuclear neutrophil offers the first line of defense against invading pathogens in our body. I would tell students they can just call it neutrophil or even simply white blood cell. At the same time, I also tell them the full pronunciation, rather than just while blood cell, would impress their patients when they become a pharmacist. The students would invariably follow such advice.

I also told them not to get confused "amorphous" in the context of polymorphism phenomena with the word, "amorous." But who knows: some students may make such mistakes during their practice as a pharmacist, like orgasm versus organism. When I introduce the word, xenobiotics, I would ask them never, ever, to become xenophobic, which then led us to words like hydrophobic and hydrophilic, and such bad word as pedophile. As I recall now, it was quite ironic for a guy who barely spoke English when he left Korea teaching new English terminologies to American kids.

In information theory, so-called Shannon Entropy defines the limit on how well a set of data can be compressed for an ideal communication, or in maximizing the signal-to-noise ratio. The theory is highly mathematical, which I will never fully understand, but I do remember the following story about the origin of the name, Shannon Entropy. One day in the 1940s, a mathematician, Claude Shannon (1916–2001), attended a party, probably some gathering of like-minded people, and explained to a physical chemist his new discovery of what has become the foundation of information theory, and asked him to coin a word for the concept.

The listener not only understood the concept but also was clever enough to suggest Shannon call it entropy. According to the chemist, one main advantage of using the word, entropy, is that it is conceptually elusive and represents an intangible quantity such that not many people would understand it not to mention challenging Shannon. Using an esoteric word may lose your audience but will undoubtedly trigger awe among them.

The other night I watched a "B Movie" where a 16-year-old son discovers that his father, revered by the small-town residents and idolized by the son himself, was, in fact, a serial killer in his secret pervert life. With help from his friend whose mother was also a victim of his killing spree, the son kills his own father. In the memorial service, the son delivers a eulogy that is completely devoid of the true personality of his father. It remains secret even to his mother. Likewise, in gangster movies, absolute loyalty seems preferred to being a rat as the alternative may well be a violent death. Such silence is necessitated by the given circumstance.

More antonyms of the above proverb may include: "Speech is silver, but silence is golden," "An empty wheelbarrow makes more noise (Entry #10)," and "Silent prayers are well replied by God." Relative to these axioms promoting silence, the above proverb seems to encourage verbal expression, just as I advocated in the opening paragraphs of this essay. The dichotomy in these two extremes is, I suppose, a matter of degree of silence and depends on the given situation. If in doubt, it would be always desirable walking in the "middle" of a road. (05/07/2021)

335. A man with a sword is felled with a sword.

칼 든 놈은 칼로 망한다.

A man who has killed another man with a knife will most likely get stabbed to death. Or a man with a bad intention to harm others will get hurt in the same way. That is, "You reap what you sow." The proverb implies that history, especially tragic ones, repeats itself. The modern history of Korean presidents may illustrate its key point.

The Republic of Korea was inaugurated on August 15, 1948, three years after the end of the Second World War. Syngman Rhee was the first president. His administration, which lasted for 12 years, had never been popular, suffering from a dismal economy, political suppression, and corruption. Subsequent to the so-called April Revolution, primarily caused by university students, Lee had to flee to Hawaii in 1960. He died of a stroke in 1965.

Park Chung-Hee successfully appointed himself a supreme leader through a military coup in 1961 and had stayed in power for 18 years, shaping modern Korea into what we have now. He had ruled the country with an iron fist till he was assassinated by none other than his own Korean CIA director in 1979. Park's regime was followed by another military coup d'état by Major General Chun Doo-Hwan. It effectively dashed for another eight years till 1988 a hope of establishing a government through a democratic election process. His authoritarian rule was met with ferocious protests by university students and labor unions. His political opponents were often arrested for no obvious justifications. In 1980, the infamous Gwangju Massacre took place, in which almost 600 innocent demonstrators were killed by the military regime. In 1996, Chun was convicted of treason, mutiny, corruption, and sentenced to death, which was later commuted to life imprisonment.

Roh Tae-Woo was also from a military background and yet elected via open election mainly because the opposition leaders Kim Dae-Jung and Kim Young-Sam failed to form a unified opposition. After he retired, was charged with mutiny and treason in 1996, and was sentenced to a 22-year jail time. His bigger crime was the corruption during his presidency: he was scheduled to repay illegally gained wealth of W24 billion (22 million U$). At 88 years old, he is currently spending most of his time in hospital.

Korea enjoyed a relatively peaceful decade between 1993 and 2003 with two Kims as presidents. Kim Dae-Jung (1924-2009), who succeeded Kim Young-Sam, even won the 2000 Nobel Peace Prize for his effort for reconciliation with North Korea and Japan. Roh Moo-Hyun took over the five-year presidency in 2003 from Kim Dae-Jung. After he stepped down from the presidency, numerous aides and government officials were investigated and charged for bribery. Roh was also suspected of bribery, attracting much public attention. In May 2009, he committed suicide by jumping from a cliff behind his home. It was a prevailing perception that his successor, President Lee Myung-Bak, overzealously ordered the politically motivated corruption charge, which eventually led to Roh's suicide. Lee Myung-Bak served from 2008 to 2013. Five years after he stepped down, he was convicted of bribery, embezzlement, and abuse of power, and sentenced to 15 years in prison. He was also ordered to pay a fine of over 11 million dollars (13 billion won).

Park Geun-Hye was inaugurated in February 2013 as the first female president in Korean history. Just into her first year of presidency, a tragic disaster of biblical scale struck the nation: a ferry named *Sewol* with overloaded cargoes sank, drowning some 300 passengers including more than 200 high school students on a field trip. See more in Entry #3, "Thread through the eye of a needle, not around the body." Her incompetent handling of the disaster was the beginning of her downfall. Beginning in 2016, a corruption scandal, later coined as *Choi-Soonsil-gate*, triggered the country's biggest political turmoil in decades: See Entry #95, "Shaking the tree when one is up on it." In 2017, she was impeached and is in prison now, serving a 25-year sentence.

In the past 70 years, the Republic of Korea has seen 10 presidents. Except for those two Kims from 1993 to 2003, every president has faced a tragic ending in their life or political career. One was killed, the other killed himself, and the rest ended up in jail and hefty fines. There has existed a perception of retaliation by a new president of the old one they succeeded. The current President Moon Jae-in will retire next year. His "fate" would be interesting to watch.

All said, these presidents should have understood the above proverb and practiced lenience to their predecessors. (05/09/2021)

336. Temptation to have red-bean gruel.

팥죽 단지에 생쥐 들랑거리듯 한다.

This proverb says, "You are behaving like mice swarming all over the pot of *paat-jook* (팥죽)." The latter is red-bean gruel. It depicts certain addictive and rather undesirable behaviors. Now, detailed explanations are due: first, I don't believe we have rats or mice in Korea. One-letter word, 쥐 (pronounced *juee*), takes care of both species. The mouse we have in Korea is bigger than the mice we see here in the States, say, in my previous lab, and much smaller than the rats of the New York City subway. But one thing is common: they eat almost anything, particularly the *juee* loves *paat-jook*, or 팥죽.

Paat-jook is prepared by boiling rice and red beans. The taste is adjusted only with salt but prolonged boiling in low heat brings out the inherent taste of red beans, somewhat sweet and very soothing. An important component is rice-ball, slightly smaller than a typical meatball in spaghetti. The final product is similar to grits in texture and usually consumed around the winter solstice. Since the preparation entails a rather elaborate procedure requiring some effort, people tend to fix a large quantity and store it in a jar in a cold place. That is where mice hang around with ceaseless hope to taste it.

We do not fully understand why nocturnal moths are attracted to an artificial source of light, getting very close to burning themselves sometimes. One explanation is that a distant light source such as the moon serves as a reference point in their navigation, while city lights such as lamp posts cause them a great deal of confusion. Some evidence supports the hypothesis, but we have to admit that we cannot decipher every habit of every animal species. Mice running around the pot of *paat-jook* must be for the same reason as butterflies or bees hovering flowers. So long as their behaviors do not directly affect us in negative ways, we just let them be as such.

In contrast, some human behaviors are not so innocuous or tolerable. Today, the U.S. House Republicans ousted Liz Cheney from their leadership simply because she spoke the truth as to the 2020 election results. She has never altered her conviction that Donald Trump is "bad news" to Republicans and the nation. It has irritated every Trump supporter in the nation. The voice vote took only 16 minutes. Here is Cheney's warning: "We cannot let the former President drag us backward and make us complicit in his efforts to unravel our democracy..... Down that path lies our destruction and potentially the destruction of our country." Last night, after the vote, her Republican colleagues fled the conference room like mice scurrying away when the owner of the *paat-jook* shows up.

Jeffrey Epstein was convicted as a sex offender and committed suicide in jail while waiting for a court appearance. He was a well-known socialite and financier. An elite social circle was always present around him not so much because they needed his financial advice but because he seemed to have access to underage girls for sex. At least that was the perception people have maintained. Many prominent people were his acquaintances: Trump, Bill Clinton, Alan Dershowitz, Woody Allen, Harvey Weinstein, Rupert Murdoch, Michael Bloomberg, Richard Branson, Katie Couric, Michael Jackson, Alec Baldwin, the Kennedys, et al. It is recently said that Melinda Gates has been quite leery about Bill Gates' association with Epstein. This is the A-list of who-is-who. Why have these people been swarming around Epstein like moths near a lamp or mice around the pot of *paat-jook*? One time, their association with him was a kind of "batch of honor," but once Epstein was convicted, they fled like those Republican congressmen from Liz Cheney. They behave as if they have never met or heard of him.

Sex, money, and power to the man are what the magnet is to needles. The 7th century General Kim Yu-Sin used to frequent a brothel in his youth so often that even his horse knew where to go after a night fell. The high testosterone in his body started the habit but later used his manly prowess in unifying three small nations in Korean Peninsula for the first time in our history. See Entry #45, "Could sparrows skip a grain millhouse?" As to money being a magnet, earlier I introduced Bernad Madoff who embezzled tens of billions of dollars from his acquaintances through a large-scale Ponzi scheme: See Entry #4, "You steal a needle now, then soon a cow." Examples of power corrupting politicians are too numerous to list here but the behaviors of Republicans toward Trump must be a good one, including the episode described above. The question is why these people compromise the principles they once had on those occasions. (05/13/2021)

337. A mud of clay holds water.

굳은 땅에 물 고인다.

This proverb is something to do with saving money. Money comes and goes following one of the following three scenarios. First, when the income is greater than the spending, money would accumulate. This is the financial state that people would like to have. The extra money in the bank for a rainy day offers them peace of mind. This is the situation the proverb refers to. That is, rainwater lingers for a while on clay mud as puddles of water.

Water quickly disappears on the porous sandy ground as in ocean beaches. This is analogous to the second scenario where the spending is faster than the income. Here, it would be just a matter of time to see the bank account dwindling down to zero balance. How long it would last depends on the difference in the rate of spending and income, and how much money there is now. Finally, if someone spends money at the exact same rate as they bring money in, the balance in their bank account will remain constant in a steady state.

The above simple kinetic principles become complicated as soon as we introduce a new expenditure like a home mortgage, car payment, insurance premiums, monthly energy and water bills, service fees for wi-fi, TV cable, cell phone, etc. These things often follow selling a home and moving to a new location. Recalibrating the future is an effort to keep the ground solid so that one can continuously "hold water."

A quick Korean syntax is warranted before we try to apply the above proverb in characterizing a human personality. In English, a single adjective can complement the subject in a sentence as well as modify an immediately following noun. For example, the word "beautiful" can be used in both "The girl was beautiful" and "a beautiful girl." In our language, however, a given adjective changes depending on how it is being used: "The surface is hard, 굳다, or *good-da*. But in the case of "a hard surface," it is 굳은, or *good-eun*." The above proverb talks about a hard ground and thus uses the adjective, 굳은, or *good-eun*.

When we say, "So-and-so has a sloid (굳은, or *good-eun*) spine," we mean that the person is a man of integrity and principle. Here, the meaning of those words, 굳다 and 굳은, are closer to firm, secure, strong, and determined, perhaps to the extent of stubbornness. Thus, the above proverb could have a different meaning, nothing to do with money. It may state that a person with a determined mind can achieve something extraordinary.

Liz Cheney introduced in the previous essay, Entry #336, is one such person. If you recall, her father Dick Cheney served as the vice president under George W. Bush from 2001 to 2009. Most of the time, I did not agree with her father's nor her conservative Republican stands on various issues. But I must confess my admiration of her courage to speak the truth in the face of her own political peril. I wish her well and hope she comes back to the political arena to straighten up their party, just like the Korean President Kim Dae-Jung.

In 1973, almost 25 years before Kim became president, he was kidnapped from a hotel in Tokyo by South Korean CIA agents. This was the price he had to pay for his constant criticism against the authoritarian regime of then-President Park Jung-Hee. They took him, with his hands tied behind the back and blinded, to a boat moored on Japanese water and were about to throw him overboard for certain demise. At this very moment, a Japanese patrol plane, which had been tracking the kidnappers, landed on the water and rescued Kim. Apparently, the US ambassador to Korea made a special request to the Japanese government for such action.

Soon after Park was assassinated in 1979, another military man Chun Doo-Hwan took over the government in rather dubious means. In 1980, Kim was arrested and sentenced to death on charges of sedition and conspiracy by Chun. This time, Pope John Paul II intervened, asking Chun for clemency. Now Kim's sentence was reduced to 20 years in prison. He was soon forced into exile in the US. After he was allowed to return to the homeland in 1985, his political career took off in earnest, and eventually served as President from 1998 to 2003. He won the 2000 Nobel Peace Prize for his work for human rights in South Korea and his effort for reconciliation with North Korea. He has been referred to as "Nelson Mandela of Asia."

In my dictionary, Kim was a man with a solid spine just like Liz Cheney. Like Kim, Cheney can come back with renewed vigor. Both were more than just solid to hold water. (05/15/2021)

338. Tadpoles in a well.
우물 안 개구리.

How much of this world or the vast night sky with billions of stars in the mysterious black universe and beyond can you see through a tiny pinhole? What can you see in the whole span of the Midwest prairie while driving at the center of a moving circle? How can one know about this planet Earth and people therein if they do not read, think, and feel for anything, while never stepping outside the place they are born and die? Or is this not an important question in their lives?

When we do not know what we do not know, we cannot even form a sensible question. Simply put, we cannot know that we are ignorant. And yet, we often behave as if we are the people who know it all. Call it active ignorance, or "no brain, no pain:" see, Entry #114, "A one-day puppy isn't afraid of a tiger." So, this proverb is asking what those young frogs in a small pond know about anything.

Bangtan Boys, also known as BTS, have just become the first Asian entertainers to appear on the cover of *Rolling Stone* magazine in its 54-year history. Earlier the group was elected by *TIME* magazine as the Entertainer of the Year 2020. They have appeared in most of the major music shows in the world and grabbed numerous awards. They are the idols of their fans called the Army, more for their optimistic message of life in general than their good looks and talents alone. What they have achieved in promoting the image of contemporary Korea is priceless, erasing the old and often sad images of Korea.

Conscription requires Korean male citizens between the ages of 18 and 28 to perform compulsory military service in the duration of 18 to 20 months. It also stipulates that athletes who win medals in the Olympic Games are exempted from the obligation. In the past decade, approximately 250 exemptions were granted. According to a new law that was passed in December 2020, a two-year extension is now possible for notable K-pop artists such as BTS. At present, nobody seems to know for sure what will happen to those seven members of BTS when they reach 30 years of age. One or two members of the group will become 30 in two years.

Stubborn and overzealous Korean bureaucrats - call them tadpoles in a small pond - may send them to the military service, effectively putting down one of the best ambassadors we have ever had to the world. Besides, BTS is supposedly contributing more than U$ 5 billion to Korea's economy every year. Approximately one out of 10 tourists to Korea cites BTS for their main reason for the visit. Narrow-minded people with a narrow field of vision would order them to fulfill the mandatory service under the name of national security. President Moon Jae-In and his administration can issue a special exemption for BTS but it is not certain as the following episode suggests.

Moon lost in his first bid for the presidency in the 2012 general election to more conservative Park Geun-Hye. Soon after she was impeached and removed from the presidency, Moon was elected president in 2017 and is now to step down in 2022. He favors a peaceful reunification with North Korea, which many Koreans of the older generation consider impossible. His soft approach with appeasement towards North Korea has been irking the majority of citizens. He has been walking a tightrope, trying to please China as well as the US, while keeping a side glance toward Japan. The net result of his foreign policy has been thus far a zero-sum game.

Moon favors a dramatic reform of chaebols. Nobody seems to know exactly how he has acquired the notion that breaking up big corporates is good for the nation. Does Moon try to emulate the antitrust scrutiny against Microsoft in the late 1990s or the recent fine imposed on Google by European antitrust regulators? Does he really worry about unfair business competitions among high-tech industries? I honestly do not know but it has been my perception that Moon's dislike of wealthy chaebol families could be rather personal.

Under Moon's watch, de facto Chair of Samsung, Lee Jae-Yong, was arrested and jailed for some dubious charges spilled over from Park's political scandal, *Choi-Soonsil-gate*. See Entry #95, "Shaking the tree when one is up on it." Those fanatical prosecutors and judges involved, who were undoubtedly encouraged by Moon, were tadpoles in a small pond. There is no other way to describe these people with a pea-sized brain and seeing the rapidly changing world through a tiny pinhole on the wall that is separating them from the rest of the world. Is Moon, by any chance, mimicking his idol Xi Jinping harassing Jack Ma, Lee-equivalent in China? (05/17/2021)

339, A rabbit startled from his own flatus.

토끼가 제 방귀에 놀란다.

Rabbits are the prey of foxes, badgers, wolves, lynxes, and the like. They are also harassed by dogs, snakes, hawks, eagles, and kids. Because they are always at the receiving end in the animal hierarchy, they must be constantly aware of their surroundings to detect potential danger. They have developed a wide field of vision as well as powerful eyesight. Their long ears also allow them to detect predators from far away. It is thus no wonder that their behaviors are nervously cautious, and our ancestors thought that they are easily startled by the sound of their own farting. What would this proverb try to tell us?

A child who knows he has just committed a "crime," say broke a precious porcelain vase, bursts to a heartfelt, albeit self-induced, crying in the loudest voice they can muster so that his mother can hear. This is part of a built-in self-defense mechanism for preempting an expected punishment. Call it instinct. The proverb describes a person on the edge with a heightened state of alert to the surrounding. Any small noise, including the sound of his own escaping flatus, can frighten him. This interpretation reminds me of the following incident.

Soon after I graduated from college, I started to work for a pharmaceutical firm as a developmental scientist. It must have been 1966. The research and development group of the firm was with their manufacturing facility in An-Yang. Since the town was too far for daily commuting but close enough to Seoul where we lived, most of the unmarried employees stayed in a kind of dormitory on the company premises and would come home during weekends only. One night, just about to go to bed, we heard a loud booming sound coming from one of the manufacturing buildings. We all knew that something exploded but exactly what we did not know.

We were about to run outside to see what was happening. That was when one of my contemporaries, an engineer, entered the dormitory room breathlessly with a face as white as white marble and shivering in that hot summer night. He was not able to utter any sound but just standing at the entrance with teeth rattling. Everyone was asking him what happened, but he was just pointing outside with a shaking arm. We rushed outside to a small building that was still lit.

There was a series of reaction vessels in the room, each with a stirrer at the top. They were made of some sort of steel and had a sealed "jacket," through which steam can pass so that one can heat the content. One of the smaller ones, approximately 100 liters (26 gallons) in size, which was holding what appeared to be plain water, was gushing out steam and dripping water through a hole obviously created by the explosion we heard earlier. The hissing noise of the steam and wet floor were the next thing I noticed.

His boss, another engineer, who happened to stay overnight in the An-Yang facility also arrived at the same time as we did. He quickly closed off the steam valve and some level of normalcy returned. Then we noticed the man who had caused the mess was standing by himself at the corner of the room, still trembling but very quietly.

He appeared to be very much awed by the force of steam that punctured a hole in a steel tank. Several minutes later he seemed to be relieved realizing that he was not killed by the shrapnel or something from the explosion. And yet, his posture, with both hands folded in front and eyes downcast, was one of apologizing as well as expecting some serious punishment. While we were cleaning up the mess, he was led by his boss to a small conference room. Later we learned that he was opening the valve of steam incrementally to see how it changes the temperature of the water in the tank. It explained why we discovered a laboratory thermometer in the room.

It was the last time we saw him as he was soon fired. Apparently, he had tried other "idiotic experiments" during the short period of his employment and his boss had simply seen enough. Nobody seemed to know, or care to know, what happened to him after the incident. But I still remember what I witnessed on that night in the An-Yang facility. This young engineer was the personification of the rabbit surprised by his own farting sound, a loud explosion.

The more I think about the unfortunate incident now, the more I feel sorry for his misfortune. He did not run the experiment with any malicious intention. It just started with an understandable curiosity but with a quixotic approach. Albeit started quite innocently, he got himself fired in the end. Some sixty years later, I wish that his life has turned around for a better direction since then. (05/21/2021)

340. Nonsense from a well-fed man.

익은 밥 먹고 선소리한다.

We often hear, "you are what you eat," suggesting that eating well is good for your wellbeing. In the proverb, a well-fed man symbolizes a man with an outstanding familial pedigree especially in terms of educational background and social status. Now, such a man carries on foolish talks, *sun-sori*, or 선소리. We may wonder "what is eating him?" or "what did he eat?" Or "he must have taken the wrong medicine this morning." The crux of the above proverb is nothing to do with the meal he had but everything to do with his strange behavior, certainly unexpected from him. "How can a man of such high social status always babble such rubbish?"

On May 12, a Republican House Representative from Georgia, Andrew S. Clyde, declared that the January 6 assault on the US Capitol was a "normal tourist visit." Immediately, a video taken on that day appeared in news media, which showed the same guy, with mouth agape, rushing toward the doors to the House gallery and helping barricade them to prevent rioters from entering. Why did he barricade the door to "tourists"? In support of Clyde, on May 19, a Republican Senator from Wisconsin, Ron Johnson, claimed the Capitol siege on January 6 was a "peaceful protest." What is wrong with these people? For crying out loud, five people were killed in the insurrection. Even a kindergarten child would understand the meaning of the word, "peaceful." What are they eating or what was eating these people?

In the past four years, "America was run by a sociopathic con man with a dark magnetism who enveloped a huge part of the country in a dangerous alternative reality" (quoted from Michelle Goldberg on the 05/21/2021 issue of *the New York Times*). This is the man who explored with reporters at a TV briefing the possibility of using Lysol as a cure for COVID-19. Lysol is a disinfectant commonly used in a household. Its manufacturer immediately asked consumers not to use them for COVID-19, either to mock the man's brilliant idea or to protect their own legal liability later. This man still insists that his presidency was stolen in a fraudulent general election last year. *Sun-*

sori, or nonsensical statements, from this man are too numerous to record on this page. Are Korean presidents any better?

One of the toughest jobs for Korean presidents is how to deal with North Korea, an unpredictable and cantankerous regime with nuclear power and long-range missiles. In essence, there are three possible approaches: one is to appease them with aids, the second is threatening them with rhetoric and display of military muscle, and the third one would be the combinations of the first two as-needed basis. Pouring into the North with money, medicine, and other sustenance is impossible, for South Korea, albeit richer than the North, is not that rich. As to the second option, South Korea is weaker than the North in military power and North Korea is aware of it.

On March 26, 2010, a South Korean warship, 88m (96 yds) long and weighing 950 tons, was hit by a single torpedo from a North Korean submarine off Korea's west coast. It sank along with 46 sailors. The Korean President Lee Myung-Bak said, "I know a lot about the ship. They are prone to breakage," implying that the torpedo attack may not be the real cause of the accident. (Lee was once the head of Hyundai Engineering and Construction, including the shipbuilding division.) This statement not only discouraged those officials in the government who were anxious to start a thorough investigation but also angered citizens who firmly believed it was caused by the North.

More than a decade later, in March this year, President Moon Jae-in implied that the ship could have run aground. The conclusions of these two presidents did not sit very well with Korean people who have firmly believed it was the ploy of the North. To them, what those presidents said was merely *sun-sori*. After spending a fair amount of time going through articles and reports available in the public domain, I am convinced that the true cause of the sinking will remain unknown forever. What made people angry was not so much about the truth but the perception that the leaders of the nation cannot stand up against the aggressive behaviors of North Korea.

Moon has approached North Korea with appeasement. He seems to have abandoned the idea of "conquering" the North via rhetoric backed by military prowess. He mumbled not long ago, "I could have offered a medal of honor to Kim Won-Bong for his valor in the campaign of independence of Joseon from Japan. The problem was that Kim led the invading North army in 1950. It was another *sun-sori* from another well-fed man. (05/22/2021)

341. Denuded pheasant.

털 뜯은 꿩 모양이다.

Pheasants, especially males, are good-looking birds with long tails, colorful feathers, and wattles. But then, what would you expect to see if we pull out all feathers after the head is cut off? You must have seen a turkey or a chicken after their feathers are removed exposing pale pink skins with hundreds of pimples all over the body. It looks pathetic and that is exactly what the above proverb is alluding to a person who suddenly has lost everything valuable. Just imagine a man with high standing in a community who has lost his family and friends through gambling and become an alcoholic. People who used to know him may say to one another that he was like a denuded pheasant. Fictions are full of such people and even Bible depicts a prodigal son returning home wasted (Luke [15:29–30]).

I have always admired Bill and Melinda Gates for their charity work in developing countries as well as their stand in climate change. Then, seemingly out of nowhere, we heard that they are getting a divorce. The news was still a matter of their personal choice and most people followed the story from a respectable distance. One most recent revelation was not so ordinary though: as it turned out, Bill Gates has not been such a saint that everyone has assumed. His resignation from Microsoft's board of directors apparently came after his romantic relationship with an employee was unearthed. It is now rumored that he might have been forced to resign by the board members, although a spokesperson for Gates said, "There was an affair almost 20 years ago which ended amicably. Bill's decision to transition off the board was in no way related to this matter. In fact, he had expressed an interest in spending more time on his philanthropy starting several years earlier."

Does retirement mean "losing feathers?" After the epiphany of "all dressed up but no place to go," I have realized that I have become indeed invisible and perhaps useless in society, invisible because nobody seems to acknowledge my presence wherever I go. People, especially younger ones, appear to be particularly in a hurry whenever they deal with old people and show unwarranted irritations whenever we ask for some simple questions unless the business at hand is monetary in nature. This is certainly a generalization, but kindness is in a short supply towards older folks.

I cannot blame anyone really as I was probably the same way when I was much younger. Let's say I am in the middle of some delicate experiment in the lab and a colleague of mine who has recently retired pokes his face through a half-open door to say hi. He may say that he is visiting someone else and drops by to see how I am doing. He means well and it is the type of visit too casual to inform me in advance. Seeing me busy on the bench he may just depart saying he would see me later, he may come in standing beside me watching me doing an experiment, or he may start a casual conversation. Either way, my response would not be like what I used to be with a glass of beer with him at some social gatherings. Depending on the mood, my body language may well be considered cold, which I may regret later.

I used to know quite well a recently retired professor of physiology in our medical school, well enough to ask him if he would be kind enough to teach my graduate students how to cannulate the portal vein of a rat. Tapping the portal vein that carries blood containing the digested nutrients as well as absorbed drug substances from the entire gastrointestinal tract provides an important piece of information on the drug the rat has taken orally. Although the name "vein" implies otherwise, the portal vein has some serious pressure, and thus attaching a cannula is not something a chemist can do routinely.

Without any hesitation, he showed up in my lab and a few students learned the surgical procedure from the most experienced physiologist one can imagine. Afterward, I wanted to compensate his time, but he refused to accept any consulting fees. I just took him to a cafeteria and bought him lunch. He seemed to rather appreciate the occasion so that he can convince himself that his experience and skillset still can benefit young people. It was an excellent outcome for everyone involved, and now I see why many retirees start a consulting business while they can.

So, is retirement the same as "losing feathers?" It depends on the retiree. There is no need to retreat from the bustling world as I have been doing in the past eight years, but it would be wise to gauge the need for your service before jumping back to the fray. That is, try to go where your presence is appreciated. (05/24/21)

342. Your eyes are your glasses.

자기 눈이 안경이다.

In a collective society like Korea in the past, homogeneity in opinion usually overrides an individual's, as in "what's good for the goose is good for the gander." Collective mannerisms based on tradition, or *hyung-sik* (형식), are deeply engrained in the mentality of Koreans. Any deviation from these norms is frowned upon. Wearing a watch on the right wrist, for instance, would attract curious looks from others: see Entry #177, "Get the land, then build the house." Thus, how others would think of me becomes an important question we constantly face before any decision is made.

Similar to "Beauty is in the beholder of the eye," the above proverb asserts that it is ultimately you who would define what-is-what. This includes your own life. This assertive stand seems to be at odds with what is presented above. It is certainly rare, but we have come across such self-centered assertiveness once in a while. For example, we saw a proverb saying that you do not have to accept what appears to be an outrageously lucrative offer if you do not like it: see Entry #232, "Don't want to be the governor of *Pyung-yang*."

Possibly ruffling feathers, you may reject the offer of the governorship of *Pyung-yang*. Similarly, you may marry a girl everybody thinks bad news. But, in the end, she turns out to be an angel. At a first glance, both instances appear to be a lost opportunity. The reason behind your decision, either rejecting what appears to be a lucrative offer or accepting what appears a bad deal, would vary, but I would say wisdom or even intuition would play a role.

Yi Seong-gye (1335-1408) became the first king of the Joseon Dynasty, Taejo, after he successfully overthrew the 400-year-old Goryeo Dynasty through a military coup. However, he was so disgusted with the power squabble among his sons from two wives, he abdicated only six years later. This historic event, quite well known to Koreans, would be another example where one wishes to fade away to obscurity from an almighty power.

Yi had five sons with the first wife, the last one of which had helped his father found the new nation more than any other siblings.

This son, Bang-Won, who later became the third king, naturally assumed that he would succeed the throne. King's second wife and one of King's close aides had a different idea: they conspired to install one of her two sons as the second king of the nation. This development did not sit well with Bang-Won.

Bang-Won immediately had his men kill the two sons from his stepmother as well as the previous collaborator of his father. This violent domestic upheaval took place while King Taejo was "alive and kicking," only in his 60s. He was disappointed by the vanity of power and fragile nature of humanity, after appointing his second son as his successor, he self-exiled to Hamhung, the town where he was born. Historians believe that it was Bang-Won who installed one of his older brothers as the second king, a proxy king, lest he is misunderstood as a power-grabbing monster.

Two years after the second king was enthroned, the fourth son tried to become king. As if he had been waiting for some excuses, Bang-won himself got involved in removing everyone and became King Taejong. Speaking of Joseon Tragedy, this is it. Two footnotes to the history: Bang-won sent emissaries to Hamheung several times to lure his father back to the palace in Hanyang, current Seoul, but King Taejo presumably killed the messengers every time, expressing his determination not to see his son again. This story was introduced earlier in Entry #194, "Messenger on a one-way journey." Later, King Taejo did come back to Han-yang and lived the rest of his life there. He died in Changdeok Palace and was buried in Guri, Gyeonggi Province.

A similar case was the abdication in 1936 of King Edward VIII from the British throne, which allowed him to marry Wallis Simpson, an American socialite who had divorced her first husband and was seeking a divorce from her second. There was no way for the prime minister of the United Kingdom would approve of his marriage to a divorced woman with two living ex-husbands. It was just politically and socially unacceptable. As it became apparent that he could not marry Wallis while remaining on the throne, he abdicated. In this case, love was, of course, the cause of Edward's decision to give up his throne. It was a reign of 326 days, the shortest in U.K. history. All said, it appears fitting that the abdication took place in the land where *Romeo and Juliet* was written. (05/27/2021)

343. The full moon also wanes.

달도 차면 기운다.

On the early morning of yesterday, May 26, 2021, the full Super Flower Blood Moon arrived here in the western part of the continent. It was called the supermoon with the moon closest to the earth. At the same time, there was a partial lunar eclipse, casting the shadow of the earth upon the moon. It made the light to an orange-red color, thus referring to the moon as a blood moon. I had planned to wake up at 3:30 AM, but my laziness got the better of me and slept through till 5:30 (so much of my willpower). Then, last night I looked up the moon and what I saw was still awesome but not like what I had seen in the pictures uploaded on the web. With time, the moon will slowly but surely undergo its phases as if nothing happened the other night.

So says the above proverb, implying that everything has peaks and valleys with time. Can you visualize the almighty Roman Empire from what you see in modern Greece, how can we imagine the arrogance of the Japanese Imperial Army prior to the Second World War from present Japan still struggling with COVID-19 and pressure from the summer Olympics Games, what happened to British Empire and Commonwealth of "the sun never sets," where are the indigenous Indians nowadays who once roamed the vast land of North America, do Chinese still claim that their country is in the middle of the planet Earth or "Middle Nation (중국)," as they used to say, is France still the magnetic core of the modern culture, etcetera, etcetera. Why, even Korea once ruled the huge territory of Manchuria.

However, the crux of the proverb appears to be more concerned with the ebb and flow of an individual's fortune rather than a nation's. It is thus analogous to Entry #2, "Sunny spots and shade change places." A chaebol's fortune or the wealth of a family seldom lasts beyond three generations while a penniless man can hit a jackpot to become an instant millionaire. We, Koreans, tend to attribute such cyclic nature of fortune to fate, or *un-myung* (운명). This mentality of passivity might have originated from the central premises of Buddhism such as the cycles of rebirth. From an egalitarian viewpoint, it is also fair to share such up-and-down fortunes, in spite of the widening gap between the rich and the poor in every society.

Every marriage is a mystery that no one including close friends and even parents can truly understand until something dramatic happens. Although the married couples divorce for the best interest of each party involved, the third parties invariably receive the news as a sad, if not failed, one. This is how the syndicated columnist Ann Lander who had offered solutions and advice for all sorts of personal issues broke the news on her own divorce in 1975:

> The sad, incredible fact is that after 36 years of marriage, Jules (her husband's name) and I are being divorced. As I write these words, it is as if I am referring to a letter from a reader. It seems unreal that I am writing about my own marriage.

About a month ago, Bill and Melinda Gates, one of the richest couples on this planet, announced that they are splitting after 27 years of marriage. A joint statement posted on Twitter reads:

> After a great deal of thought and a lot of work on our relationship, we have made the decision to end our marriage. We have raised three incredible children and built a foundation that works all over the world to enable all people to lead healthy, productive lives. We continue to share a belief in that mission and will continue our work together at the foundation, but we no longer believe we can grow together as a couple in this next phase of our lives.

Jeff and MacKenzie Bezos jointly announced their divorce via Twitter in January this year, saying they decided to split "after a long period of loving exploration and trial separation." The couple married 25 years ago, the year before Bezos founded Amazon. Reading this news now, I cannot stop reexamining the above proverb. What is going up will return to the ground, once full becomes empty, beautiful flowers dry up to the wrinkled papery thing, money comes and goes, drought follows monsoons, etc. Come to think of it, life itself consists of the beginning and end, or birth and death. It is indeed both saddening and enlightening. (05/28/2021)

344. A village calf remains a calf, never a bull.
동네 송아지는 커도 송아지다.

Every morning you see your face in the mirror while shaving, without much noticing another wrinkle under the eye or sunspot on the cheek. Friends you see all the time do not change. For you, their children are always kids even when they become, say, 50 years old. Of course, there are changes but you just do not recognize them. You ask your 10-year son to jump over a pine seedling you have just planted every morning, rain or shine. Could he become a recording-breaking high jumper in the future? If you let him lift a calf every morning, would he eventually become a world-class weightlifter?

You, as a child, witnessed the birth of a calf in the village with much awe and wonder. And you and the baby calf have developed affection since then. To you, the calf is the same calf, however big a bull he has become. Then one day, all of a sudden, you ask yourself who this stranger in the mirror is and who that humongous bull is. They look familiar with the crooked smile and tilted lips on the mirror and swinging tail of the bull trotting toward you as if he has just found his long-lost brother. Likewise, there will be a morning your son cannot jump over the pine tree and can no longer lift the calf.

I left Korea in 1967. Since then, I have visited Seoul several times. Each time, the city I had left no longer existed. For those who have continuously lived in the town, the changes must have been very slow in coming, but the Seoul I was visiting could not have been more foreign to me. During the 2008 visit, I took one day off from those "babysitters" and ventured out alone to look for the old house we used to live in. Call it a sentimental journey. The place my parents settled down just after they had fled North Korea was a small townhouse in Seogye-dong (서계동), Yongsan-goo, less than two miles southwest from the City Center. The address was 33-24 Seogye-dong.

From the second floor of the house on a hillside, I used to watch trains coming and going at the Seoul railroad terminal. On a cold day, I would see a burst of steam coming off the locomotive then I hear its whistle a second later. That was the same spot where, during the airstrike by the US airplanes at the peak of the Korean War, my oldest brother wrapped with heavy blankets would yell whenever a plane was about to bomb the trains. The rest of our family all huddled together inside a crawl space downstairs to avoid flying objects from explosions while hearing the high-pitch noise of the bomber planes. They were the fighter-bomber version, F-86H Sabre, produced by North American Aviation. After the air raid, it was not uncommon to find some shrapnel in our yard, even inside our house landing after breaking windows. In between the air raid, my buddies in the neighborhood and I used to go down to the train station just to look around. It was always dead silent under the bright sun in the blue sky.

Now, I got off the city bus at the Seoul train terminal and started to walk heading south. Less than a mile, I took a right turn to a tunnel under the railroad, a huge architectural wonder to a six-year boy. It was always cool and echoes were bouncing off the moist wall. Then, I took another right turn to a narrow and winding path that eventually led me to a broad street that I still remembered. Again, heading south a bit, I was supposed to climb a steady uphill on my right, away from the train station on a narrow passage. That is where I completely got lost, having circled a few blocks.

It was a hot day in May. To cool off my head and rejuvenate my determination, I took a lunch break at a small restaurant. The place was bustling with college kids. There must be one close by. If so, it must have been a new one as I did not remember it. The owner of the place, an old fellow with a threadbare apron, confirmed that I was indeed in Seogye-dong, but was not of further help when I showed him the address of the old home. A glass of beer I had with the lunch made the situation worse to bear in the afternoon: sweaty body and frustrated spirit. Those narrow passages I was exploring looked familiar and yet not quite the same roads I was looking for.

I just could not find a small playground in front of our home, the center of the neighborhood. That is where we held an entertaining evening for North Korean soldiers. I felt strangely close to them as they spoke the same dialect we used at home, but my mother hid my older sisters. Instead, my brother sang "오빠 생각 (*Thinking My Brother*)" for the soldiers sitting in a circle with an open fire in the middle. The boy who sang the song into the crisp fall night with clarity has now been dead for more than a decade. These memories are almost 70 years old, but I know they are correct: the feeble light of the tunnel and the song sung by my brother. What has changed is the surroundings. (05/31/2021)

107

345. A drum in the neighborhood.

동네북이다.

When a child wets the bed overnight for the first time in his short life, his parents would send the boy out to neighbors to borrow salt. Tradition is that the boy covers the head with a fanning basket of bamboo that is used in sorting grains. Everyone in the neighborhood except the boy knows about the accident the boy had last night and laughs at him mercilessly. However cruel it may sound, the boy eventually realizes that they have somehow known that he wet the bed and that they, often including his buddies, enjoy themselves upon his misfortune. He thus learns a lesson not to wet the bed through a public humiliation, which he will never forget. Now that he understands the cryptic message of the ritual, he would join the other side to enjoy the misfortune of other first offenders.

We can say that the boy became a drum that everyone in the village can strike as they please while casually walking by. Why salt, not sugar or even eggs? Why, of all things, a winnowing basket on the heard? I cannot tell you why, but it suffices to say they are part of the tradition that every kid in Korea eventually gets to understand. We are all humans. We all make mistakes. Some are serious and some are trivial, each with varying degrees of embarrassment and penalty. In my case, most often it is to do with alcohol consumption, like when I entered a lady's room at a bar, an event that my friends refused to forget: see Entry #44, "Embarrassment lasts longer than poverty."

The public humiliation of a famous person is usually associated with sex scandals, bribing, or lying. The 42nd President Bill Clinton's impeachment by the US House of Representatives started with his affair with a White House intern, Monica Lewinsky: see Entry #201, "No means yes in bribery." About 25 years earlier, the 37th President, Richard Nixon, resigned rather than going through the impending impeachment. He lied about Watergate Scandal: see Entry #68, "Lies become bigger, but food supplies smaller." In July last year, the mayor of Seoul, Park Won-Soon, committed suicide after he was accused to have sexually harassed his secretary. I suppose that suicide was his way to avoid public humiliation: see Entry #280, "Scratching other people's legs."

As a nation, the US has had its own share of embarrassing history. Here I would like to highlight only those events related to racial discrimination. Unlike other topics where one's embarrassment can be considered a badge of honor, in these examples there cannot be any other interpretations. The so-called Indian Removal Act was established in 1830 by President Andrew Jackson's administration. Over the two following decades, it forced migration of indigenous Indians of five major tribes (Cherokee, Muscogee, Seminole, Chickasaw, and Choctaw) from their homelands to areas to the west of the Mississippi River. During this forced relocation of over 60,000 to the Indian Territory, they suffered from diseases and starvation. The tragic event is now called the Trail of Tears. This is in addition to "having stolen America" from them.

Yesterday, May 31, was the 100th anniversary of the Tulsa Massacre. Mobs of White citizens of Tulsa, Oklahoma attacked Blacks and burned down their booming businesses of the Greenwood District of the city, known as "Black Wall Street." The incident began when a 19-year-old Black shoe shiner was accused to have assaulted a 17-year-old White elevator operator at a nearby building. It spread rumors of possible lynching, eventually triggering a full-blown battle between the races. We do not know exactly how many were killed but it should be close to 200, including some Whites. In one estimate, over 100,000 Blacks became homeless with total property damage in $33 million of current value. Both Black and White residents have kept silent about the massacre. The incident was largely omitted from national and local histories till 2001 when the final report from a commission was published.

In 1942, at the peak of American hatred of the Japanese subsequent to the Pearl Harbor Attack in late 1941, approximately 120,000 Japanese-American citizens were incarcerated in concentration camps in the western interior of the country. The 32nd President Franklin D. Roosevelt ordered the actions. Although the official justification was to mitigate security risk, the internment is now considered to have been based on racism. After many court battles, in 1988, President Ronald Reagan officially apologized for the internment on behalf of the US government, allowed reparation, and admitted that the US government actions were based on "race prejudice, war hysteria, and a failure of political leadership." (06/01/2021)

346. Raising the floor lowers the ceiling.
마루가 높으면 천장이 낮다.

If you raise the floor a bit for whatever reason, you will find the ceiling is getting closer to you. Of course, it does, duh. The implication is that if you have both good and bad sides to a matter, you cannot have both ways all the time. Although occasionally one can have a lucky break (see Entry #304, "Take a pheasant as well as her eggs"), the give-and-take paradigm eventually averages out everything.

The First Law of thermodynamics says that, when the energy in a form of heat, for example, comes into from the surrounding, its total energy still remains constant. Energy can be transformed from one form to another, but can be neither created nor destroyed. We see a fork operator lifting heavy lumbers on a pallet in Home Depot. Here, mechanical energy is transferred from the machine to the lumber, which now possesses gravitational potential energy. Just imagine what is going to happen if it falls to the floor from the second-story height. Likewise, one could state that the total wealth on this planet Earth is constant: if one nation becomes richer, there must be or could be another nation becoming poorer.

Could humanity and its surrounding nature be continuously more prosperous and happier? If we consider them as an "isolated system" the answer is certainly no. The only way to satiate our bottomless greed is by exploiting nature to ever-increasing greater extents. Even in this practice, something must give in. Think of the irreversible climate change and its impact on the continuously deteriorating environment we have been witnessing in the past several decades. This not only has caused many serious problems the world is facing now but more importantly may terminate humanity as we know now in the near future.

There has been much outcry among the conservatives in this country on illegal immigrants from Central America like Guatemala, Honduras, El Salvador, Nicaragua, and even Mexico. These complaints are baseless: the fact is that for the long run they actually contribute to the US in terms of economic growth, increasing tax revenue, reducing offshore jobs fleeing from the States, lowering the prices of goods and services, and the welfare of their motherland.

Although illegal immigrants are less likely incarcerated than native-born Americans (M. Landgrave and A. Nowrasteh, Cato Institute, 03/15/2017), the perception that they are a significant source of crime in this country has persisted and rendered the issue to become a political one. Trump administration approached the issue with the "Great Wall" on the border with Mexico, while the Biden administration with more shelters and lenient immigration laws. Recognizing the softer tones from the Biden administration, more people have arrived at the southern border: this spring there were more than 100,000 apprehensions including children.

Migration is usually attributed to violence, poverty, and drought. Of these, the drought has been the main and fundamental cause of the problem. Without seasonal rainfall, the natives cannot grow corn and bean, the mainstay of the Central American diet. During the 2018 drought, 2.2 million farmers suffered crop losses, leaving 1.4 million people without food. How can anyone close the door when they are facing the death of starvation at your doorstep?

Severe drought and malpractice in dryland farming during the 1930s brought the prairies of the Great Plains, the Interior Plains of North America, what has become known as the Dust Bowl, or wind erosion. More than 500,000 Americans became homeless. Many migrated west, particularly California, looking for work. The exodus was the largest migration in American history: approximately 3.5 million people moved out of the Plains states during the decade following 1930. The widespread hunger and poverty were the subject of *The Grapes of Wrath* by John Steinbeck, the folk music of Woody Guthrie, and the photographs by Dorothea Lange.

Closer to home and at the present time, severe drought caused by global climate change is ravaging the entire Western half of the US. Lake Mead, the source of water of this area, is so drained of Colorado River water that the States Nevada and Arizona may have to cut the water supply. Without any fundamental remedies to reverse climate change, we may have to look for some other places to survive. The seemingly sudden explosion of the commercial space industry appears to offer those who can afford a second home on moons and Mars. (06/03/2021)

347. A flaw in a gem.

옥에 티가 있다.

I understand there are five major flaws we must look for carefully before purchasing sapphires and emeralds: a crystal flaw, a cavity or crack, a flaw called "bearding," needle inclusions, and carbon spots on the surface. The discussion on "Diamond Flaw" in Wikipedia is divided into two major sections: 10 external flaws and 11 internal flaws. These lengthy treatments of the subject indicate that it is indeed rare to find a perfect gemstone.

The above proverb, in direct translation, reads "There is a flaw in jade, or *ock* (옥)." The jade, usually green in shade, is considered as the "imperial gem" in Asia and used in many common objects like hairpins, earrings, finger rings, and other jewels including various decorative items. If such highly regarded jade has (always) a flaw, surely no person or, for that matter, nothing on this planet would be perfect. "No gold is without its dross," "There are spots even in the sun," or "The best cloth may have a moth in it."

Midang Seo Jeong-Ju (미당 서정주) (1915 - 2000) is considered one of the greatest Korean poets in modern time. His poems have been translated into Japanese, Chinese, English, French, Spanish, and German. A legend has it that his work was even considered for the Nobel Prize in literature. On the next page, I introduce one of his poems, *Beside the Chrysanthemum* (국화옆에서), translated by the 2004 Manhae Prize winner, David R. McCann.

In contrast to his highly acclaimed fame as a poet, there has been some blemish in his personal life: he was quite eager, whenever convenient, for accommodating and flattering the contemporary political climate. The public display of his affection towards Japan while Korea was under their occupation disappointed his readers. After Korea became an independent country in 1945, he behaved as if he were a running dog of authoritarian Korean presidents: Syngman Rhee, Park Jeong-hee, and Chun Doo-Hwan. In short, he has been accused of having betrayed fans to obtain personal gain at any cost. As much as he has been admired for his artistic taste and contribution to modern Korean poetry, he has been a traitor to many Koreans.

112

한 송이의 국화꽃을 피우기 위해
봄부터 소쩍새는
그렇게 울었나 보다.

한 송이의 국화꽃을 피우기 위해
천둥은 먹구름 속에서
또 그렇게 울었나 보다.

그립고 아쉬움에 가슴 조이던
머언 먼 젊음의 뒤안길에서
인제는 돌아와 거울 앞에 선
내 누님같이 생긴 꽃이여.

노오란 네 꽃잎이 피려고
간밤엔 무서리가 저리 내리고
내게는 잠도 오지 않았나 보다.

*To bring one chrysanthemum
to flower, the cuckoo has cried
since spring.*

*To bring one chrysanthemum
to bloom,
thunder has rolled
through the black clouds.*

*Flower, like my sister returning
from distant, youthful byways
of throat-tight longing
to stand by the mirror:*

*for your yellow petals to open,
last night such a frost fell,
and I did not sleep.*

People often go to great lengths for perfection. Why? The other night, my wife was boiling oxen tailbone at low hear for a very long time, something like six hours, to prepare the broth for 곰탕, or *gom-tang*. After the heat was turned off, she let it cool to room temperature, which takes another several hours. Then the whole thing goes inside the refrigerator. The next morning, she tried to remove the solidified fats floating at the top: it was not solid enough to be picked up with hand but soft enough to be scooped up with a spoon. She claimed that we used to have a spoon with mesh, just for this type of work, but could not find it in all kitchen drawers. In the end, she decided to use a spoon in a foul mood. I just stayed away.

In the beginning, the work proceeded smoothly as she was able to take out the big pieces easily. I would have stopped when about 90% of the fats were removed, but not my wife. Not only small pieces were more difficult to remove but also they were much softer now: they were almost like oil droplets. I wanted to tell her that there is a point beyond which the outcome does not improve as much as the effort. But I did not, lest a major argument should start. (06/07/2021)

348. The more you bang the drum, the more noise you create.
북은 칠수록 소리가 난다.

Here is another obvious observation turning into a proverb: of course, you are surrounded by silence if you don't do anything with a drum, but you will hear more drumbeats if you keep on banging the drum, duh! A standard interpretation is that you make a situation worse if you keep working on it. It is, in this context, the same as "A hole gets bigger whenever you work on it," Entry #234. In that essay, I introduced Watergate Scandal as an example, which eventually led to the resignation of the 37th President Richard Nixon in 1974. The culprit of the tragic outcome was his continuous attempts to cover up the initial, somewhat trivial, break-in of an office.

In a similar vein but slightly different interpretation, I would like to submit a case where what appears to be a spectacular success, banging the drum, that is, is followed by a tremendous amount of headache, or noise. This story has not been well known outside the Korean history book. On June 25, 1950, the Korean War broke out with a sneaky invasion of North Korean armies across the 38th parallel. Their advancement was so swift that in a few days, the government of the Republic of Korea had to flee at a lightning speed all the way to Busan Perimeter, a southeast corner of the Korean Peninsula.

In September 1950, General MacArthur, then the commander-in-chief of the United Nations Command Forces executed a brilliant military maneuver of launching an amphibious attack at Incheon, a harbor very close to Seoul. It allowed the UN troops to rapidly move north, even capturing the capital city of the North, Pyongyang in October. Unfortunately, the maneuver also cut off a large number of the North Korean troops from supply lines as well as any direct contact with the retreating main force. It trapped as many as 25,000 North Korean soldiers within the rugged terrain of Mount Jiri, one of the biggest mountains located in the center of the Korean Peninsula.

These battle-experienced stragglers organized their own rank and file to form a formidable resistance against the efforts by the South Korean army to eradicate them. They kept a low profile during the daytime. In the night, they attacked the police stations and public buildings in a bold manner. More menacingly, they climbed down to nearby villages not only to harass the innocent civilians but more importantly to confiscate foods and domestic animals for their own survival. The villagers would follow the orders from the South Korean army during the daytime but surrendered to North soldiers during the night. For those civilians, it was a matter of life or death. The mopping-up effort by the South Korean army took more than 30 months, till the armistice day, July 27, 1953.

During the wee hours of June 28, 1950, the third day of the Korean War, the three bridges over the Han River - the one for regular traffics and the other two for the outbound train to Incheon and the northbound train from Busan - were all destroyed by South Korean soldiers to slow down the North Korean army. According to a US military advisor, approximately 50 cars were destroyed or plunged into the river and 500 to 800, mainly policemen and military personnel, were killed. A saddening part of the story was that the South Korean soldiers failed to destroy two other bridges, - the inbound train to Seoul from Incheon and the southbound train for Busan. Dynamites just quit. For the ensuing two days, the American B-26 bombers also failed to destroy them. These failures allowed the North Korean tanks to cross the Han River in a few days.

Equally saddening was the fact that President Syngman Lee, after a special train carrying him had escaped Seoul on the 27th and now safely relocated in Daejeon, made a public announcement that the UN had already determined to fight off the invading enemy and that military and civilian supplies were on way to Korea. His comforting words changed the mind of many refugees to turn around and come back to Seoul. Once the military brass realized that Lee fled Seoul, they also ran for their dear lives to the south before ordering their subordinates to destroy bridges.

The majority of citizens including our family and South Korean soldiers were trapped in Seoul, along with abandoned military armaments. According to a briefing by Brigadier General John Church to MacArthur on the 29th, the size of the South Korean army was reduced to about 25,000 from 98,000. In the end, Lee and his cronies were able to find a scapegoat for the fiasco in Colonel Choe Chang-Sik, a military engineer. He was summarily executed in Busan. Twelve years later, in 1964, Choe's widow appealed for a new trial, in which he was found innocent posthumously. (06/10/2021)

349. Even a river dries up if used.

강물도 쓰면 줄어든다.

A river usually collects water from rain, a drainage basin, melting snow and ice, and springs. The water flows through its courses such as valleys of mountains or lower lands of plains and ends at a mouth that could be an ocean or another river. The river is the source of fresh water and food, offers means of transportation, provides both mechanical and electrical energies, serves as a border, and even presents various recreational activities. It is thus not surprising to find that major cities and civilizations have been situated along rivers. Left alone, the river tends to destroy what humans have built around them, or even dries up itself, especially under severe droughts.

Nature changes in her own ways, sometimes mysterious but harmonious or horrific but understandable, so long as humans do not get involved. It can bring about a storm or inferno on a biblical scale but always seems to bounce back to a renewed beauty. By definition, natural disasters are all man-made because it is humans who consider it as such whatever a given natural change might be. Once we begin to exploit nature under the name of development, or greed, disasters are bound to occur unless we take care of whatever we have done to nature, rivers in this particular proverb.

The above proverb is telling us that even an almighty river can "lose water" if we (ab)use it, implying that we should not take advantage of anything given to us simply because there is plenty, of water in this case. That is, once we humans manipulate the river, we will have to provide the utmost care afterward, just to please nature if nothing else. It is a matter of respect that nature deserves. Better yet, we should ask ourselves beforehand if what we are about to do with the river is well justified. A simple economic payback cannot be an excuse, but we do all the time.

In the past century, the US built more dams than anybody else in the world to obtain hydropower, irrigation of agriculture, flood control, water supply, and other purposes. Since the 1950s, however, these dams have become a headache to the municipality involved and to the public and thus more than 1,700 dams have been removed (see www.americanrivers.org/DamRemovalDatabase). The following may highlight the main reasons for the recent disfavoring of dams.

First, dams prevent natural fish migration, limiting access their spawning habitat. Dams invariably slow the river, resulting in stagnant water pools. They would disorient fish as well as increase the duration of migration. Since the water is released depending on our needs, it destroys or alters the reproduction cycles in many species. In all cases, dams change the original function of the river altering the pattern of sediment, riverbed, gravel, logs, and food for fish and other species. In essence, it changes the whole ecosystem. Finally, the water quality changes due to fluctuations in temperature and oxygen levels.

This summer, Lake Mead on the border of Arizona and Nevada is so much drained of the Colorado River that we are facing potential rationing of water in Las Vegas. Famous for the home of Hoover Dam, constructed during the Great Depression (1931–1936), Lake Mead provides millions of people across the Southwest. We still have several feet to go before rationing is inevitable and Hoover Dam's electric output is jeopardized. Then, we are also somewhat "comforted" by the fact that other Western states like Utah are suffering more than we do.

We moved to Las Vegas from Chapel Hill, NC, in May 2018. With more than 2,000 miles of the move, changes in climate and terrain were like day and night. As late as in May, we see snow caps on Mount Charleston of 12,000 feet; we can expect the daytime high during the summer months above 110°F (43°C); days without any rain would stretch more than a half year; the relative humidity hovers around a single digit; birds I see now are strangers and so are flowers like petunia, snapdragon, dusty miller, starflower, etcetera.

Of all these changes, the most remarkable is the scarcity of water from rain. During the winter months, we have some: indeed on February 21, 2019, we even had snow accumulated on the ground all day. I do not remember when we had rain last time but I do remember I quit counting after 200 days up till March this year. Just yesterday, California had a flood while here in the Western states have suffered a continuous drought and wildfire. Scientists attribute such extreme weather to global warming that is in turn caused by the atmospheric greenhouse effect from excessive use of fossil fuels. (06/12/2021)

350. Prairie after mountains.

태산을 넘으면 평지를 본다.

Once you go over a mountain, you will come across a vast area of flat land, implying that happy days would follow a period of hardship. Of course, it all depends on the nature of the hardship one has gone through. One sleepless night preparing for a final exam is hardly the hardship it refers to here. If you have a regular day job to support not only your livelihood but also higher education through night classes, you would be the subject of the above proverb. There are so many rags-to-riches stories, I will not bore you with another one. Instead, I would like to introduce Eugene Garfield (1925 – 2017), who used to earn a living driving a taxi in New York City during the nighttime while studying chemistry at Columbia University.

Current Contents was a weekly magazine published by Institute for Scientific Information, which was founded by Eugene Garfield in 1956. The booklet, of about 5" x 7" in size and printed on low-quality paper, was simply a reproduction of the title pages from several hundred scientific journals. The beauty was that it offered subscribers a rapid review of updated publications: journals cited were only one week old. Surveying the weekly booklet used to be my Saturday morning ritual: once I found interesting reports in my field, I ordered a reprint. It would take about a week to have them in the mail.

Reprints are provided by the journal publisher to the senior author of the report and thus on a much better-quality paper than the paper we commonly use in a copier. The reprint usually comes with the author's complimentary words along with the signature. If you digest the papers and file them away for over 30 years, your brain and file cabinet become brimful. I attribute my satisfactory career to this exercise of going through *Current Contents* every week. How can one contribute to the progress in science without knowing what others are up to? With the ready access to online services nowadays, what I am writing about must be a scientist's life of the gone era.

Eugene Garfield was born as Eugene Eli Garfinkle in New York City to a Lithuanian-Italian Jewish family. His BS degree in chemistry and a degree in library science were from Columbia University in 1949 and 1953, respectively. His PhD thesis submitted to the Department of Linguistics at the University of Pennsylvania in 1961 was about developing an algorithm for translating chemical nomenclature into chemical formulas. He developed several innovative bibliographic products, including *Current Contents*, the so-called Science Citation Index (SCI), and other citation databases. He was also the founding editor of *The Scientist*, a news magazine for life scientists, another magazine I used to read all the time.

How can we assess the impact of a given research paper on the advancement of science, especially in medical science? This question had been around for many years, but the SCI could well be the first quantitative measure of the impact. A basic premise was how often your publication is cited by other scientists. This sounds unfair because the mere number of your publications may not truly indicate how much you have contributed to science in general. As it turns out, the SCI also identified what journals are important to have your publication in. Prospective employers like universities ask how many papers you have published in such prestigious journals as *Nature* and *Science* rather than the total number of publications.

The above approach did not satisfy every scientist. Indeed, there are several issues that may deserve further discussion. For instance, a widely-used method of analysis will be quoted every time it is used. A case of the point was so-called Lowry's procedure for protein assay, which was developed in 1951. It measures the concentration of total protein in a sample and was based on simple chemistry but has been quoted more than 300,000 times thus far. Does the procedure thus deserve a high score on the scale of impact factor? Maybe.

In 2007, Professor David Colquhoun at the University College London declared that Eugene Garfield has done enormous harm to true science. He ridiculed the assertion that the impact factor "has the advantage of already being in existence and is, therefore, a good technique for scientific evaluation" by saying, "you can't get much dumber than that. It is a 'good technique' because it is already in existence? There is something better. Read the papers." All in all, it is sad to see the competitive nature of humanity spilling over to the realm of science. Soon, someone may devise a means to quantitatively compare Chagall's painting with Andrew Wyeth's, or fictions by Ernest Hemingway (1899–1961) versus those by André Gide (1869–1951). (06/13/2021)

351. Flowers from a dead tree.

죽은 나무에 꽃이 핀다.

Here is a dead tree which we have never thought would produce flowers, not to mention new leaves. Then, one day out of nowhere, it shows a new bud shooting out of what appears to be a dead branch. The above proverb says that often time what we have abandoned surprises us with something new and unexpected, like the resurrection of Jesus Christ. People call them miracles, but the truth can be stranger than any fiction. I picked up the following two-day-old story from the *National Public Radio (NPR) Daily Newsletter*.

In brief, a commercial lobster diver says he escaped unscathed after nearly being swallowed by a humpback whale, which whale experts describe as rare but plausible. If the story reminds you of Jonah's stay in the belly of a whale for three days and three nights [Jonah 2:1-11], you are not alone.

On the morning of June 12, 56-year-old Michael Packard was scooped up by a whale while he was diving off the coast of Provincetown, MA. "I was in his closed mouth for about 30 to 40 seconds before he rose to the surface and spit me out," Packard later wrote on Facebook. "I am very bruised up but have no broken bones." He was pulled out of the water by his crewman and rushed back to shore, where he was transported to Cape Cod Hospital. He walked, albeit with a limp, out of the hospital that afternoon. He is still recovering from soft tissue damage.

According to his own account, he was about 45 feet down in the water when he suddenly felt "this huge bump and everything went dark." He feared he had been attacked by a shark. "Then I felt around, and I realized there were no teeth and I had felt no great pain," he said. "And then I realized, 'Oh my God, I'm in a whale's mouth, and he's trying to swallow me.'" Packard was still wearing his scuba gear and breathing apparatus inside the whale's mouth, which he said was completely dark. He thought about his wife and sons.

After about half a minute, the whale rose to the water's surface and began shaking its head from side to side. "I just got thrown in the air and landed in the water," Packard recalled. "And I was free, and I just floated there ... I couldn't believe I got out of that." This was confirmed by a witness, a crewman Josiah Mayo, who saw that the whale burst to the surface and toss Packard back into the sea. Lobster divers typically go out in pairs, with the crewman tracking the diver's movements underwater by following their air bubbles. Packard said that his mate "came right over to me and got another guy to help pull me aboard." That other man was Joe Francis, a charter boat captain who happened to be nearby.

"I saw Mike come flying out of the water, feet first with his flippers on, and land back in the water," Francis said. "I jumped aboard the boat. We got him up, got his tank off. Got him on the deck and calmed him down and he goes, 'Joe, I was in the mouth of a whale.' " While the two men witnessed Packard's escape, Packard noted that they didn't see the whale scoop him up in the first place because "he ate me when I was down on the bottom."

Two whale experts told NPR that interactions between humpback whales and humans are rare, and that the whale most likely engulfed Packard by accident as it was opening its mouth to feed on small fish. One expert, Iain Kerr, the chief executive officer of the nonprofit Ocean Alliance, explained that humpback whales are known for lunge feeding, in which they open their mouths, accelerate and "take in 10 SUVs (sports utility vehicles) worth of water and fish and then everything else." He said that whales are typically very aware of their surroundings. But in this particular case, it's entirely possible that as the whale lunged toward a school of fish, "it's a one-in-a-million shot that Packard just got rolled into the mouth."

Kerr continued: Because humpback whales have a small esophagus, Packard could not have actually fit in the whale's throat. Still, he is lucky to be alive. "With the type of forces that are involved here with animals this large, it could have gone 20 different ways that could have killed him. For example, had the whale closed its mouth out of fear, it could have broken Packard's neck or back. To be clear, the whale did not want him in its mouth." Kerr compared the situation to an open-mouthed biker accidentally inhaling a fly. The other researcher, Dr. Jooke Robbins, the director of Humpback Whale Studies in Provincetown, speculated that the whale would have had to open its mouth and potentially use its tongue to push Packard out. He doesn't expect to hear about any more encounters anytime soon.

Such events are extremely rare, both experts stressed. Perhaps as rare as a dead tree produces a flower. (06/14/2021)

352. Slapping face follows enticing.
어르고 뺨친다.

Human history is rich with bad people with bad intentions who are luring others to do something for their own benefit. This proverb describes a situation where a man entices another person to do what he wants but then changes his tune to a nasty one, in fact, striking the person's cheek. A typical example may be a womanizer luring an innocent girl and quickly abandoning her soon after she gets pregnant, or a conman embezzles money from a lonely widow living at a nursing home. I suppose the bad person could be a woman also. An interesting word here is *uh-reu-go* (어르고), an adverb derived from a verb *uh-reu-da* (어르다). A best English word for it may well be: appease, lull, humor, or fondle, but I am using "entice" and "lure."

After the United States withdrew from Vietnam, in July 1976, North and South Vietnam were merged to form the Socialist Republic of Vietnam. The leaders of the new government then began to retaliate against those collaborators of the US. They were bona fide enemies of North Vietnam. Approximately two million South Vietnamese fled across the South China Sea to countries throughout the region risking their lives in crowded boats. These "boat people" forced the US to scramble to find them a home. The US alone ended up receiving more than a million refugees.

Although a large number of South Vietnamese, estimated as many as 400,000, were sent to re-education camps where many endured torture, starvation, and disease while being forced to perform hard labor, there was a consensus that mass executions did not take place. Despite this comforting report, we are left with this lingering thought if we, Americans, could have done more to those one-time our friends. After all, did we not entice them to collaborate with us, say, spying on the North Vietnamese and sharing intelligence they gathered with us? Did they not fight along with us for whatever justification we have professed? Inconvenient as it may sound now, they were once our war buddies.

On April 13, President Biden announced that he will withdraw all American troops from Afghanistan by the 20th anniversary of the 9·11 Attack that drew the United States into its longest war. The war has cost trillions of dollars in addition to the lives of more than 2,000 US service members. At least 100,000 Afghan civilians have been injured or killed. Many Americans are now deeply troubled with the possibility that the new Kabul government could jeopardize gains made over the past two decades in health, education, and women's rights.

The immediate concern is, of course, the safety of our troops during the withdrawal and accordingly the Taliban was warned against attacking departing US forces. Following the mantra, "in together, out together," the troop withdrawal will be coordinated with NATO. There were what appeared to be courtesy visits to NATO by Secretary of State Antony Blinken and Defense Secretary Lloyd Austin. The decision was in exchange for Taliban severance of all ties with al-Qaeda and agreement to begin negotiations with the Afghan government toward a cease-fire and peace accord.

Thus far, we have not seen any plan or discussion on the "fate" of our Afghan collaborators, should the Taliban take the charge of the country. Being surrounded by rugged mountainous terrain, there will not be any "boat people," but there will be a large number of refugees.

Sex or money is one of the best tools to lure a respectable gentleman into a compromising position. It may be followed by some serious blackmailing. A wealthy real estate executive Charles Kushner, who had been suspected of tax evasion, learned that his brother-in-law was cooperating with federal authorities. As part of revenge and witness retaliation, Kushner hired a prostitute to have her meet his brother-in-law in a New Jersey motel room that was equipped with a hidden camera. He then sent the recording sent to his own sister. The plot did not work, and Kushner pleaded guilty.

At that time, in 2005, the former New Jersey Governor Chris Christie was the US Attorney who negotiated a plea agreement with Kushner. Later Christie said that the episode was one of the most loathsome, disgusting crimes he ever prosecuted. Moving fast forward, in December 2020, ex-President Trump pardoned Kushner as part of a late-hour clemency spree. The White House justified the pardon by citing Kushner's charitable work since he completed his sentence in 2006. But then, everybody remembers that Jared Kushner, Charles' son, is Trump's son-in-law.

So much slapping and enticing were happening that my head spins lately. (06/16/2021)

353. A big snake climbing over a wall.
구렁이 담 넘어 가듯 한다.

You are watching a huge snake climbing over a sturdy stone wall. It is a remarkable scene, something you do not see every day. It is a thrilling experience with some level of awe as well as fear in you. The snake seems to take her sweet time. Although within a few seconds the snake is gone, you feel it was like a long minute. The snake moves in stealth and yet purposefully without disturbing anything. It is hard to believe that the wall had a visitor a few minutes earlier.

The initial investigation of a spectacular crime or an accident by law enforcement invariably receives sensational coverage in the mass media. However, with little progress in solving the crime or identifying the cause of a tragic accident, the episode begins to fade from people's minds. Years later, to the few people who still remember the incident, the incomplete police work would look like "a snake climbing over a wall." This is particularly true with Koreans, although they are quite persistent in following the progress of an investigation of a scandal. No other nations surpass the Korean's initial zeal and appetite toward a scandal, especially a juicy one. They are like a hungry dog holding a piece of T-bone steak.

Around midnight of June 9, 2020, the dead body of Seoul City mayor, Park Won-Soon, was found in a remote wooded area of a mountain in the north of Seoul. Without any foul play found at the scene, the death has been considered a suicide. Indeed, there was a letter to his daughter, which many people considered a suicidal note. Just one day prior, his former secretary had accused him of a sexual offense. She had been often asked to take care of intimate matters of Park's life, like handling his underwear when he took a shower at his office. More damning was that he used to send inappropriate texts and photos of himself in underwear as well as late-night messages in obscene language. See Entry #280, "Scratching other people's legs."

On several occasions, Park had apparently warned his aides of anticipated bad publicity involving legal litigation from his secretary. According to his secretary-in-chief, Park was ready to resign. Despite this piece of supporting evidence, many people subscribed to a conspiracy theory that he was murdered by his political rivals. The

124

mayorship of Seoul is often considered a stepping stone for a better and higher position in the Korean government such as the presidency. A theory was that Park's rivals preempted his candidacy in advance. It was a plausible explanation, but the curiosity slowly faded from people's minds, like "a snake climbing over a stonewall."

At this writing, nobody is talking about the death of the mayor except for a few lawsuits involving defamation of the mayor's family and the accuser, his former secretary. Even this new development appears very much in the context of the Me-Too movement in Korea.

Korean parliament election was held on April 15, 2020. All 300 members were subject to the election. The ruling party, the liberal Democratic Party, won it in a landslide. Out of 300, they took 180 seats, guaranteeing them an absolute majority in the assembly. Although political pundits attributed the spectacular victory to the initial success in controlling the COVID-19 pandemic by the government, many Koreans believed in systematic voting frauds. Their claim was largely based on a statistic-based analysis of voting records. The statistical inference is not as convincing or as powerful as some direct physical evidence such as outright concoction of the voting results or fraudulent voting practice. Because of the rampant COVID-19 infection, large-scale demonstrations were not only banned by the government but also have fizzled out themselves.

To this day, nobody seems to know what really took place in the election. Considering small margins in the election outcome throughout the country, if there indeed existed a fraud, it must have been some type of systematic fraud. It certainly appears to justify some serious statistical analysis. Now, more than a year later, we just shrugged it off, saying that it was like "a big snake climbing over a wall" and hoping that the next time would be different.

As a footnote, I spent some time to find convincing evidence for the fraud in numerous reports posted on the web. One seemingly reliable source cited a scholastic eForensics analysis of the election by a political science professor at the University of Michigan at Ann Arbor. Then, I noticed that the link to this publication did not show anything. And yet the publication was heavily quoted by many online posts. I was not able to find the paper on his University website either. Yesterday I sent an email to the professor asking for the reprint of the report, but I have not yet heard anything from him. Did someone fabricate a story? The whole thing seems fishy. (06/18/2021)

354. A wealthy family at the expense of three villages.

부자 하나면 세 동네가 망한다.

This proverb says that, while a family becomes richer with new money, the folks in three villages will suffer from poverty. As I implied in Entry # 346, "Raising the floor lowers the ceiling," if someone gets richer, somebody else is bound to become poorer. This suggestion was derived from a thermodynamic law of energy conservation. In a positive spin, the proverb also implies that to achieve a meaningful goal, many people may have to sacrifice their routine activities. Quite pessimistic as it may sound, the quintessential element of humanity is the competition for survival and a better life. In practice, it translates to cut-throat societies and wars between nations.

Besides such serious global issues as the disparity in wealth and climate change, we still have numerous regional conflicts. Going out of a whim, I am listing them at random without much elaboration: Hamas-Israel conflict, Chinese persecution of Uyghur Muslims, the dictatorship of Myanmar, African immigrants in Southern Italy, Yemen civil war, suppressed people of North Korea, central American immigrants at the southern border of the US, China-Taiwan conflict, Russia-Ukraine war, Iran-Iraq tension, Afghan-Taliban fight, India-Pakistan border squabble, ill-guided Trump supporters, humanitarian crisis in Somalia, Ethiopian government's treatment of Tigrayans, Turkey-Syria war, China-Hong Kong clash, even the "chicken fight" between Korea and Japan.

Wherever we look nowadays, there is blood, hatred, and anger spilled over to the street in any corner of this planet Earth. "Can we, can we get along?" is what Rodney King asked during a TV appearance on May 1, 1992, during the riot subsequent to his brutal beating by Los Angeles police forces. From a historical perspective, differences in religion, culture, and custom may be the justification of most international feuds. However, the immediate cause of many wars could be the national greed fueled by private corporates run by overzealous managers and unsatiable stockholders.

In the First Opium War (1839–1842), Great Britain in support of her private company, the British East India Company, forced the Chinese Qing Dynasty to open its trading policy so that a large amount of opium can come into the land. This was against Dynasty's wish to stop the Company from selling opium to private traders who smuggled it to China. As far as one can tell, the behavior of Great Britain at that time was as bad as, if not worse than, some of the Central American countries maintaining a blind eye for exporting illegal drugs to the US in recent years. Note that Great Britain was successful in opening the Chinese market forcefully with her almighty navy force. It was delivering 4,000 chests, each 77 kg of opium per year.

In the Second Opium War (1856–1860), besides Britain, France and Russian Empire joined the fray, akin to a gangrape of present days. Once again, their modern military forces brought the Chinese to kneel with their head bowed. Qing Dynasty, a paper tiger by now, was compelled to offer Europeans favorable trade concessions, including the legalization of the opium trade and easier transport of cheap laborers, coolies. Most of all, China had to give up the sovereignty of Hong Kong over to Great Britain.

As discussed in detail in entry #317, "Beating the boulder with an egg," the so-called Ostwald Ripening in physical chemistry explains the disappearance of small corner stores and dominating presence of humongous corporates like Amazon, Walmart, Barnes and Noble, Costco, etc. I, for one, miss very much those small dime stores in the neighborhood. Likewise, powerful nations seem to last for a while whereas small countries appear to struggle to exist under constant pressure from a neighboring nation like Ukraine by Russia. In short, the above proverb and Ostwald Ripening are the same and one.

Sad to say, constant struggles for the existence of a weaker nation against the lurking threat from powerful nations are indeed the hallmark of human history. Think of Korea. On the other hand, one may naively think that a weak nation, once becomes a powerful one, may remember what they have suffered and decide to show compassion to others based on empathy. It is hardly the case. Based on the history of the Opium Wars alone, I can clearly see the current determination of the Xi Jinping government of China never to become a weakling again to kneel down to any nations in the future. Their defiant attitudes on many global issues are easy to understand if we try to understand what humiliation they have gone through. (06/22/2021)

355. Placing persimmons and pears at a *jesa*.

남의 집 제사에 감 놓아라 배 놓아라 한다.

Jesa, 제사, is a kind of religious ritual where participants remember the deceased with reverence. It can be a big event as in a National Memorial Day, or more commonly a small domestic gathering of intimate family members alone. Nonetheless, the ritual follows a certain *hyung-sik* (형식), or formality and fixed procedure, just as the Catholic Mass has. There is an altar with a picture of the deceased surrounded with full of fruits. One of the most essential steps is of course formal salutations of direct descendants as well as friends. These are the "must" items. Within a traditional framework, however, an individual *jesa* can vary depending on the family tradition.

As said above, *jesa* is primarily an affair of individual families. How to run the ritual is really their prerogative. Nobody is supposed to poke their nose in this solemn event. The above proverb says otherwise: someone asks the head of the family to place persimmons here and pears there on the table at the altar. It would be unwarranted meddling. The proverb advises us not to interfere with other people's business.

Often, there exists only a blurred boundary between advice and meddling. Those in the receiving end can be quite defensive such that anything you say becomes meddling or nagging. A mother's inquiry about her daughter's status of dating can start innocently enough they can have enjoyable lunches. But then the mother becomes a bona fide intruder in her daughter's life. The daughter may call it meddling. On the other hand, there are people who listen to everything others have to say like a dry sponge soaking up water. Here, the advisor can go far into the space of the dead-quiet listener.

Varying degrees of personal involvement can exist in each one-to-one interaction, ranging from suggesting to coercing, to blackmailing, to even *pro quid quo* and threatening. A wealthy mother can wield a lot of sway over her financially struggling daughter. Or it can backfire and terminate the otherwise amicable relationship and the poor father or her sibling may have to step in. Or it can become deadly serious once the law gets involved.

Mickey Rooney, a great actor of the gone era, someone whose estate could have been worth hundreds of millions when he died in summer 2014. Instead, he endured beatings, humiliation, and poverty at the hands of his eighth wife and one of her sons, both accused in 2015 of elder abuse. At the Senate Special Aging Committee, Rooney tearfully testified that he had been a victim of the elder-abuse to the extent that he was stripped "of the ability to make even the most basic decisions about my life," leading to an "unbearable" and "helpless" daily existence. Rooney's attorneys filed court papers in their petition for a conservator to protect him and recover his assets. (From the 10/21/2015 issue of *The Hollywood Reporter* after modified)

Britney Spears was a pop idol during the late 1990s and early 2000s with provocative choreography. Since 2008, she has been living under a conservatorship with her father as a legal guardian. This happened after a few mishaps that were captured by the ever-present paparazzi and aggressively covered by the media. She had been taken to a hospital by ambulance a few times for involuntary psychiatric evaluations amid a series of public struggles and concerns around her mental health and substance abuse. Today, Spears is to appear at the Superior Court in Los Angeles to address who should control her finances and her personal life. Most fans are anxiously waiting for the end of guardianship.

Last year, the Korean pianist Paik Kun-Woo was accused by his in-laws of having abandoned and left his wife, a well-known former actress Yoon Jeong-Hee, in Paris. He appointed their daughter, a violinist living in Paris, as a guardian of Yoon as the latter has been suffering from Alzheimer's Disease for several years. Earlier the conservatorship was approved by the French authorities.

In all the three cases above, the publicity was inevitable as the people involved are all celebrities. I then wonder how many ordinary families would go through such an ordeal. The crux of the matter is that a judgmental call is always involved. If the person who receives guardianship can truly handle their own affairs, others are simply meddling the life of another human being. The true motive of guardianship could be money might be involved as in a film, *I care a lot*, where a crooked legal guardian drains the savings of old folks. This would be certainly more than advising where a pear or a persimmon goes at the table of *jesa*. (06/23/2021)

356. Licking a watermelon.

수박 겉핥기.

If you lick the outside skin of a delicious-looking watermelon, what do you taste? What would you find on a sun-drenched monolith of rock after a dog passed by? What do you see after a snake climbed over a stone wall as in Entry #353? Nothing, or, as they say, "zero, zip, zilch, nada." The superficiality involved in licking a watermelon without being able to taste what is inside is the subject of the above proverb.

Simply because you were asked to, you could complete a job assigned to you without asking why you are doing it. I do not know if a given job makes people work rather mechanically or if people who do the job half-heartedly make the job appear boring. If one rather absolutely respects and follows an order, such questions may be irrelevant, but I cannot stop asking. Industrial automation inevitably makes workers a mere part of the assembly line in manufacturing factories. We can still view on *YouTube* such a change as portrayed by Charles Chaplin in *Factory Work*.

Moving fast forward, one of the major complaints of the Amazon warehouse workers is the constant surveillance of their "productivity." Amazon apparently tracks workers' every movement inside its warehouses. Employees, who work too slowly or are idle for a bit too long, risk being fired. The company seems obsessed with satisfying customers in the most efficient way, and their zeal to achieve the goal has resulted in record growth and spectacular profits.

Tenured professors in academia tend to relax a bit to become less competitive and productive in their scholarly research especially when they begin to lose interest in what they have been doing. Jeff Bezos, Amazon's founder, also believes that a permanent workforce could become lazy and create mediocrity. Indeed, the company's own data showed that most employees became less eager over time. To remedy the situation, for a while he adopted a short-term-employment model, which would mean little opportunity for advancement of the employees. Most of all, Bezos believes in the use of technology in hiring, monitoring, and managing workers.

Under such a pressured and mechanized working environment, employees are bound to barely lick the surface of a watermelon. They may not even have time to wash outside first. The guru of mindfulness, Thich Nhat Hanh, urges us to find and enjoy some meaningful time even during washing dishes: see Entry #3, "Thread through the eye of a needle, not around the body." I do not know if it would be possible to find peace during the frantic working hours at the Amazon warehouse.

Superficially completed works invariably bring about a disaster later. The big news this morning was the partial collapse at 1:30 AM of a 12-story condominium building near Miami, killing at least one person and approximately 100 missing under the rubble. We will not know the exact cause of the collapse for a while, but some kind of structural defects are suspected. The building is only 40 years old. Albeit leaning, the Tower of Pisa has survived over 800 years.

About a week ago, I had several email correspondences with my contact at the Korean publisher of this book series, Volume III. It was my responsibility to make proper arrangements for online promotion and advertisement of the title.

Author: Where did the ad show up?
Mr. J: It appeared in *book.naver.com*
Author: I'm having a hard time finding them. Can you give me the link?
Mr. J: Here they are. (A web address was offered.)
Author: How long would these announcements stay at the sites?
Mr. J: Four weeks.

Since Seoul and Las Vegas follow a 14-hour time difference and since a weekend was involved in the above email exchange, it has taken a week to obtain the above information. My first boss at the industrial position almost 50 years ago told me that successful communication is based on empathy: voluntarily offer all information to the other party that I believe they might be interested in. It was one of the best pieces of advice I have ever received in my life. The young man Mr. J needs to pay attention to our communications. Or must I have been more specific in my first email? It would be boring for Mr. J to preempt all my inquiries since he must be facing this sort of questions day in day out. For him, my question was one of the hundreds he deals with. But for me, it was a one-time inquiry of paramount significance. If he is the type who licks the watermelon as he was asked, he may stay at the current position for a while. (06/24/2021)

357. Three-inch togue ruins five-foot body.
세 치 혀가 다섯 자 몸 망친다.

This proverb introduces two units for length: *chi* (치) and *ja* (자). The former, approximately 3 cm, is one-tenth of the latter, 30 cm. I simply translate them to an inch and foot, respectively. The proverb says that the tongue, only three-inch-long, can destroy the five-foot body, emphasizing once again the importance of *maal*. It is one of the most popular topics we find in Korean old sayings. See, for example, Entries #1, 10, 15, 23, 180, 199, 209, 250, and 275. In fact, the title of the first volume of this essay series was one of them: *The tongue can break bones*, almost the same as the above.

Why were our ancestors so careful with *maal* or what you say? I am quite sure of Chinese influence on it. They were trenched with wisdom and philosophy derived from long-standing Confucianism. After the Tang dynasty collapsed in 907 and before the Song dynasty unified China in 960, there was a great deal of turmoil with many tribal nations, commonly referred to as *Ten Nations in Five Generations*. During this period, a scholar named Poong-do (Korean pronunciation) shrewdly survived numerous factional infights to his way to a premier position in one of the remaining nations. His political skill must have been akin to that of Machiavelli several centuries later in Italy. Poong-do's thoughts on *maal* are presented below.

口是禍之門 (입은 재앙을 여는 문이고): Lips are the door to calamity,
舌是斬身刀(혀는 자신을 베는 칼이니): the tongue is the knife slaying you.
閉口深藏舌(입을 닫고 혀를 깊숙이 간직한다면): Tongue deep inside the mouth
安身處處宇(어디서나 거뜬히 몸을 편히 하리라): will keep you in eternal peace.

In short, our ancestors thought, and I was accordingly taught, that silence is indeed best for my interest. We were discouraged to open our mouths. In contrast, in this country, parents and teachers encourage us to speak our minds. While Americans teach how to speak while our parents taught us not to speak at all. Both philosophies have merits depending on circumstances. I am not here to call for a judgment one way or another.

In both cultures, the lesson we are to learn is what you have said would have a consequence you have to live with throughout your life. Our ancestors took a passive approach and decided to avoid all grave consequences simply by keeping mouths shut. You will not be blamed for nothing said. Indeed, Poong-do survived the political chaos of his time quite well with few words and a bowed head. Americans eagerly express their thoughts and opinions but supposedly with utmost care lest the consequence drags them down to deep trouble afterward. The fifteen-minute fame on cable news and social media is simply too much a temptation for many people.

It is said that nobody cares to remember long-gone lies by public figures. This is not true in my case, although surviving memories are somewhat selective. In 1988, Al Sharpton, one of the most prominent civil rights activists of our time, made big headlines throughout the summer describing how a 15-year-old African American girl Tawana Brawley was raped by a gang of white men, smeared with feces, and stuffed in a garbage bag. One of the assailants, according to Brawley, was Steven Pagones, a New York prosecutor. Sharpton decried a coverup and suggested the involvement of the Ku Klux Klan, the Irish Republic Army, and Mafia.

As it turned out, it was all faux. Pagones sued Brawley and her advisers including Sharpton for defamation, and won the case. Later, Sharpton's former aide revealed that Sharpton had never been concerned about Brawley but was using the case to "take over the town" or making them "the biggest niggers in New York." Lately, whenever I see Sharpton on TV, I just change the channel. A poll taken at that time showed that 85% of whites believed that Brawley was lying while only 34% of blacks did, a prelude to the O.J. Simpson trial in 1995.

Just yesterday, a New York court suspended the former New York City mayor Rudy Giuliani from the practice of law because he lied to "courts, lawmakers and the public at large in his capacity as lawyer for former President Donald J. Trump." This man and Al Sharpton should have followed Poong-do's teaching and kept their mouth shut.

Nowadays we are constantly bombarded with so much new "breaking news" that I sometimes cannot distinguish what is true and what is fake. Besides, such a fast pace of news cycles appears to accelerate the rate of lies. (06/25/2021)

358. Time is medicine.
세월이 약이다.

"Time heals all wounds," says this proverb. Living is homeostasis in our favor. At some point in our lives, the equilibrium tilts toward the surroundings and we become ill. With time, some survive and others succumb. Either way, time serves as the ultimate cure.

All feelings of the past stay in memory: some last long, others fade quickly. Fond memories tend to last long: my name displayed along with other applicants who had passed the entrance exam to Kyung-gi Middle school in 1955, the first extramural research grant in 1992, and my own wedding ceremony belatedly in 1996?　Sad memories also linger for the rest of our lives. The memory of the mother, longing to be exact, was most intense immediately after her passing. Although I have continuously missed her, I think of her less often nowadays. Again, time will do that.

In 2018, my wife June Cho resigned from Duke University out of frustration, anger, resentment, impotence, and more. She had lost legal litigation against the University in a court battle. It all happened only three years ago, but what is the point of regurgitating unhappy old memories throughout our lives. Time is indeed medicine. When we breathe the last breath, nothing will matter.

Early 2015, she began to have acrimonious interactions with the Vice Dean of her School of Nursing. It was a gradual development as she could not recall any single eruption of shouting match. It is not uncommon that administrators in academia, once deciding to give a professor a hard time, can make the professor's life miserable and ruin the career in many subtle ways that they can justify on the paper. See also Entry #317, "Beating the boulder with an egg."

In her case, the Vice Dean started to interfere with the research project my wife had just started with a great deal of enthusiasm with a brand-new research grant that was transferred to Duke from her previous position at the University of Alabama at Birmingham. I cannot tell how the "bad blood" began between them, but in every turn, my wife had to defend her work in minute details, wasting much of her time and labor. In all cases, the University ruled in my wife's favor, which perhaps irritated and angered the Vice Dean more.   At some point, my wife felt that she had enough of the nonsense and decided to submit a formal grievance report to the University. That was when the waves of retaliation from her School administrators began in earnest.

The "harassment" from the Vice Dean and her cronies including their concocted claims were all well documented as evidence, but it was not sufficient enough for the University Grievance Committee or the federal Equal Employment Opportunity Commission to make a ruling in her favor. In the end, her charge was submitted with as many as 26 pieces of evidence to the NC Middle District Court, where a judge dismissed the case for a lack of evidence. The most maddening part was our realization that the court of law is little to do with truth and justice but more with the law itself. By that time, I had already retired and hence we could move to another university of my wife's choice. Within a short period of three years, we have now forgotten all about that particular chapter of our life.

Time, as we perceive now, will cease to exist when we die. The following is from an essay, *How to Die* by Kim Hoon (김훈), a 74-year-old contemporary Korean writer:

The other day, I went to a crematory for a dear friend's funeral. There was a queue of hearses and buses at the front of the building. As a coffin was lowered to the furnace, the "incineration" light was blinking under his name. Forty minutes later it said, "completed," followed by 10 minutes of "colling." A decade ago, it used to take about 100 minutes but technology has now advanced: ash, less than a gallon, was poured onto a conveyor belt. An employee collected the ash in an envelope and handed it to the family. His oldest son carried it in a jar hung on the neck and led the funeral procession. Not many people shed tears. Kids in the waiting lobby were playing video games on their cell phones while enjoying ice cream.

The ash bid adieu in absolute silence, showing nothing to the bereaved family and friends. Yet, the absurdity of this abrupt ending looked proper and even offered peace. The dead cannot describe death for our benefit. We, the live ones, cannot experience death. Then, I realized how heavy our lives are and how light death is. (06/26/2021)

359. Wearing a silk dress in the dark night.

비단옷 입고 밤길 간다.

Stargazing is something I have wanted to do in the past several years, but I needed a dark sky first. Now that I am living in a desert town of Southern Nevada, there should be many places to visit for a dark night sky. I have not yet solved the logistics involved such as where to stay overnight, but I have investigated a few potential places. Death Valley National Park, which is only a two-hour drive away from here, is highly recommended for stargazing. They suggest a trip around the annual Death Valley Dark Sky Festival. If I can drive a few more hours, I can visit Tonopah, the world capital of stargazing.

I understand that in places like Tonopah, you cannot see anything beyond a few yards in a typical night. Then, why would one wish to dress up in fancy clothes to go out to a dark night? After all, nobody can see what you are wearing anyway. This is the question behind the above proverb, saying that one's behavior depends on circumstance: we should not, for instance, be rowdy at a funeral parlor or in a museum. However, a more common interpretation of the proverb describes a situation where you have nothing to show although you have invested a great deal of effort and time into something.

Thermodynamics is concerned with the initial and final states, not so much about the process the system has undergone between the two states. The return of a boomerang represents a zero-sum event although it might have flown in the air for a while. As I mentioned earlier in Entry #108, "Licking fingers after pulling a dried pollack," one of the most frustrating occasions that a research scientist experiences is when a project sponsored by a federal grant (i.e., tax money) fails to produce any positive results, significant enough to disseminate to others through publication. It is not exactly a failure as the investigator eventually learns what went wrong, a valuable lesson in itself.

I have wanted to see a professional journal available, which is devoted to reports of "failed" experiments so that others can learn from the failure. I sure have had many failed research projects and frustrating hours of my students, for which I apologize belatedly.

There is a trade magazine called *Journal of Irreproducible Results*, but it is primarily for parody and humor.

In this highly competitive world, the successful outcome tends to justify means, often marginally ethical ones. "Losers" appear to have no place in our society. Here, I am using the words, success and failure, from an objective viewpoint, but those folks who have been enjoying spectacular success and fame may not be very happy by and in themselves. Unhappy millionaires may be a dozen a dime but so seems successful scientists. As a scientist, I must confess that often my own works looked fantastic to others but more often they look awfully trivial to me. I often wondered if the feeling of triviality was just a reflection of my own inferiority complex or humbleness.

Kurt Gödel (1906–1978) was one of the most respected logicians and mathematicians in his lifetime. During later years at the Institute for Advanced Study at Princeton, however, he believed that he had not achieved the goals that he had set out for himself. He firmly considered himself a failure and believed that the Institute would fire him any day. He thought he had done nothing significant because he thought he was not talented enough. In reality, he worked on his own field in his own way, as most pioneers do. In his mind, however, they were not fashionable enough and he felt guilty for not being productive as he did as a young man in Vienna.

Gödel was Einstein's closest companion at the Institute. Einstein himself confessed that his own work by then did not amount to much, but he came into the office "just to have the privilege of being permitted to walk home with Gödel. "They were an established Princeton sight, the almost comically mismatched pair making their way home each afternoon across the sweeping lawn of the institute grounds, opposite in almost every personal trait. Einstein with his unruly hair, baggy sweater, and suspenders: looking "like a good old grandpapa while Gödel was solemn, serious, rail-thin, immaculately dressed on the hottest summer's day ...."

Even his great work, *the Incompleteness Theorem*, was no longer a consolation. All of his contributions, Gödel sadly observed, were of a negative kind – proving that something *cannot* be done, not what *can* be done. In the end, Gödel succumbed to debilitating paranoia: he would eat only food that his wife prepared for him. Eventually, he starved to death: Read *Journey to the Edge of Reason* by Stephen Budiansky. (06/29/2021)

360. The sky seen through the eye of a needle.
바늘 구멍으로 하늘 보기.

I am not sure if anyone really knows how big our universe is. One crude estimate from the Big Bang Theory is that the universe must have a minimum diameter of 23 trillion light-years and is still expanding. If you care to calculate the figure, here is the speed of light: 300,000 km/sec or 186,000 miles/sec. What would you observe if you see this vast space through a tiny pinhole the size of a needle's eye? One's attempt to do so is their prerogative, but when they start to behave as though they understand everything about the universe and force others to believe them, some serious troubles begin.

What we learn from a given observation depends on the person, like blind men describing an elephant. Add the factor of time: you have the history interpreted in as many ways as historians. The first-century Roman Emperor, Nero, is portrayed as a tyrant and has been accused of having an incestuous relationship with his mother, of killing his first two wives, and of being generally evil enough to burn down Rome while fiddling (remember Peter Ustinov in the 1951 movie *Quo Vadis*?). Now, the British Museum offers an alternative narrative of a young man who became emperor when he was not yet 17 and was driven to suicide by his adversaries at 30. The museum director says that charges against Nero have been "based on manipulations and lies that are 2,000 years old and very powerful. In reality, he was trying very hard, and he was dealt an extremely bad hand." See Farah Nayeri in the 05/26/2021 issue of *the New York Times*.

The history of Nero and Rome is so old that however one may interpret them it bears little practical significance in our current lives. Nobody is going to raise the hell out of ancient history with a raised jugular vein and white-knuckled fists. The most recent incident, the attack on the U.S. Capitol on January 6, has been universally condemned and treated as such by the law enforcement personnel. However, there have been some politicians who watched the insurrection through the eye of a needle. Even with such a narrow viewfinder, they should have watched the videotapes and shut up their mouths for good, but instead, they have been disseminating their "noble" opinions as if everybody else was wrong.

A Republican senator from Wisconsin, Ron Johnson, said that the attack on the U.S. Capitol was not an insurrection but a largely "peaceful protest. I condemned the violence, but to say there were thousands of armed insurrectionists breaching the Capitol intent on overthrowing the government is just simply false narrative." Paul Gosar, another Republican House member from Arizona, chastised the FBI for having the nerve to ask the public's help in tracking down what he called "peaceful patriots." Not to be the second fiddle to these "ground-breaking" observations, Andrew Clyde from Georgia said, "If you didn't know that TV footage was a video from January the sixth, you would actually think it was a normal tourist visit." Are they describing the universe as seen through the eye of a needle?

Biased opinions are often from skewed observations, which can be formed by misinformation. It is further aided by hatred of other people who do not agree with their belief or by the anger from within themselves against perceived injustice upon them. In Entry #114, "A one-day-old puppy isn't afraid of a tiger," I introduced the concept of active ignorance and described how dangerous an actively ignorant person can be. When those like-minded people get together, they encourage and believe in each other forming a herd mentality that could collectively produce a brutal force. By this point of thought development, they know everything better than anybody else: see Entry #78, "Three shoemakers can outsmart Einstein." This brief analysis is one way to look at the January the sixth insurrection.

Is examining something via a pinhole always a bad practice? Not at all. However, it should follow a broad survey of the field. It is a desirable exercise of focus to aim for depth rather than breadth. When we gaze at a particular star with a telescope, first we will have to use a low magnification to find the general area where your target is. It is just a matter of saving time in settling on the target.

Before I retired, I had offered my share of reviewing grant proposals for the National Institutes of Health. Just like other old reviewers, I always tried to give a favorable score for new investigators. However, I could not be always generous when these young and ambitious investigators tried to do everything under the sun. When there was no focus, there is very little I could do. It is indeed a good practice to select an appropriate aperture in a camera for the desired field of depth. (07/01/2021)

361. A ship with multiple captains climbs up a mountain.
사공이 많으면 배가 산으로 올라간다.

The interesting word in this proverb is *sa-gong* or 사공. It means an oarsman or a rower in a small boat like a ferry. It thus says, "If there are too many oarsmen in a boat, it can and will likely climb up a mountain. To modernize the nuance, I am just using the words "captain" and "ship." It would be equivalent to: "Too many cooks spoil the broth." The proverb has been quite popular in Korea and was in fact introduced earlier in passing in Entry #12, "Hands and feet should work together in a burglary." At that time, I said I am surprised to see that the US Congress, with 100 senators and 435 House Representatives, has not yet flown to the end of this universe, not to mention Himalaya.

Diversity is always desirable in, among many aspects of our lives, deriving the best decision, cultural understanding, education of empathy, releasing racial tension, etc. Just imagine how boring a monotonous society would be. Accommodating diversity is particularly rewarding after an initial helter-skelter is all satisfactorily resolved in a renewed sense of a common goal. Working together in a team sport is an essential part of winning, as in rowing in unison. Individuals may be ordinary and often weak entities but, they can be strong and victorious as a whole. And yet, as the above proverb says, we often spend way too much time emphasizing differences between us, usually on trivial matters, rather than in finding a common ground.

I now wonder what makes some people willing to work with others in earnest while other people always show cold shoulders to any plea for cooperation. If I may generalize, self-confident people seem to be more willing to collaborate even with those whose opinions often differ from their own. They seem to have abundant space in the room for accommodating different views and ideals. They are generally more outgoing in human interactions and optimistic in life. People flock around such individuals with positive outlooks.

People I usually find difficult to work with are those who tend to be self-righteous with an analytical mind. Often, they are a great speaker and maintain excellent persuasive power, perhaps at the expense of becoming poor listeners. Korean churches in this country, for example, are a good place to find those who seem to "know all." This is perhaps because the social gathering at a Korean church is where elderly parishioners can fully express themselves in our mother tongue: see more in Entry #167, "Flapping wings under a blanket."

In the case of a competitive sports game, working together comes by easily since participants in a team have one common desire: defeating the other team to move on to the next round of the tournament. One could say it is a matter of survival. In a similar token, if the world finds a common goal or common enemy to defeat, can we have a unified world, United Nations in a true sense? Many nations who have been fighting each other will become allies to deal with a common threat: it would be a matter of survival.

The Unidentified Flying Object (UFO) may serve such a purpose well. Just last week, the US government confessed in a much-waited report that they do not know anything about the UFO but at least they acknowledged its existence. As far as the Pentagon is concerned, there is no evidence that any of the UFO episodes are associated with some secret American weapons programs or unknown technology from Russia or China or extraterrestrial visitations. But they did not rule out any of these possibilities, either.

The document released by the Office of the Director of National Intelligence concluded that some of the episodes reported show technological capabilities that are unknown to the United States: for example, objects are moving at an extremely fast speed. Such technology must be also beyond the capabilities of Russia and China, the report concluded. Once again, UFO is a fertile ground for world peace. Both Russia and China will draw the same conclusion, which by default implies the existence of extraterrestrial visitations.

China and Russia will be working with the States to solve the mysterious UFO phenomena. The UFOs are now from our common enemy! Forget about wars and conflicts in Afghanistan, Ukraine, North Korea, Iran, and every corner of this world. Maybe, just maybe, some smart leaders can tie the UFO business to the change in global climate also. In due time all nations on this beautiful planet Earth will unite to develop one frontline of defense against these invading enemies. Let us just hope that those wise heads of state like Biden, Putin, Xi, et al. seize this opportunity for world peace. As stated in Entry #290, "Charcoal briquettes burn better together." The UFO may bring all of us together to become one *sa-gong*. (07/04/2021)

362. Eat the liver of a flea.

벼룩의 간을 내어 먹는다.

This proverb is the same as: "Skin a flea for its hide." It illustrates a situation where someone tries to take away something from a person who does not have anything. Just after Korean War, most families suffered from poverty. However, tax collectors were as active as before. I remember when they confiscated my mother's sewing machine and how sobbing my mother was. It was one of a few valuables she had, or our family owns. I must have been seven years old. I still recall the impotence I felt deep in my bone. It was akin to extracting the liver of a flea for dinner. A few days later, we somehow managed to get it back, but I resented the seemingly cruel tax collector as much as the poverty our family lived in.

What are the things that one can lose or give up only under a most strenuous circumstance? A random list may include religious belief, valuable possessions including money and real-estate properties, domestic safety and security, health care, right to education, the pursuit of happiness, mobility right, etc. These are all under the umbrella of basic human rights in terms of liberty and freedom. An autocratic nation can deprive them of individual citizens. This is only if citizens are aware of such concepts as, say, the right to happiness.

Citizens, gather 'round your loudspeakers, for we bring important updates! In your kitchens, in your offices, on your factory floors – wherever your loudspeaker is located, turn up the volume! In local news, our Dear Leader Kim Jong Il (Kim Jong-Un's father) was seen offering on-the-spot guidance to the engineers deepening the Taedong River channel. While the Dear Leader lectured to the dredge operators, many doves were seen to spontaneously flock above him, hovering to provide our Reverend General some much needed shade on a hot day. Also to report is a request from Pyongyang's Minister of Public Safety, who asks that while pigeon-snaring season is in full swing, trip wires and snatch loops be placed out of the reach of our youngest comrades. And don't forget, citizens: the ban on stargazing is still in effect. (from *Orphan Master's Son* by Adam Johnson)

If a new generation of North Koreans do not know what they are missing simply because they are ignorant, how can we tell them that they are being robbed of something most basic in humanity? Their older generations who may still remember the taste of freedom must disappear soon if not already put into prison. Just look at the situation in Hong Kong: children are now facing the early stage of indoctrination of Communism, while most of the older activists, especially journalists, are already in prison, possibly subject to re-education programs. As with the 1989 Tiananmen Square protests, the current struggle to recover the freedom they once enjoyed will slowly fade into memory lane. That is the brain-wash at its best.

The former president Donald Trump used to brag about his ability to avoid paying taxes and fought hard to hide his tax returns from prosecutors and from Congress. Now, we know that he paid no income tax in some years with massive write-offs. His strategy was making property seem less valuable for tax purposes and more valuable when he wants to appear wealthy. So far, Trump has not been formally charged for tax evasion. For that matter, he may never be charged for tax evasion.

However, on the 24th of June, the prosecutors from the office of the Manhattan district attorney filed 15 felony counts against the Trump Organization for a tax scheme stretching back to 2005. The indictment also alleged that the Chief Financial Officer Allen Weisselberg of the Organization has evaded a total of more than $900,000 in federal, state, and city taxes during this period and that he received approximately $130,000 in state tax refunds to which he was not entitled.

Trump has been calling the investigation into his tax practice a witch-hunt and his lawyers will fight for their money at the court vigorously in coming months. While news outlets will have field days, ordinary citizens will be left with a puzzling question as to how such a crime has never been exposed before. But we know something was fishy when a financial wizard Warren Buffett paid taxes at a lower rate than his secretary. This household is in a tax bracket close to the 30 percentile. Why is the Internal Revenue Service trying to cut out "the liver of a flea" while it lets a big and fat fish swim freely mocking the public openly? (07/05/2021)

363. A sheet of paper is lighter when lifted together.

백지장도 맞들면 낫다.

How much would a sheet of paper, say, 8.5" x 11" in size, weigh? Not much, and one can easily lift with two fingers. And yet, the above proverb says it is always lighter if people lift it together, perhaps not so much to save the energy but in the spirit of collaboration. Your job is much more fun if there is another person working with you. The "parable of the arrow," introduced in Entry #290, "Charcoal briquettes burn better together," also said that one plus one could be more than two in synergy.

Why do we cooperate with other people? The major reason for helping each other must be some sort of implied reward, although some altruistic, high-minded motives can be in play also. Such an urge as compassion for the needy is so fundamental in humanity that it needs not to be from religious teachings. I suppose that most human interactions are within these two boundaries, one calculated act and the other blind compassion.

In the case of animal behaviors, one can design experiments to address some basic issues involved in the "cooperative pulling paradigm." The simplest device would be a reward placed on a platform to which two strings are attached. It is too heavy for one animal to pool but two of them can do it together. More sophisticated devices to test more complicated hypotheses may require a higher level of intelligence. We often watch such experiments in a Public Broadcasting Service TV program that involves dogs, wolves, chimpanzees, and even birds like ravens.

The key to their success is, of course, an understanding of cooperation and the ability to perform intentional coordination to achieve a goal. The more I read about these experiments, the more complex conclusions I encounter, especially in terms of their relevance to human cooperative behaviors. As more individual chimpanzees discover a new way to obtain food through cooperation, researchers find that the competition among them also increases. Dominant apes displaced others, monopolizing the device used in the experiment. Those bullies freeloaded as well as took the food others worked for.

The competition gradually leads to fewer cooperative acts. Dominant individuals are unable to recruit partners and abandon the test apparatus, which entails aggressive protest from others, and freeloaders are punished by third-party arbiters. With time, the ape group manages to restore and increase levels of cooperative behavior by various enforcement techniques. When the researchers repeat this experiment with a new group of chimpanzees who have not yet established a social hierarchy, they again find that cooperation overcame competition in the long run. Novice chimpanzees learn quickly from elders, albeit with limited understanding of the task.

Much of animal behaviors was exactly what we would expect from humans or vice versa. I am sure though that such resemblance in behavior would disappear as the test animal is further away from homo sapiens in the evolutionary tree. I would also think that the necessity of cooperation depends on the nature of the goal. The ultimate reason for working with others remains the same: reward.

I used to volunteer for a soup kitchen, serving breakfast for the needy. We had to be at the facility by 5:30 AM, which is not a trivial feat during the dark and cold winter mornings, to prepare meals in advance. One memory I still cherish is that I would be in an upbeat mood throughout the day I served them. Everything was agreeable on that day. If this isn't a reward, what is? Altruistic works by Albert Schweitzer in Africa or Mother Teresa in India are attributed to their religious conviction: however, one can argue that it all led to the feeling of self-reward. The same conclusion can be made in all cases of working together for a noble cause.

In the business world, the words, cooperation and competition, sound like an oxymoron. In fact, too much cooperation between competitors can bring an anti-trust suit from the government if not other competitors and consumers. Monopoly comes mainly from patent protection. Even in this case, the Biden administration decided in May to waive the right involved in COVID-19 vaccines as the move would enable more companies to get into the vaccine-manufacturing business, easing supply shortages and helping with the monumental task of vaccinating the whole world. Because of this decision, I may not gain as much as otherwise from the Pfizer stocks I own, but I don't have any problem as it was the right thing to do. (07/06/2021)

364. Cats cleansing their faces.

고양이 세수하듯 한다.

This is how I wash my face over a basin. With both hands, I scoop running water directly from the faucet and splash it onto my face. Then I would vigorously rub the face with both hands up and down with or without soap. If I feel ambitious, I also go over the back of the neck as thoroughly as I can. Excess water during this maneuver drips along the elbow onto the benchtop. When it is over and dry up the face and the arms with a towel, I invariably feel great just looking at the clean face in the mirror. If I am in hurry (maybe an excuse), then I leave the puddles of water around the sink as it is. It is a mess.

Cats do not have the luxury to use tap water. They wet the inner part of the paw with the tongue several times and rub the face with the thoroughly cleaned paw: right paw for the right side of the face and left for the left side. Like us, they keep their eyes closed during the cleaning. Unlike us, however, their face moves more than paw. Occasionally, they also go through the bottom of the paw with the sandpaper-like tongue as if there was something lodged between nails. I am not a cat person, but I must admit that a healthy cat knows how to keep their body always clean and shiny, although they do not enjoy any wet bath offered by people.

As thorough as it may sound, cats washing their faces in this proverb metaphorically represents a person who works on an assignment quite superficially with minimal effort. This expression is likely from what appears to be the cat's minimalistic approach to washing their face: like when a kid washes the family car because he was asked to. It is different from washing and waxing your own car on a warm spring day with a pending date in the evening.

For a change, you feel like tidying and cleaning the front yard, perhaps unconsciously expecting some word of praise from your mother or even from your neighbor for the good deed that is never expected by anyone. Now, as you are about to grab the broom, your mother yells at you, "why can't you sweep the yard instead of lying down doing nothing!" Your good intention disappears in a heartbeat. You will certainly lose the enthusiasm and sweeping the front yard becomes a chore you will do like a cat washing his face.

146

Washing a car or sweeping the floor is a simple task, but the quality of the outcome depends on the mood of the person. Why do people finish shoddy work, which may affect many lives later? Would it be the result of honest mistakes or deliberate planning? The results, loss of lives and property, might be the same; however, society and the law may treat them differently depending on the cause.

On June 29, 1995, one of the fanciest department stores in Seoul, Sampoong Department Store, collapsed or "pancaked," killing over 500 people and injuring about a thousand. The building was originally designed for a residential apartment building with four floors. During construction, however, the head of the project, Lee Joon, decided to change the plan for a large department store. This new plan cut away several support columns to install escalators. Besides, they added another floor, the fifth one.

The building was completed in 1989 but later expanded bits and pieces without much scrutiny and tests for safety. Several hours before the collapse, amid customers complaining about building vibration from air conditioner systems, they realized that collapse of the building was imminent. At an emergency meeting, the directors suggested to Lee that all customers should be evacuated, but Lee refused to do so for fear of revenue losses. Lee himself left the building just before the collapse. Later he was sentenced to a 10-year jail term. See also Entry #179, "Save a penny, or *pun* (푼), to lose a fortune?"

Several thousands of miles away and 26 years later, a 12-story condo building in Surfside, FL, pancaked in the middle of the night - just like Sampoong Department Store. For the past two weeks, rescue crews have moved tons of concrete and recovered dozens of bodies. Beginning yesterday, the searchers are no longer looking for survivors. Their mission was changed from "rescue" to "recovery." As of this writing, the death toll has risen to 60, with 35 victims identified. Eighty people are still classified as missing.

It could take months to determine the cause of the collapse, but there are already some clues, including design or construction flaws. Inspectors talk about major structural damage to the concrete slab below the pool deck and numerous cracking and crumbling of the columns, beams, and walls of the parking garage. Putting aside all the expert analyses, we can safely conclude that the common cause of both collapses was saving money. (07/06/2021)

365. Bad news travels faster,

나쁜 소문은 빨리 퍼진다.

I do not know why it is the case, but it may just be my perception: people are usually misers in praising or congratulating others when an occasion calls for. It was not always easy to congratulate colleagues who had just received a big research grant while I had been struggling for a few years. Was it out of envy or jealousy? Or the feeling of my own failure? Not that saying a few congratulatory words costs anything on my part. When a colleague receives a grant, our department chair used to announce the good news at our faculty meeting, handing in a bottle of champagne to the grantee.

When I did receive the bottle, it used to put me in an awkward situation as if I did not deserve it or any congrats from my colleagues. Now that I am retired, I can talk about such a moment in the past tense. I might not have been generous in praising or congratulating others, but I can say for a record that I did not speak ill of others behind their back. In fact, I used to avoid those who spread ill-intended gossip as I was afraid that I could be the next victim of their sharp tongue. It was simply a matter of self-defense. In essence, the above proverb is saying the same: in general, opinions criticizing others travel faster and more widely than the words of praise.

In Gresham's Law of "bad money drives out good," the good coin with a face value greater than the commodity value (i.e., the value of the metal used in the coin) disappears in the circulation while bad coins with a commodity value considerably lower than its face value dominate. This is because people spend bad coins, keeping the good ones for themselves. In an analogy, we can state that useless stories are more abundant at a given time in any society. Just look at what is being circulated on the internet-based social media and other platforms of anonymous "free expressions." I have just come across another fake news that Kim Jong-Un died of a cerebral hemorrhage. I do not know how many lives he has but we even saw his funeral several months ago. Close to home, millions of Americans believe that Donald Trump is the legitimate president and that COVID-19 vaccines developed by hard-working scientists are of little use but with many side effects.

I am now only a few years away from becoming an octogenarian. No news from old friends is no longer good news. A long silence makes me wonder if everything is alright with friends with whom I have maintained the frequent exchange of news. Friends might have complained about his body weight, high cholesterol, sleep apnea, blood pressure, teeth, overactive bladder, arthritic knees, hearing problem, dry eye (in my case), etc. When any one of these is getting worse, the suffering friend may find it "why bother" to write a note to me, which is exactly the cause of my concern.

Before various electronic means became widely available, we had two ways of communication: a phone call and letters. Most often, they would deliver real news. Not anymore: they are either unsolicited calls or printed ad materials for you-name-it: furniture sale, cremation appointment, new grocery store, car insurance, hearing aids, denture, credit card, shopping club, realtor, termite control, etc. When printed X-Mas newsletters started to arrive, announcing how well their family has been doing, what a wonderful summer vacation they had together, which daughter married whom, etc., I begin to realize that more impersonal letters would materialize in the future. Gone are the days you draw X-Mas cards yourself and write real news with your own hand in cursive letters. It was painstaking but receiving such ones was such a great pleasure and hence I used to do the same.

Nowadays, more personal communication is via cell phone: texting, Kakao Talk, and email. I do not have an account with Facebook, Instagram, Tick Talk, and all other online social networks. I just don't see much benefit in joining the crowd. More than 150 high school classmates are currently participating in a Kakao Talk chatroom. As we have lived more days than days to live, we do have more memories than plans. Most of the posts are thus about the events that occurred almost a half-century ago. This is particularly true for those classmates having lived in this country. Even this sharing of memories seems to max out. More frequent is a simple announcement of departure from this world of a classmate along with the arrangement of the funeral and memorial service. We are curious about the cause of death, but it is seldom announced. We just shrug it off saying, another one has left us. It becomes the occasion to ask myself how long I would live, but more importantly how I ought to live the rest of my life. At least it is a plan. (07/09/2020)

366. Chicken and cow glancing each other.

닭 소 보듯, 소 닭 보듯 한다.

They, cow and chicken, neither hate nor love each other. There is nothing for them to share or fight against: feeds, temperament, size, habit, playing field, movement, activity, etc. are all different. One thing common may well be that they share their owner. But the farmer respects their independence. The cow goes to the field with the farmer in the morning while chickens are fed by the farmer's wife. The only time they come across would be the evening hours: by then each will be ready for a well-deserved rest. If apathy is an active form of disregard, it is not the proper word to describe their lack of interactions. They simply do not mean much to each other, period.

One of my favorite equations in a physical chemistry textbook is the so-called Lennard-Jones (L-J) Potential. In Entry #34, "A man in love salutes his in-laws' horse post," I used it in describing human interactions. The following is an excerpt from the essay.

It describes the energy associated with two atoms as a function of the distance between them. When they are far away from each other, as in two total strangers, there is no energy involving the two atoms. As the two approach each other, they develop some sort of attractive force with its total energy lower than the sum of the energy from each. There is an optimal distance with the lowest energy (and hence a most stable state) between the two atoms, or a desirable relationship in a couple by analogy. Interestingly, according to the L-J Potential, the total energy involved shoots up exponentially as they come too close, rendering the system extremely unstable.

In analogy to the L-J Potential, the chickens and the cow are figuratively far away with neither attractive nor repulsive force upon them, although they may cohabit on the same premises. The eye-to-eye contact would require some effort from both animals. The cow will not have any problem looking down, but chickens have to look up to the cow. This would require some effort, as they are usually accustomed to pecking ground for grains. They may say, "why bother."

A high school kid has been eying on a particular girl at a party all night, but she does not seem to acknowledge his presence. He tried to catch and hold her glance in his direction for a few seconds, but, alas, it has not happened so far. He can tell his friends later that she was like a chicken around a cow. The car salesman who has sold you a car does not recognize or pretends that he has never met you when you bring the car in for service. The busy waitress who has served you the dinner seems to have forgotten you. In both cases, you would be a cow among chickens.

A socially ill-treated class is formed not only by the color of skin but by demographic factors such as wealth, gender, age, religion, education, political inclination, birthplace, etc. There is no point in going over again what we all know: "money lets you open all doors." Discrimination based on gender has become less of a social problem lately. In fact, the issue has become expanded to a broader range of subjects involved in LGBTQ (lesbian, gay, and bisexual, transsexual/ transgender, queer). More recently, two more letters were added: I for intersex and A for asexual, no matter what they mean.

In agriculture-based, slow-paced societies, the older generation was treated quite well with reverence. Regardless of whether they deserved it or not, my generation, for instance, seldom stood against the teaching and advice from the elder, especially our own parents. In a modern, "fast-and-furious," society based on computer technologies, my generation has been standing still amidst new developments. We become bewildered even in a simple task like ordering a hamburger at a fast-food joint. To the younger generations, we seem to be perpetually struggling with any new technology platforms of any kind. Among our contemporaries, the use of emoji or idiotic abbreviations used in Kakao Talk is frowned upon, but that is exactly how we become obsolete and isolated from the rest of society.

Of other factors listed above, one's birthplace can indicate not only familial pedigree but also status on a global stage. Many North Korean defectors to the South were initially welcomed, but not anymore. Japanese passport is said to be best accommodated in the world. If you are Japanese, that would be something you can brag about. The demography seems to assign a group of people to the class, which may collectively see others like a cow towards a chicken. It is an unfortunate observation I have made throughout my long life. (07/11/2021)

367. Even a flea has a face to carry around.

벼룩도 낯짝이 있다.

The principal of the high school I attended believed in pride in each of us that was associated with the high esteem of the school. I guess it originally stemmed from the fact that we were smart kids, intelligent enough to have passed the highly competitive entrance exam for admission. At any rate, the school was recognized as such by all parents who had children of our age. At that time, perhaps unlike nowadays in Korea, kids entering a prominent preparatory school was one of the most important dreams of their parents as it likely opens a door to elite universities.

Every morning, the principal exalted the word, pride, in our school-wide gathering. Impressionable age we were in, his sermon had perhaps the greatest impact on our lives. Oxford dictionary defines pride as "the quality of having an excessively high opinion of oneself or one's own importance." It is "the justified love of oneself," as opposed to false pride or narcissism. One positive influence of his teaching and our teachers, especially those alumni of the same school years ago, was that we are a specially "chosen" cohort of students with a bright future. They bestowed chips upon our shoulders. Maintaining such status throughout our lives has inevitably mandated supportive data in actions and behaviors. Since we are graduates of this highly revered school, we cannot behave like a jerk from other so-so schools. As I look back, it has placed a heavy burden on all of us.

This is where the above proverb finds relevance. Even such a minuscule and worthless creature like a flea has a face, or pride. How can you be otherwise as a human being! For crying it loud, you are a graduate of this high school. How could you do this (or that)!

However, the pride engrained in each of us seems to have exerted more harm than the benefits implied above. First, if a circumstance allowed, we tended to become arrogant and self-righteous. We behaved as if we know all. In many instances of interactions with others, we often were smarter and better informed, but we needed not to behave like a nerd. Many of us were also self-centered, if not outright selfish. We wanted to be at the center of the universe, whether it is warranted or not.

I have always considered the word, pride, in a positive connotation. Call it the result of brainwashing. Gradually, however, I began to realize that the usage in opposite nuance is in fact more common as in "pride comes before a fall." Indeed, "it can refer to foolishly and irrationally corrupt sense of one's personal value, status or accomplishments." I now wish our teachers warned us of its dangerous underside. They could have simply taught us the importance of self-esteem without invoking others as a reference.

Although not everyone in their milieu was so elegant, of course, the chance grouping of these girls conferred on all of them a certain grace, elegance, and agility, a disdainful pride that made them seem of a completely different species from the girls in my world. They seemed to me to dress in an extraordinary way that I wouldn't have known how to define, and …. [from Young Girls by Marcel Proust (1871–1922)]

The necessity of "saving one's face" or "maintaining pride" in public is not only from educational level as shown above but also from a family name, nationality, social status, and other circumstances one is under. If you are from a well-respected family, the last thing your clan wishes to see is you bring disgrace to your family name. Just like in old Europe, the so-called *ga-moon* (가문) you were born with plays a critical role in your early life in Korea. "For Pete's sake, you are a grandson of so-and-so!" How can you do this! People who recognize your name must have a certain level and type of expectations.

You cannot be a cheapskate if your parents are a millionaire. If you have a PhD degree in chemistry, others may expect you to be familiar with a certain subject. Since I am from Korea, albeit many decades ago, people ask me about BTS, the Korean pop music group I am not familiar with at all. Or they immediately begin to tell me about an uncle who served in Korean War.

In short, if you have a "face," which you do, then you are supposed to do at least something we, all humans, are to do. There will be many disappointed folks if you do not behave as expected with a person with a "face." If you are a president of this country, for instance, citizens expect you to do your job with decency and integrity. Even a flea has a face and behaves as fleas do. (07/13/2021)

368. Licorice to a medicine man.
약방에 감초.

Without being too technical, I can state that anyone in any organization, say, an employee in a private company would belong to one of the following three categories. In the first category, the employee is absolutely needed and indispensable for the good of the company. Without them, the company suffers a great deal in finance as well as in morale. They may possess the important technical know-how relevant to the company or could be a member of management. They are well compensated and regularly awarded. Their retirement party is quite a send-off event and remains a legend. Needless to say, I tried to be such a member as an employee at two different jobs: one at a pharmaceutical firm and the other at a university. I am not in a position to say that I was successful for the effort.

Employees belonging to the second category are those who are not terribly missed even when they are no longer around. They do commendable jobs, nine to five, day in day out, five days a week. Their daily performance is nothing extraordinary but adequate enough to remain employed. My profession was never of clocking a timecard and yet sometimes I was aware of the stagnant state I was in. My hunch is that most of the employees with nominal authority and responsibility must belong to this category.

The third category consists of people who should not be where they are now. They are the cancer of the organization. They create a toxic environment that will slowly lead the organization and its people to chaos, from which they may not fully recover for a long time. In a twisted logic, this group of people is justified to exist as they serve as a reference for the first category. In most instances, we don't know what to do with these bad people, but all we can do is minimizing their influence on the rest of us. It is difficult though if such an individual is sitting at the Whitehouse and continuously supported by a large number of people belonging to the same category.

Before we go back to the above proverb, we need to quickly review the role of licorice root, *gamcho* (감초), in the traditional herbal medicine in Korea. As described in detail in Entry #42, "Good medicine is usually bitter," the folk medicine was usually prepared by slowly heating up various components, all derived from nature, in water for several hours. The ingredients ranged from dried fruits to exotic animal organs like the gallbladder of a bear. The whole thing is then filtered through a sheet of porous fabric like hemp cloth. The filtered solution was invariably black and tasted awful. To cover the bitter taste, the medicine man always added licorice root.

The above aphorism says that there is no apothecary practicing herbal medicine that does not have licorice root. If they do not keep dried thinly sliced licorice root, they are not practitioners of herbal medicine. Because of its popularity in old medicine, a person who gets involved in nearly everything, or "has a finger in every pie," is commonly referred to as *gamcho.* Most likely they would belong to the first category introduced earlier. They are usually extroverts, friendly to anyone, have a bottomless quantity of ideas and opinion on any topic, present at every party you attend, very good at organizing charity work, somewhat noise but generally well tolerated by peers, generously offer their time and effort.

If we consider *gamcho* analogous to the indispensable keystone that is holding a stone arch work, we can say that Osama bin Laden was a *gamcho* in al-Qaeda. Like a keystone, without him, his organization is no longer a major threat to the Western world. Al Capone, the *gamcho* behind the Saint Valentine Day Massacre, was imprisoned in 1932, effectively undermining the crime syndicate of Chicago.

In some instances, the *gamcho* remains hidden from the public. Many benefactors of charity work, for instance, stay anonymous for various reasons. In 2020, the Centre for Addiction and Mental Health in Toronto received an anonymous donation for $100 million, the biggest donation for mental health research in Canada's history. In 2007, the University of California San Francisco was the recipient of a $150 million anonymous donation for its cancer center. We will never know who these anonymous *gamcho* were.

It was Park Chung-hee (1917–1979) who successfully carried out the military coup in 1961 with a small band of loyal military comrades. He will be remembered as a strong leader or even hailed as a national hero who had modernized Korea. The coup was nominally carried out by then Army Chief of Staff, but it was Park who held the power behind the scene, a hidden *gamcho.* (07/14/2021)

369. Jumping with a dagger between teeth.
칼 물고 뜀뛰기한다.

You would remember a scene in a pirate movie of a one-eyed jack with a cutlass in his mouth jumping from one ship to another on a swinging rope. Imagine a kid skipping a rope with a knife between the teeth. However you may look, it is a very dangerous move you would not recommend your kid to try. But some people show such reckless behavior perhaps for "enjoying" the thrill involved or demonstrating their braveness to others. No matter, it is quite entertaining for onlookers, like watching a gladiator facing a hungry lion, perhaps secretly wishing some tragic ending.

Evel Knievel (1938–2007) was a stunt performer and entertainer. Throughout his career, he attempted more than 75 ramp-to-ramp motorcycle jumps. The initial publicity was from the jump over the fountains at Caesars Palace in Las Vegas in 1967. He tried the longest jump thus far, 141 feet (43 m), but ended up with a crash. After the daredevil show, Knievel became more famous than ever. In 1971, he set a new world record by jumping 19 cars with his Harley-Davidson XR-750. The record survived for 27 years.

His promise to jump over the Grand Canyon never materialized since the US government refused to allow it. Instead, he tried his act at the Snake River Canyon in southern Idaho, where he failed to cross the canyon and almost got drowned. He performed in 1975 at Wembley Stadium in London, trying to jump over 13 London buses but crashed again. During his career, Knievel had suffered more than 433 bone fractures. In one of his last interviews, he said:

You can't ask a guy like me why I performed. I really wanted to fly through the air. I was a daredevil, a performer. I loved the thrill, the money, the whole macho thing. All those things made me Evel Knievel. Sure, I was scared. You gotta be an ass not to be scared. But I beat the hell out of death. [...] You're in the air for four seconds, you're part of the machine, and then if you make a mistake midair, you say to yourself, "Oh, boy. I'm gonna crash," and there's nothing you can do to stop it, not at all.

Every day we live with a certain level of risk. It is part of life, although we do not like those risks beyond our control. We will have to live with possible loss or failure, believing "fortune favors the bold." Risk-taking is subjective: just look around to see how people invest their money. It also depends on an issue involved: taking a vaccine against coronavirus is a no-brainer, while surgically removing a few facial wrinkles may require some self-persuasion.

All companies take a risk one time or another for greater profits, say, with a new line of products being developed by company scientists and engineers. Market analysis is done to avoid undue risks. Here, conservative managers may go for mimicking other existing products with minimal modifications but for a maximal advertisement of putative improvement. Such a complacent approach might have forgotten that the consumers do have the final say. In the long run, they will quickly lose the competition with an innovative product from some small but aggressive companies.

Take Dyson vacuum cleaners as an example. James Dyson, then an employee of Hoover, recognized the superiority of the bagless cyclonic vacuum technology, and approached Hoover for further development and licensing. Hoover did not want to license the design, allegedly because the vacuum bag market was worth $500 million. In effect, Dyson was a threat to their profits. This was happening early 1980s. See how the two companies stand in the current market. There have been many imitators of Dyson vacuum cleaners: the consumer-products maker Amway lost a court battle to Dyson, and you see in Home Depot many vacuum cleaners from other manufacturers that look suspiciously similar to Dyson. True to the word, pioneer, Dyson took plenty of risks while financially struggling. In the end, however, it all paid him a well-deserved dividend.

War is an extremely risky business. The victor may put the leaders of the losing nation on a war tribunal, and they can be executed. Just think about the Nuremberg Trials after World War II. Even the nation that won the war often looks like a loser in terms of human casualty and economic devastation, not to mention ruined infrastructures. For what and whose benefits do we start a war? It is very much like dancing with a dagger in the mouth. (07/17/2021)

370. Meet the lover, pick the mulberry as well,
임도 보고 뽕도 딴다.

If you are to meet your date in the field of mulberry plants, you have two things going for you. First, you get to see your girlfriend or boyfriend whom you have not seen for the past several days. The longing is about to be over, and your heart is full of excitement and happiness. What better event is there? Secondly, during the stroll, you may pick and nibble mulberry fruits, *bbong* (뽕*). They are now well matured to purple to black with a sweet flavor in taste. Your lips may become stained as such, but this is all part of the fun. So, the above proverb describes the prospect of achieving more than one job with one move, like going to the post office and dropping by a grocery store on way back home. It would be equivalent to: "killing two birds with one stone" and Entry #304, "Take a pheasant as well as her eggs."

Merits of multitasking have been greatly exaggerated in recent years as our lives have become more hectic in a fast-and-furious mode. Blame the cut-throat society fueled by rapidly advancing technologies. Nowadays, people do not seem to have a moment of pause to smell the roses anymore or simply to be mindful of the surrounding. When was the last time you wandered around a flower garden or sat on a park bench enjoying a book or listening to birds singing?

If a blacksmith heats too many irons in his fire at once, it cools the fire and none of them will get red-hot properly: thus, the expression, "too many irons in the fire." If a cowboy tries to heat too many branding irons in an open fire, he may not be able to brand his calves as fast as he might have thought. You may not catch any rabbits if you chase two simultaneously: see also Entry #31, "Dig one well at a time."

I have been advising young people to take "one firm step at a time," avoiding the fad of multitasking. Admittedly, I have become old and slow at multitasking myself, but that is not the reason for the advice. It is simply the right way to complete a job that will remain satisfactory for many years to come. Besides, "haste often makes waste." Trying to be too smart often backfires.

Stealing gangsters' money even using some violent means is very appealing as they cannot report the loss to the police. So long as you disappear from those scumbags, like in an isolated tropical island, you will be more than okay. Along the way, you might have killed a couple of bad guys, or have exposed some crooked cops to the public, it would be a bonus. So, everybody, except those gangsters, should be happy. It thus makes sense why there are so many thriller TV dramas based on this basic theme. Throw in some love stories, then you have an excellent plot. In reality, however, those gangsters do not easily give up the money you stole, and most likely you or your beloved one gets murdered. When you think you are smart, it is time to remember that there are more people who are smarter.

Korea, being small and militarily weak, has been now in what appears to be a perpetually precarious state of foreign affairs. After the Second World War and particularly after Korean War, Korea has been a staunch ally of the US. However, lately, especially during the Trump administration, Koreans seem to question the commitment from the US for future security. Current President Moon seems to have been attempting to maintain a delicate balance between China, Japan, and the US. Besides, he must appease North Korea with nuclear armaments. It has not been and will not be an easy task to please everybody all the time. Maybe Moon should have recognized that gone is the day you can meet your lover as well as pick some delicious mulberry at the same time. (07/21/2021)

---

*As pointed out in Entry #173, "Listen to the elder, rice cake will come to you," many Korean consonants, such as (b), (j), (d), (g), (s), and (z) can be doubled up to designate hard sounds: for example, the pronunciation of (b) in "bag" is different from those in "boy." Lately, Koreans seem to offer a new set of English characters for these hard sounds: for instance, (bb) in pronunciation of "bag." In Entry #173, I used (dd) in *ddeok*, or rice cake. That sound is not what you pronounce in "dog." If we follow this convention, *bong* (뽕, or mulberry fruit) should have been written as *bbong* in the above proverb. I do not know if this convention has been formally sanctioned in English but it points out that English-speakers often find it difficult to pronounce such words as *ddeok* and *bbong*. Although the convention has not yet been officially endorsed by all parties involved, I will continuously use doubled Korean alphabets as in *bbong*.

371. A thief finds his legs asleep.

도둑이 제 발 저리다.

Criminals, especially first-time offenders, must feel some level of remorse for the criminal acts they committed. Al Capone might have been so much acclimated to the violent atmosphere that he might not have felt anything after killing several rival gangsters as in Saint Valentine's Day Massacre in 1929. But imagine a teen-aged girl shoplifting for the first time and her mental agony during her sleep.

In the above proverb, repentance manifests itself as sleepy legs. Tingling and numb sensation from the leg is usually from excessive pressure on nerves due to prolonged crossing of legs. What is it got to do with a guilty conscience? I cannot tell. That is just the way Korean proverbs are. As sleepy legs are benign and temporary, the girl who did shoplifting for the first time likely moves on for bigger items after overcoming her own remorse. That would be the beginning of bigger problems down the road. On the other hand, most of us can forgive a criminal who suffers from penance from their admission of the wrongdoing. We could even admire the courage of these people for their public confession.

Some political operatives, or consultants in a fancier word, tend to let the objective dictate means: they would plot and carry out nearly anything, for instance, to win an election, or reclaim a lost election as we have recently witnessed. They appear to be blinded by overzealous ambition toward a hefty goal. Lee Atwater, a political strategist for Republican Party, died in 1991 at the tender age of 40 of incurable brain cancer. Before he died, he had become a Catholic, and he issued several public letters in an act of repentance to individuals whose political careers he had harassed. In essence, he tried to come clean and free, confessing all the dirty tricks he had performed.

My illness helped me to see that what was missing in society is what was missing in me: a little heart, a lot of brotherhood. The 1980s were about acquiring – acquiring wealth, power, prestige. I know. I acquired more wealth, power, and prestige than most. But you can acquire all you want and still feel empty. What

160

power wouldn't I trade for a little more time with my family? What price wouldn't I pay for an evening with friends? It took a deadly illness to put me eye to eye with that truth, but it is a truth that the country, caught up in its ruthless ambitions and moral decay, can learn on my dime. I don't know who will lead us through the '90s, but they must be made to speak to this spiritual vacuum at the heart of American society, this tumor of the soul (from February 1991 issue of *Life* magazine via Wikipedia).

Early in his career working as a campaign consultant for a Republican congressional candidate, Atwater spread rumors that the Democratic opponent was a sympathizer of Communists, and had undergone psychiatric treatment, etc. These accusations were all concocted. His candidate went on to win the race. We could now say that Atwater was the grandfather of all misinformation and fake news of our time. He also apologized to Michael Dukakis for his role in using Willie Horton as the centerpiece during the 1988 presidential election. Horton committed a capital crime during a weekend furlough from the prison, which Dukakis could have stopped as the governor of Massachusetts. George H.W. Bush overcame Dukakis' 17-percent lead in early polls to win the election by landslide margins.

In the contemporary world of pop music, noteworthy are the apologies in February this year from Justin Timberlake to Britney Spears and Janet Jackson. In essence, he confesses that he could have done much more than the way he had treated them for their professional growth as well as in personal lives and that he benefited from a system that condones misogyny and racism. His voluntary and public statement speaks volumes about his character.

Toward the end of the Vietnam War, morale declined and disciplinary problems grew among American enlisted men, not to mention the anti-war sentiments in the country. Even Robert McNamara (1916–2009), then the secretary of Defense, submitted a confessional note to President Johnson: "The picture of the world's greatest superpower killing or seriously injuring 1,000 non-combatants a week, while trying to pound a tiny backward nation into submission on an issue whose merits are hotly disputed, is not a pretty one." It was as much an apology as we, American citizens, wished to have received from him earlier. It could have prevented the bloody war much sooner than 1973. (07/23/2021)

372. Old sayings are without flaws.

옛말 그른 데 없다.

Old sayings, proverbs, aphorisms, maxims, adages, idioms, and dictums are all time-tested: otherwise, they could not have survived. The wisdom and the perceived truth therein must be relevant at any time of any culture of humanity. Cynical interpretations or some modifications are possible, but they would be rare and arise only on exceptional occasions. A Haitian proverb, "The fish that is being microwaved doesn't fear the lightning," reveals its modern age quite honestly. Thus far, I have introduced 372 Korean proverbs in a series of four books, which should attest to the essence of the above statement. Maybe we ought to take this opportunity to examine Korean proverbs more in-depth.

Origin

The oral history of Korea goes back for five millennia. The Korean alphabet Hangul was not, however, available until it was invented and promulgated by King Sejong (1397–1450). Although the traceable history of idioms preceding the 15th century had been recorded in Chinese characters, I suspect that they could not have been very popular among our ancestors, since most of them were simply illiterate in Chinese. The ordinary citizens, or 서민 (seo-min), who shared barely-won happiness and various adversities in their lives, invented and used the proverbs. These proverbs are the collective consciousness of the Korean people, which eventually defines who we are now.

If there is a unique feature in Korean old sayings, it would be gentleness, often with humor derived from the everyday lives of average citizens. They are as if the sharp edges have been worn down through continuous use over many years. They are rolling hills under the blue sky peppered with lazy white clouds, never the Alps or the Himalayas under a windy snowstorm. They are small, gentle streams and the peaceful sound of a lullaby, never the deafening thunder of Niagara Falls. The gentleness and subtleness that I identify Korean proverbs with must be from not only seo-min's life but also the geography and terrain of Korea. Without too much further ado, I will instead let these proverbs speak themselves.

Interpretation

The beauty of proverbs lies in their simplicity. Spoken and written in plain language, any child can memorize them as soon they learn to speak. However, the deep-rooted meaning of these idioms evolves as we get older. Most likely, children hear a given proverb for the first time from an older and thus wiser person who quotes on one occasion, and then, they hear the same proverb spoken later by others in slightly different situations. Soon, these proverbs become children's own. Each and every proverb requires a context. The events or stories one chooses for a given proverb is their prerogative, indirectly presenting their own interpretation of it.

Language and Culture

Most of the Korean proverbs use declarative sentences as in, "The tongue can break bones," while others adopt a form of rhetoric questions with some level of subtlety: "Have you ever seen hairs without skin?" In Entry #45, "Could sparrows skip a grain millhouse?" I attributed the popularity of this approach to goading listeners to their own answers. It is Korean style.

Because proverbs are so much a part of the language and culture, understanding Korean proverbs mandates an understanding of both. That is precisely why Korean proverbs offer the best platform for understanding Korean culture. Proverbs are both poetic and traditional, and recorded in a "formulaic" language, often with archaic words. One of the most challenging tasks in my endeavor has been how to keep alive those rhymes, perfect in Korean, in English. "Soybean" and "red bean" do not convey the phonetic nuance of "*kong* (콩)" and "*paat* (팥)," respectively: see #9 and #152.

Antonymous Proverbs

There are many proverbs that appear to contradict each other. Clean water is desirable in Entry #41, whereas #129 says that fish cannot survive in clean water. Ignorance is bliss in #102, while #121 promotes education. Regardless of the fact, it would be your fault if you get misunderstood (#22). In #49, however, it is emphasized that you reap what you sow. In #67, big animals are from big forests, while a dragon is born in a small stream. (07/27/2021)

273. Fixing the barn after the cow escapes.

소 잃고 외양간 고친다.

This is equivalent to an English version, "closing the barn door after the cow (or the horse) has bolted." In the Korean version, the animal escapes through a broken door or wall while the Western version is through an open door. Either way, the proverb is asking "What good is it to fix the barn after the cow escaped?" For many possible reasons, it is worthwhile to repair the barn: if nothing else, the repaired barn with a fresh coat of red paint would look nice.

On January 6 this year, hundreds of rioters attacked Capitol Police and Metropolitan Police Department and eventually breached the halls of Congress, all to stop the certification of the 2020 presidential election. It was a blatant effort to subvert the democratic process of this country by means of brute force and violent assaults. Almost seven months later, the US House Select Committee is holding its first hearing with four officers who defended the Capitol.

One officer described how rioters attempted to gouge out his eye and called him a traitor as they sought to invade the Capitol. Another told of being smashed in a doorway and nearly crushed amid a "medieval" battle with a pro-Trump mob as he heard guttural screams of pain from fellow officers. A third said he was beaten unconscious and stunned repeatedly with a Taser as he pleaded with his assailants, "I have kids." A fourth relayed how he was called a racist slur over and over again by intruders wearing "Make America Great Again" garb. (from the 07/27 issue of *the NYTimes*)

Of many questions to be addressed, who spurred the attack will be most interesting. "All of them, all of them were telling us, 'Trump sent us,'" Aquilino A. Gonell, a U.S. Capitol Police sergeant, testified this morning as he tearfully recounted the horrors of defending Congress. How was it possible for a sitting president to incite the riot just to stop the certification step for US Congress for newly elected president Joe Biden? On the other side of the bench, Republicans boycotted the hearing, behaving as if the horse has already bolted and thus no need to investigate the riot any further.

Liz Cheney, one of a few Republican House Representatives who had sided with the group for the impeachment of Trump, has maintained that the riot was a "cancer on our constitutional republic" if Congress failed to hold accountable those who were responsible. As the special House committee began this morning, she urged lawmakers to find out "what happened every minute of that day in the White House." She said, Trump's "every phone call, every conversation, every meeting leading up to, during and after the attack." How much of her wish will be achieved by the Committee remained to be seen as the proceeding continues. Needless to say, her participation in the inquiry has drawn serious scorn from party leaders.

Preventive measures, including routine maintenance work for buildings and infrastructures, seldom attract much attention from the public and are not what you may say "sexy" until something tragic happens like a bridge falling and a train derailing. Had Washington's law enforcement successfully prevented the riot in advance to mere scuffles on a confined street, we would not have had the opportunity to review what was going on in the head of the previous president and his lieutenants at the White House. In the hindsight, we may say it was a blessing in disguise, particularly if something significant and noble comes out of the House hearing.

When I worked for a pharmaceutical firm, my lab was on the 7th floor of a nine-floor research complex. Because of building vibration, albeit minute, we could not use a very sensitive balance to measure a small quantity, say, a few micrograms of a potent drug substance. One microgram is 10^{-6} grams and 3.5×10^{-8} oz. On such occasion, we used an analytical lab in the basement, in which one corner of the lab was isolated from the rest of the building. I cannot overemphasize the importance of accurate weighing in any chemistry experiments, and the company maintained a crew of technicians whose job is checking balances throughout the company.

There was a guy whose job was changing light bulbs in all buildings of the company. Then there were people whose sole job is to do with water, gas in the lab, security of experimental data, lab safety, etc. But for these support personnel, we could have a succession of accidents all the time. Did I constantly be grateful for their service? Do I always appreciate the ever-present sun? (07/27/2021)

374. Deep water attracts fish.
물이 깊어야 고기가 모인다.

The word, water or *mool* (물), is one of the most common words one can find in Korean proverbs: seven out of 100 proverbs presented in Volume II, *Easier to See Jeong* (Love) *Leaving than Arriving*, contain the word. In Entry #125, "Blood is thicker than water," I attributed the strange behaviors of water, compared with other liquids, to the extensive hydrogen bonding between water molecules. Science aside, what our ancestors noticed about water must have been how water adapts the shape and the size of the groove it passes through without any "complaints." Its seemingly limitless ability to accommodate the surrounding was the crux of many Korean proverbs. Here is another example of its metaphoric attributes: deep water is full of big fish while shallow water is with minnows.

One possible interpretation is that a man of virtue is always surrounded by loyal friends. However, its reverse statement does not seem to be always correct since a man crowded by people is not necessarily a man of virtue. A powerful or wealthy man is often seen with a good size of the entourage. In most instances, the crowd, eager to please their leader, hang around only as long as their mutual give-and-take interest lasts. They are like flies on a drop of honey.

During the early years of the Trump administration, the turnover of political appointees was at a truly record-setting rate. They were either dismissed by Trump because he did not like them or they resigned after experiencing what appeared to be a frustrating time with Trump: just to name a few quite significant positions, White House Chiefs of Staff Reince Priebus and John Kelly, White House Communications Director Anthony Scaramucci, Secretary of Health and Human Services Tom Price, National Security Advisors Michael Flynn and H.R. McMaster, National Intelligence Director Dan Coats, Secretary of Defense James Mattis, Whitehouse Press Secretary Sean Spicer, Attorney General Jeff Sessions, Secretary of State Rex Tillerson, FBI Director James Comey, and more of the like.

Trump had four Chiefs of Staff: besides Reince Priebus and John Kelly, he had Mick Mulvaney and Mark Meadows. Of these, Meadows seemed to get along with Trump best as Meadows did everything he was asked to do, including rejection of the 2020 election outcome. By comparison, President Obama had only three Chiefs of staff during his eight-year tenure. During his first term, Rahm Emanuel served for 619 days. He left Whitehouse to run for Chicago Mayor. Bill Daley only committed to serving until Obama's re-election. During his second term, Denis McDonough stayed for 1,461 days.

Just the other day, on July 25, Tom Barrack, who was a major fundraiser for Trump's 2016 campaign and chairman of his 2017 inaugural committee, was indicted for illegal lobbying. He was the latest in a long list of indicted or convicted high-level Trump associates. Paul Manafort, chairman of Trump's 2016 campaign, was convicted in 2018 on charges of banking and tax fraud along with his aide and deputy campaign manager. Steve Bannon, a special counselor to the president, was charged with criminal conspiracies to commit wire fraud and money laundering. Michael Cohen, Trump's longtime attorney and fixer, pleaded guilty in 2018 to tax fraud, bank fraud, campaign finance violations, etc. He later became a whistleblower. Roger Stone, another Trump confidant, was convicted in 2019 on seven counts of witness tampering, obstruction of justice, and lying to Congress. Michael Flynn, who served as Trump's national security adviser, pleaded guilty to lying to FBI investigators.

Most of these charges centered on abuses of power for political or personal gains. Trump is clever enough to have his subordinates do the dirty work and thus most likely will not suffer the same debilitating shame over the considerable crimes of his inner circle. As president, he scoffed at most of their indictments and offered pardons for many of their convictions. Although he succeeded in erasing some of their criminal records, the record-breaking criminality of his administration will still remain intact for the history of this nation. He certainly worked in shallow water populated with minnows, playing a kingfish himself. What else can we say?

I cannot stop comparing those Trump's cronies with the devoted fans, "Army," of the Korean BTS band. One of the primary reasons for the dedicated fan base is the respectful attitude of the performers towards the Army: the band, for instance, has never delivered a performance in mimicry, be it in the studio or live on stage. In return, the Army pours their affection to BTS. The depth of their mutual adulation is far from the relations we witnessed in the Trump cabinet.   (07/31/2021)

375. The dragon is easier to draw than the snake.

안 본 용은 그려도 본 뱀은 못 그리겠다.

The dragon exists only in our imagination and thus anybody's drawing of a dragon is as real as others'. No one can argue about which is a better presentation. Snake is a different story: everyone has seen a few snakes in their lifetime and thus has a definite idea as to which drawing looks real and best. One can write a scholarly tome on contemporary abstract paintings, say, by Mark Rothko or Jackson Pollock, but they depend mainly on our imagination. To untrained eyes like mine, they are like reviewing drawings of a dragon.

More realistic paintings, such as those by Norman Rockwell or Andrew Wyeth, are easier to appreciate because we are familiar with the subjects of their paints. A Thanksgiving dinner of a big family, the famous scene of Rockwell's painting, is something we all experience and easy to identify ourselves with. Wyeth's *Christina's World* or *Winter 1946* provokes some darker stories that would require some imagination. Some of M.C. Escher's artworks call for a somewhat different type of imagination, close to fantasy. Then, of course, there are renaissance paintings and those by impressionists we all love.

According to the above proverbs, realistic paintings are more difficult for an artist to draw albeit easier for us to enjoy. That is probably because there can be too many critics, who would say "No, that doesn't look like a snake at all!" What can average Joe say about *Number 17A* by Jackson Pollock, which was sold to a private collector at a price of $200 million? The crux of the above proverb could be that we can easily develop a certain imagination or fantasy, but difficult to reveal a truth or the fact of a matter.

The infection by delta variant of the coronavirus SARS-CoV-2 has been a hot issue lately. Just the other day, on July 30, the headline of a CNBC article read: "CDC study shows 74% of people infected in Massachusetts Covid outbreak were fully vaccinated." Earlier another article appeared on June 25 in *the Wall Street Journal*. It introduced a study from Tel Aviv indicating that there was no difference in infection rate between vaccinated and unvaccinated groups among the newly infected people in Israel.

At first glance, this is not what we, fully vaccinated people, have been expecting and sounds rather alarming. And yet, we all know for a fact that the hospitalization rate or the mortality rate of the fully vaccinated population is extremely low. These two seemingly contradicting reports are creating some confusion among the learned population. Here, I would like to submit a possible explanation. The attempt is in reflection of what is implied in the above proverb: truth is hard to come by while speculation can be a dime a dozen.

Whether a person is infected or not is usually determined by a PCR (polymerase chain reaction)-based, fully automated test that is readily accessible nowadays. It is sensitive and specific. In essence, it directly detects the presence of the genetic code of the virus. Amplification of a diagnostic signal is an integral part of the procedure. If a quantitative analysis of viral load is required, one just looks at how much amplification is involved. The routine test uses such bodily fluid as saliva. The procedure is used in most epidemiological studies. Here, a positive test result means "infection."

The coronavirus enters our body through the lung epithelial cells on the lung surface upon binding on its target, ACE 2 (angiotensin-converting enzyme 2). The cell membrane to which the virus is attached invaginates, a process called receptor-mediated endocytosis. Ideally, to prevent infection, this is the step we must block, like sentries stopping intruders at the gate. To the best of my knowledge, vaccines currently available do not generate antibodies of IgA type that could prevent virus particles from binding their receptor ACE 2 on the cell surface. The keyword here is "cell surface."

What we produce upon vaccination would be antibodies of IgM followed by IgG on booster injection. These antibodies bind viruses that have already infected systemically. The antibody-virus interaction is similar to the key-lock pair in that they are specific and once formed the resulting immune complex could no longer behave as the free virus would. This is the neutralization step that will stop the respiratory disease. In terms of "infection," we are all equally hapless regardless of the status of vaccination. This hypothesis is consistent with the field reports from Tel Aviv and Provincetown, MA. One could predict that the infection rate might be even higher among the vaccinated people if they behave recklessly with a sense of assurance from vaccination. A word of precaution: this essay deals with a hypothesis, which could serve as misinformation. (08/02/2021)

376. Pull a sword out to fight a mosquito.

모기 보고 칼 빼기 한다.

This proverb is similar to Entry #113, "Use a shovel for a job for *homee*?" and #124, "Burning a house down to get rid of bedbugs." Both are mocking an exaggerated response to a trivial task. Nobody with a reasonable mind would burn down a house just to kill a few bedbugs. So is the present case: why would someone try to fight off a mosquito with a samurai knife? Unless this person is in an uncontrollable rage, that is. This aspect involving anger is the subject of this essay.

We will address two aspects of anger, wrath, and rage: cause and consequence. Many events can trigger anger, to varying degrees depending on the mood at the time. Also, a given offensive act causes a different level of anger depending on the person. This morning, I learned from a newspaper article that the price of a ballgame at Yankee Stadium is listed as low as $15. However, there are additional hidden costs, through a marginally legal practice called drip pricing: $4.20 for "service fee" and $3.30 for "order processing fee," making the total $22.50. As trivial as it may sound, I cannot stand such cheating in nature. These "conmen" seem to constantly test the limit of our tolerance with no end in sight.

An incident, a maddening experience, happened to me in the early 1970s at a shoe store. I spelled out "forty" for "40" on my check. The cashier was telling me with an attitude - come to think of it now, it was close to a hate crime - that I misspelled "fourty." Was I mad and angry! Not so much toward his ignorance but my poor English skill. The long line behind me at the cash register made my explanation in broken English worse. He did not know I had been careful with "flotation" and "pronunciation," without "a" and "o."

I am also mad at and disappointed with my fellow Americans for tolerating the brazenly fraudulent acts of Donald Trump. The word, betrayal, comes to my mind. Non-vaccinated people for COVID-19 make me feel the same way. The ignorance and wellbeing of vaccine-resisting folks are not important to me personally. However, the thought that they collectively make the national lockdown of every aspect of our lives including the national economy makes me mad at them. Besides, they sow mistrust among the citizens via misinformation and fake news. In both Korea and in the States, public mistrust appears to be the main source of anger and resentment.

What is the consequence of anger? It is said that anger provokes either a fight or flight. For the former, the ultimate manifestations of aggressive anger could well be a violent vengeance, possibly resulting in the murder of the instigator. Love-triangle stories often entail a tragic ending where one party gets killed. I introduced a one-act Italian opera *Cavalleria rusticana* by Mascagni in Entry #15, "The tongue can break bones," in which a husband (baritone) ends up killing the lover of his wife (tenor) in a duel on Easter Sunday.

In the 1986 British film, *The Mission*, a successful slave trader during the 1750s, played by Robert De Niro, comes home after one of his trips of kidnapping natives in Argentina jungles to find his fiancée in bed with his half brother. In a fit of rage, he kills his younger brother. Now, out of guilt, De Niro falls into depression and seeks for penance. He follows a Catholic Jesuit priest (Jeremy Irons) in a missionary undertaking in the territory of the natives.

A person in passive anger or deep resentment can respond with hostile inaction, such as withdrawing, stonewalling, exaggerated apathy. In recent years, I have found myself harboring resentment towards Republicans on many issues ranging from immigration policy to their lack of understanding of and respect for democracy. I must confess that I do not know how long this slow-burning anger will last, but it is not a feeling that I enjoy keeping forever.

When you are angry or in a rage, your cognitive ability is inevitably and greatly hampered such that you may not be able to properly recognize and digest the surroundings. That is how this mad man pulls out a long sword out of its scabbard to kill a mosquito. Terribly irritating as mosquitoes might be when you try to sleep, such irrational behaviors will never lead to any satisfactory outcome.

While controlling anger is considered highly desirable, many psychologists also believe that suppression of anger may find another outlet, like the barber who encountered the King with donkey's ears: see Entry #82, "Say the words; chew the meat." They quote the Los Angeles Riots of 1992 as an example. When four policemen were acquitted who had been charged with using excessive force in the arrest and beating of Rodney King, sudden, collective anger spilled over to Korean Town, an innocent bystander. (08/03/2021)

377. Blood on the foot of a bird.

새 발의 피다.

I do not know if anyone, save some veterinarians, has ever seen bloodstain on the bottom of a bird's feet. The sole of humans is covered by the thickest layers of skin on the body. This is basically because it constantly bears the body weight. Underneath, we also have another thick layer of connective tissue. The bottom of a bird's feet looks even tougher than ours. Nonetheless, I suppose that birds can hurt their feet and bleed when the injury is deep. The question is though how much and how long they would bleed. Very little, this old expression says.

Open wound, when occurred, activates a certain blood clotting factor along with platelets in the presence of calcium ions. This step converts prothrombin to thrombin, which in turn helps to convert fibrinogen to fibrin. Activated platelets interact with fibrin to form stable fibrin clots with the help of another activated factor. The clots effectively plug the injured site on the blood vessel. This biochemical cascade involved in blood clots is perhaps one of the best-characterized blood chemistries.

To a billionaire, a millionaire may look like a man with one single dollar to a man with a thousand dollars. You can then say that the millionaire is a bloodstain on a bird's foot, "*saebal eu pee.*" It is often speculated that the subatomic world can be as complex as the universe, although an atom is, well, an atom: extremely small to be detected with ordinary means. The above expression, very popular among Koreans, once again reminds us that everything in our lives is relative. Or to be more meaningful, there isn't anything absolute.

In essence, "a drop in the bucket" is what *saebal eu pee* means. The English idiom apparently originates from the Bible, Isaiah [40:15]: "Behold, the nations count as a drop of the bucket, as dust on the scales; the coastlands weigh no more than powder." In this clause, nations and land are of vanity and emptiness, or *saebal eu pee*, when compared with God. That is, what we may consider extremely powerful and almighty is just *saebal eu pee* in front of our Creator.

My wife and I never considered ourselves rich, but I do not believe we are really poor either. We have saved diligently whenever we could, and with the help of a financial advisor, we have invested wisely also. My portfolio has been a bit more aggressive with stocks, but my wife has been rather cautious. I have seldom monitored the change in our accounts, but my wife does. It has not been a surprise for me to witness significant fluctuations, say, tens of thousand in six months, but her accounts have been quite steady. With such changes in magnitude in my accounts, it was hard to understand why my wife was so anxious about saving a few bucks here and there all the time. It was certainly *saebal eu pee* in my mind.

Yesterday, they had a closing ceremony for the 2020 Tokyo Olympics. The USA collected 113 medals while the Republic of Korea 20 and Japan 58. One could say that Korea's 20 medals are *saebal eu pee*, but there are many nations that did not receive any or only a single bronze medal. Their medal counts are really *saebal eu pee*. In true sportsmanship, medal count should not be important, but there is certainly the pride of a nation involved. A case of the point would be Korea versus Japan as we see below.

Given the situation with the COVID-19 pandemic and in the face of strong opposition from their own citizens, the Japanese Olympic Committee did a wonderful job in completing the event without much significant trouble. However, this feeling of mine does not seem shared by average Koreans. From the beginning, Korean news media have carried reports critical of the Japanese Olympic organizers. Their complaints ranged from flimsy beds made of compressed paper (but nobody fell through them), food quality and availability (I might be wrong, but Korean athletes were said to have food delivered to them from Korea), dirty water where triathlon participants had to swim to even weather not well predicted (no other nations complained).

These bellyaches of Koreans are certainly from the long-standing animosity between the two countries. Adding insult to the injury, the Japanese Olympians collected more medals than Korea. This was unthinkable as in the recent Olympics Korean athletes were always superior to Japanese. While our ranking 16th was the lowest since the 1976 Montreal Olympics, the Japanese really excelled this time. I do not understand why nobody from Korean Olympic Committee or no Korean citizens congratulated what the Japanese counterpart and the Japanese athletes have accomplished. The narrow-mindedness of Koreans disappoints me. (08/08/2021)

378. Waiting for a morning moon early at dusk.
새벽달 보자고 초저녁부터 기다린다.

The moonlight is of course the sunlight that the moon reflects. Since the moon rotates on its own axis for the same period of time as it orbits the earth, i.e., they are "tidally" locked, we see only one side of the moon. Since the sun's light is always from one direction, as the moon orbits around the earth, we see different shapes, or phases, of the moon every night depending on the day of the month. Starting with a totally dark new moon in which the moon is right in between the sun and earth, we go through waxing crescent, the first quarter, waxing gibbous, and full moon. From then on it goes through the waning phases to a new moon.

The moon during the months of April and May appears large as it shows most of its lighted side. Just after sunrise, we can still see the moon near the western horizon, albeit pale. Some may find it beautiful, often against the blue sky, but to me, it is just one of those natural phenomena: really nothing to get excited about.

For some reason, this person anxiously waits for a wan morning moon as early as dusk. In the morning, he may perhaps face a firing squad for a sure demise or may expect a loved one to arrive. Either way, it seems unnecessarily a long period of hours for the wait, while he has a whole night to sleep through and ponder about the upcoming event. Does this man "hurry up so that he can wait?" This proverb is similar to an Irish proverb, "Don't build the sty before the litter comes," or "Haste makes waste."

Having schooled in Korea, I was subject to numerous exams. Even admission to a middle school entrails an entrance exam. "Pass or fail" for this particular exam in 1956 was announced a couple of weeks after the exam. Names of applicants who had passed were written on a scroll of rice paper glued to a wall. If your name appears, you are in. If not, you walk home with your eyes staring at the ground and shedding some tears. As I recall now, I was not able to rationally reconcile my own two opposing minds: on one hand, I was anxious to learn the outcome of the exam and on the other hand I did not want to know the result for fear of failing to pass. It was a strange, short period as if my life was hung in the air. Like waiting for the morning moon, in the end, time had solved the quandary.

Perfect timing to an event does not happen as we hope for. Missing a plane and having to idle at an airport for several hours is not the most exciting thing to do. Sitting at a bar nibbling peanuts can kill time only so much. I do not want to be the first person to arrive at a party. I should not be too late lest I walk into a noisy room already full of drunkards. I do not know which is worse, too early or too late. If one has too much time at hand, as in the case of the above proverb, they tend to do something silly, usually things unnecessary. In a competition for drawing a snake, an idiot finishes the drawing first but, realizing others are way behind, he adds feet to his otherwise perfect snake and loses the contest: see Entry #184, "Acupuncture onto a pumpkin." In one of Aesop's fables, *the Tortoise and the Hare*, it is the hare who loses the race. He is so much faster than the hare that he took a nap: see Entry #130, "Eat slowly, even ripe persimmon."

Most maddening is when you miss the opportunity of perfect timing, and you know it. This weekend, some five thousand US military personnel arrived in Kabul to make sure of a safe departure of Americans in Afghanistan. This is ironic as American troops began to leave Afghanistan a few months ago and all to be gone by September 11, the 20th anniversary of the Attack. It would be a déjà vu of Americans in Saigon on April 30, 1975. In the early morning hours, the last U.S. Marines evacuated the embassy by helicopter, as civilians swamped the perimeter and poured into the grounds. It was the end of the 19-year-old Vietnam War. I hope that such a scene is not repeated in Afghanistan in the coming days.

In the past 20 years, we have failed to build a truly independent nation out of Afghanistan. At this writing, the Taliban is controlling the nation except for Kabul. One can spend much time analyzing what has gone wrong, but one thing is very clear: the US missed the opportunity of departure. Was it because we did not have any opportune time? It is hard to believe that the four administrations with all those wise experts in foreign affairs and military power were not able to end the bottomless and aimless war. Every president seemed to have been "passing the hot potato" to the next president. Or, the United States might have been waiting for the morning sun and the pale morning moon too long and must have slipped into a long sleep. (08/14/2021)

379. Catching a mouse without breaking a jar.

독 깨질까 쥐를 못 잡는다.

This man is about to strike with a rod a mouse hiding beside an earthenware jar, but at the last minute decides not to lest the jar be broken by mistake. So, the lucky mouse gets a break and survives for another day. The man, on the other hand, is not completely happy but he at least thinks he was prudent and would look for another chance to catch the mouse. The proverb describes a situation where one's best option cannot be carried out because of potential casualties in the surrounding.

We do not know if the mouse was clever enough to secure a safe hiding place beside a fragile but valuable porcelain vessel, but if it were true then it is in the realm of blackmailing. It is like a bad guy holding a dagger at the jugular vein of a beautiful lady friend of the protagonist in a movie, and asking her man to drop the gun. Using innocent people as a shield against a pending attack has been a wicked strategy that will not go away soon.

In May this year, the ongoing Israeli–Palestinian conflict reached another level of violence. On May 15, Israel Defense Forces (IDF) destroyed with three powerful missiles a 14-story building in downtown Gaza City. The upscale building was home to about 700 residents as well as lawyers, computer businesses, and the Associated Press (AP) journalists. Upon the protest from the AP, the IDF justified the bombing, claiming that the building also housed Hamas military intelligence. The latter did not make any immediate comment, and Israel said that it had provided the US intelligence on the strike beforehand.

A worse incident happened the next day. Another upscale section in Gaza City was bombed by 11 missiles from Israel warplanes. According to the IDF, a Hamas tunnel and underground command center were the targets of the attack. It also destroyed two residential buildings, killing 44 civilians. The IDF was somewhat apologetic about the civilian casualty this time, but we will never know the whole truth. Embedding military command centers in civilian locations remind me of the mouse hiding beside a fragile jar.

On August 17, 1975, a 37-year-old fireman named Mel Lynch was arrested in his Brooklyn apartment for having kidnapped 21-year-old Samuel Bronfman II. The latter was rescued unharmed albeit blindfolded. He was the heir apparent of one of the richest families in America who owned the Seagram Company, a huge distiller worth more than $3.5 billion today. Lynch and his accomplice, 53-year-old another Irish immigrant, confessed to the crime and showed where they had kept a $2.3 million ransom. Under the usual circumstance of this kind of crime, this is the end of the story. However, here, it was a beginning of a convoluted story, stranger than any fiction, as the defendants later left the courtroom scot-free. It was neither because their lawyer was brilliant nor there were some legal issues. It was all due to Lynch's outstanding performance.

The story unfolded with a remarkable claim by Lynch's lawyer that Bronfman had masterminded his own kidnapping. At the trial in October, Lynch confessed that he and Bronfman were lovers since they met at a bar in June 1974, and often had sex in the pool house of the Bronfman property in Purchase, NY. Lynch said that Bronfman staged his own kidnapping to shake down his family for cash and that Lynch agreed to join the plot because Bronfman threatened to inform the fire department that he was gay. Although Lynch's story had many holes such as Bronfman's desperate need for cash, the prosecutor never broached the supposed love affair. "Being called gay was much, much worse then," the retired prosecutor said in a recent phone interview. It was 1976, and the topic of homosexuality was so taboo that directly challenging the claim of an affair would be pointless. Most of all, Lynch, the notably taciturn fireman, was quite mesmerizing as a storyteller during four days on the witness stand.

In retrospect, the story involves double blackmailing: First, those two Irishmen were successful in extorting a $2.3 million ransom. Secondly, Lynch was clever enough to take a social taboo of gay life to his advantage. That Lynch's story was all a big lie came out to the public only recently, almost 40 years after the crime, in a book titled, *Let Justice Be Done* by DeBlasio, Lynch's defense lawyer. It was a deathbed confession as DeBlasio died five months later in 2020 at the age of 91. In this true crime story, there appears a few clever mice running around the valuable porcelain jar avoiding whacking. (08/15/2021)

380. Close the eyes, lose the nose.

눈 감으면 코 베어 가는 세상.

We bought a new car last year. Its Owner's Manual is a tome of over 530 pages, roughly 6" x 8" in size. Besides, there are six additional small booklets: Quick Reference Guide, Multimedia System, Warranty Information, etc. A cursory glimpse alone took an hour. One item I found new is a device that prevents tires from being stolen. Are tires being lost in a parking lot? What kind of world do we live in now? Since when did we begin to worry about someone stealing tires?

The above proverb goes one step further, describing a world that is so bad that if you close your eyes for a brief moment somebody will slice your nose off your face for a steal. I do not see any legitimate use of stolen noses, but it is beside the point; the world we live in now is a very dangerous place and so you should not blink your eyes.

I seldom locked my apartment or car up until the 1980s. Idiotic it may sound nowadays, I just didn't pay attention to such "trivial" matters. Living in a college town such as Lawrence, Kansas, or a small town like Kalamazoo, Michigan, certainly allowed me not to worry about the burglary. Possessing very few valuable items also helped. There had not been any break-ins that happened to me that could have triggered a paranoid life.

About 25 years ago, my wife and I spent a two-week winter vacation in Honolulu. It was the first time for both of us to visit the place with balmy weather, seafood, a beautiful beach with a wide-open ocean, Diamondhead on the left, and all that. We were as giddy as one can be. Just off Waikiki Beach, a friendly man with a big and colorful parrot was greeting us, asking if I want to be with the bird in a picture while holding the bird in my arm. Of course, I did but I didn't know it cost some money. That was about the extent of a rip-off I remember during the vacation. Thankfully it did not ruin our first day on the island, but, still, such incidents have accumulated in me to slowly build the self-defensive guard up.

The New York Times columnist, David Brooks wrote on June 10: "Distrust is a cancer eating away at our society. It magnifies enmity, stifles cooperation and fuels conspiracy thinking." He then proceeded to offer some practical ways to restore trust. Couldn't agree more with what he said, but we will have to know how distrust begins to develop a more fundamental approach to mitigating distrust. When I recognize that I am not well qualified to form my own opinion on a certain topic, I tend to listen to people whose explanation I can trust. They are usually scientists in a given field, church elders, writers with more emotional experiences, plumbers, technicians like IT folks, even sports analysts, et al. I am sure that most people would be the same way: that is why we have a cohort of experts in each of various fields. However, such a traditional approach to form an opinion seems to be rapidly fading away in recent years, all thanks to Google, Facebook, YouTube, and all other social network platforms. We now have a society with a whole population of know-it-all.

The very concept of trust begins with self-doubt. Why do I need expert opinions and trust them when I know as much as anyone on this planet Earth? Each of us has become entitled to shouting out our own reasonings through many portals of propagandizing and dissemination. In doing so, we might have abandoned the ability to listen and respect others' thought processes and interpretations of a given event or incident. Under the new normal, the harshest and loudest speakers seem to easily take over society. Instead of "Trust, but verify," we now say, "Trust? Why bother!"

A self-centered society of "me-first" will inevitably place one's self-interest right at the center and front. "Why do we need to or have to accommodate those Afghans in this country? Admittedly they helped us, but it was then and this is now!" This is a dog-eat-dog society that the above proverb describes. Remnant flood from Hurricane Ida, the historic drought of Colorado River and Lake Mead in the West, the wildfire beyond control in California, plus rampant COVID-19 pandemic, all make us feel like the end of this world is near.

We are so exhausted with the seemingly ceaseless barrage of these calamities that we have become the prisoner within ourselves in constant paranoid. What we offer other fellow humans seems from shallow goodwill and is based on a hollow foundation. Likewise, we feel we do not receive any genuine care or respect from others. To this end, we may conclude that we cannot and should not close eyes lest someone should steal the nose. (09/05/2021)

381. A toddler playing around an open well.

우물가에 애 보낸 것 같다.

A young mother belatedly realizes that earlier she let her toddler wander around the yard without thinking that there was a public well nearby. A traditional well in Korea, like those in other places in the world, is usually housed with a roof. Underneath there would be a pulley for pulling up a brimful basket. The opening on the ground itself is surrounded and protected by a small wall. Having brought water home every morning, the mother knows the place like her palm.

But she is also keenly aware that her son is old enough to climb over the wall but not intelligent enough to recognize the imminent danger of falling to the well. Now, the mother is rushing to the well as if her life is on the line. The worry, anxiety, apprehension, or concerns involved in such an occasion is the subject of the above proverb.　They not only bring about "grey hairs" on the head prematurely but also threaten the wellbeing of a person: see Entry #248, "Three causes of death: ruthless sun, an endless feast, and trivial worries."

Of all worries we experience ourselves or witness in others, that of a mother with her son on a battlefield would rank the highest. Imagine the parents whose son is serving in the Afghanistan War. Any unexpected knock on the door would frighten them with an unthinkable thought. Just after the Disarmament Declaration in 1953, which effectively ended Korean War, two of my older brothers had to serve the two-year obligatory conscription, one after the other.

Only a few months left before his discharge, one of my brothers was assigned to an area close to the demilitarized zone. One moonless night, this brother was leading a small band of soldiers to repel or capture any infiltrators from the North. He opened fire with a carbine rifle aiming at the bottom of a wooden boat floating down on a small river and killed a man asleep on the boat. Apparently, this man failed to respond to a shout from my brother asking for a password.　The incident terrified and aged my mother several years, who immediately said with a firm determination that she would never send her last son for military service no matter what. That is how I circumvented the conscription when my turn came along.

Ordinary people with an ordinary income worry about their financial situation ceaselessly. Even if they survive uneventfully, they closely monitor the performance of the stocks they own, for instance. Stocks, as a long-term investment, invariably outperform other conservative options like the bond market, but it can make people who constantly follow the market anxious. Thus, financial advisors recommend young people to buy stocks but forget about it for many years to come.

In 2019, I came across a research paper from a small startup company in South San Francisco, which links the invasion to the brain of bacteria that causes gingivitis to the cause of Alzheimer Disease (AD). The hypothesis was tested in a series of well-designed experiments and published in highly reputable trade journals. How would anyone suspect the association of gingivitis with AD? The discovery was astonishing as well as quite refreshing. The only thing people had been talking about was so-called amyloid plaques, which may be a consequence rather than a cause: see Entry # 62, "A pear drops to ground as a crow takes off." As soon as I finished reading and marveling at their research papers, I went to the company website to learn that I had missed the company's IPO (initial public offer). I sold all "do-nothing" stocks and purchase 520 shares of the new company's stock at a significantly higher price than IPO's. Just a few minutes ago, I discovered the price has gone up more than triple.

An illicit love affair one commits also caused anxiety to the parties involved, usually the person who initiated more than the passive, receiving party. It is from the fear that their spouse or family may discover the affair. One can expand such a case to all other crimes, leading to another famous Korean proverb that says: Entry # 43, "The beaten, but not the beater, sleeps well."

Although the level of anxiety or apprehension can vary depending on the nature of the "crime," we all have suffered from it throughout our lives. How can you cover the smell after you smoke a cigarette? Where do you plan to hide the goods you have stolen? What are you going to tell your teacher after they discover that you have created an exam? Your act may not have caused any real harm to other people, but you could suffer from the anticipated "wrath of God" not to mention the self-torture from your own regret. (09/06/2021)

382. Can you spit on a smiling face?

웃는 낯에 침 뱉으랴?

A smiling face is a universal language for friendship, peace, compromise, bonding, cooperation, and all other positive messages you would like to convey to another human being. When you encounter a stranger on a deserted mountain trail or a back alley of a big city, the best way to express your goodwill would be to bear a smile on your face. Often you may not have other options. Even a forced smile would be better than an expressionless face when one is in potential trouble. It is like a Muslim taxi driver on the street of New York City with an American flag flying high on his car just after the 9·11 Attack in 2001. The gesture would be, "I'm coming in peace."

With spitting, we get rid of unwanted substances in the mouth such as a large buildup of mucus along with saliva. In many cultures, spitting upon another person, especially onto the face, symbolizes disgust, hatred, anger, disrespect, or contempt. If spitting stands for war, a smiling face means peace. Thus, the above proverb is asking how one could spit on the person who is approaching you with a big smile or stab him with a knife for no obvious reason. Most people don't, but in some instances, they can and do.

A hate crime usually involves two parties who have never met before and is mainly based on ethnicity, disability, nationality, religion, age, or sexual orientation. Hatred arises from unhappiness and, in some extreme instances, manifests itself as a desire to destroy a target population or object. Although any demographic difference would serve as an extra excuse or justification of the attack, in most instances the major motivation of the crime is apparently for seeking the thrill involved in the act itself rather than deep-rooted philosophy. Other secondary motivations may include an ill-conceived idea of protecting the attacker's community, revenge on a long-standing grudge such as hatred toward Jews, radical social or political ideology, etc.

Of these various offenders, the so-called mission offenders would be most dangerous to a democratic society. Often, they consider themselves to be crusaders, offering some convoluted argument in their propagandizing materials for recruiting supporters and members. This kind of hate crime often overlaps with terrorism, a major threat to the contemporary society of the United States.

In October last year, the FBI arrested 13 men suspected of orchestrating a domestic terror. They were plotting to kidnap Gretchen Whitmer, the Governor of Michigan, and to use violence to overthrow the state government. Later, most of them were charged in the state as well as federal court. Then, of course, there was the horrific riot on January 6th this year at the US Capitol. The way these rioters dealt with government officials who are elected in due process is as bad as spitting on the face of our nation.

There is another dimension that we ought to pay attention to: it is the importance in the competitive nature of the actions among a given criminal cohort: "I have taken care of this many Jews. How many did you?" The more outrageous acts you have committed, the more "respect" you gain within the group and it is thus not surprising that such outlandish behavior is one of the quickest ways to become the leader of the group. This mob mentality has strengthened its hold on the nation, beginning with a self-centered mantra of Make America Great Again. Sadly, many of them believe that they are true patriots.

Hatred is an angry emotion toward certain people, animals, or ideas. Since we were born without any emotions including hatred, we must have acquired it as we grow from our environment including parents. When and how did I begin to dislike a snake? One of the most paradoxical sources of hatred is from religion: for instance, Islam against Christianity and Hinduism versus Buddhism. When a given religion becomes exclusive or develops based on hatred, it begins to sow antagonistic feelings towards people who belong to other religions. It may equate the non-believers of their religion to an evil that has to be eradicated at all cost. This may well be the ultimate cause behind the 9·11 al-Qaida attack of the World Trade Center.

Finally, for the person who was attacked by flying spit in spite of his or her best effort with a smiling face, the proverb is concerned with a deep feeling of betrayal and accompanying sadness. As I mentioned earlier in Entry #174, "My ax injures my foot," *The Education of Little Tree* by Forrester Carter was one of my favorite stories when I read it in the late 1970s. But, then I realized that the true author, Asa Earl Carter, was a notorious racist, a Ku Klux Klan member from Alabama. If it wasn't spit on my face, what could it be? (09/09/2021)

383. Without the tiger, rabbits are the master.

범 없는 골에 토끼가 스승이다.

Now that the tiger is away, a cohort of rabbits is ruling the woods. This is the crux of the above proverb. Here, the interesting word is 스승, pronounced *seu-seung*. It could mean a teacher as opposed to a pupil, master to disciple, or simply a king. Any animal in the woods could fill the vacuum created by the departure of a tiger, but why lowly rabbits? It is a case of cynicism, implying that everybody wants to be the successor of the leader of an organization once the leader leaves.

The sudden death of a chief executive officer (CEO) of a huge corporate - let's say in a heart attack - would inevitably lead to a hectic period of selecting the successor among the powers that be. In the end, it is possible that a person perhaps less qualified than others, a rabbit in the above case, may become a new leader. In this typical progression of events, what is missing is the lack of assessing if the choice was indeed the best one. This is because we do not have any "control" measure of the choice. The only exception is when the successor fails big time, where people may express that so-and-so could have been a better choice. Would there be a significant difference between a rabbit and a wolf as the new king of the woods?

The corporate performance, such as stock price, under a new CEO, may offer some measure of their performance but we still cannot rule out the possibility that the stock could have outperformed under another candidate. What about other criteria such as customer satisfaction? A wolf might be a strong leader also, but what about other aspects of the woods like the wellbeing of individual animals? Aren't they better off with rabbits as their leader?

One of the common but bizarre concepts that I have never fully understood and appreciated is that of leadership, especially when the word is used in an ill-defined context. I do not have any problem in establishing criteria for: ringleaders among gangsters, cheerleaders, church leaders, boy scout leaders, dictators, even political leaders, etc. As pointed out in Entry #145, "Thread follows the needle," at a given time, we are likely followers than leaders: this is just a matter of probability based on the fact that the leader is in a smaller number.

As in the past, my wife was struggling the other day with her annual performance review for her employer, a state university. The section dealt with leadership. Specific questions that the standardized form is raising are: "How many times did you convene or organize a (research) conference?" "What leadership role did you play in a professional organization?" "What awards have you received?" "Are you currently serving as an (associate) editor of a journal?" My wife failed to answer any of these questions in a positive manner and thus worrying about potential negative impacts on her annual report and ultimately promotion and pay raise.

She is a good scientist with a very good funding record as well as publication. As such she has never been interested in and is not good at any of the questions of the above nature. It is rare for a good scientist to be an outstanding, say, a conference organizer. Can you imagine a Noble Laureate is involved in an administrative side of academic life? In Entry #145, I wrote the following: Theories are abundant on leadership, and practical workshops are popular among youths as if there is a certain set of traits one can learn and acquire to become an extraordinary leader. Such important leadership traits as intelligence and physical appearance come with one's birth: and hence "great leaders are born, not made."

When a leader is leaving for whatever reasons, the transition to the next ruler seldom occurs smoothly, and I wonder why. In a democratic nation, we elect political leaders via voting of free will. It is by far the best way to bring in a new administration based on the majority wishes of constituents. Even with such a system based on a simple and seemingly water-tight principle of majority rule, the losing party can create havoc instead of offering a concession. Just last week, the State of Georgia recounted voting that took place almost 10 months ago. Apparently, Texas will do the same for a few key counties where Republicans have suspected some fraudulent voting.

We may vest too much expectation from elected officials, which may, in turn, make getting elected a live-or-die enterprise among some politicians. Here is what Harry Truman said: "It is amazing what you (as a follower) can accomplish if you do not care who gets the credit (as a leader)." Similarly, John F. Kennedy said, "Ask not what your country can do for you: ask what you can do for your country." (09/30/2021)

384. A dull-witted horse pulls ten wagons,

둔한 말이 열 수레를 끈다.

This thick-headed horse, perhaps less intelligent and appearance-wise less attractive than others, is nonetheless so strong that he can pull as many as 10 carts all by himself. That is what the proverb says. In Entry #243, "My mule is preferred to a neighbor's stallion," I pointed out that a Porsche is not always more desirable than an old Ford pickup truck. "Look is one thing, the function is another" is the implication of the above proverb. It somehow appears to reflect an egalitarian thought that all are born with equal potential. A Porsche would attract undivided attention from girls, but a pickup truck can haul bags of fertilizer along with plants for your garden.

When applied to human interactions, the old saying suggests that people in fine clothes who can delight and entertain others in an elegant speech full of high ideals may not be necessarily the ones you wish to go to a battlefield with. Superficial friendliness and concerns for others are often little to do with deep-rooted loyalty. As in other Korean old sayings, this one also seems to promote something that is against the prevailing trend in our contemporary society: who in this fast-moving, the cutthroat world would befriend a slow, dim-witted person? Well, we find such stories at least in fiction.

During the 1960s, there was a Korean pop song called, *the man in a yellow shirt*, or 노란 샤쓰 입은 사나이. It was quite popular, and I still remember some lines from the song:

> *This man in a yellow shirt,*
> *Though quiet, I like him a lot.*
> *Don't ask me why, but I like him.*
> *He isn't the best-looking,*
> *but I just like his body language.*
> *Why is my heart throbbing with a longing?*
> *Would he feel the same way?*
> *This man in a yellow shirt,*
> *Though quiet, I like him a lot.*

A 1994 film *Forrest Gump*, a commercial hit, which was also well received by critics, introduces several decades of Forrest Gump's life, from his elementary school till 1981 when he was narrating his story to strangers on a bench at a bus stop in Savannah, Georgia. As a kid, Gump wore leg braces to right the curved spine. He was bullied because of not only the physical handicap but also questionable intelligence. But he realizes that he can run fast when the leg braces were finally off. This was the beginning of his extraordinary life.

He is invited on a scholarship to the famed University of Alabama football team. As a member of the all-American team, he has a chance to meet President John Kennedy. As a foot soldier, Gump displays a series of heroic acts during the Vietnam War, which is recognized by the Medal of Honor from President Johnson. During this period, he also develops an outstanding skill in ping pong, which opens more chances to encounter celebrities such as John Lennon.

One may expect Gump to take advantage of these high-profile publicities for a financial opportunity and a more comfortable life, but he does not. During an anti-war protest, he meets by chance his first love Jenny who has been recovering from years of drug abuse in hippie-style life. They sleep together but the next morning Jenny takes off again although she confesses her love of him also. Heartbroken, Gump goes running for the next three years in a cross-country marathon, becoming famous again before returning to Alabama. In the end, Jenny comes back to Gump with their son. Their married life does not last long as she dies of a viral disease.

With the small fortune he made from manufacturing the ping pong paddle, he starts a shrimp company, fulfilling the promise he made earlier to his dead war buddy and inviting his lieutenant now crippled. The business is quite successful, but much of their earnings go to the family of his dead fellow soldier.

It was a remarkable movie as many historic events during that particular period are vividly recorded, including Gump's encounters with Elvis Presley not to mention various presidents. And yet, Gump was not interested in taking advantage of his "fame." Maybe he was not able to, because of his low intelligence. In the end, it was not an obstacle to his kind heart, a point the above proverb tries to convey. My only lament is that such episodes seem to be plausible only in a fictional world like in songs and films. (10/02/2021)

385. Loss is part of business.
한 푼 장사에 두 푼 밑져도 팔아야 장사.

For a short period of time in the early 1960s, for one- or two-year period at most, Korea was inundated with French Pith Helmet, one of those, beige-colored, hard hats that a jungle explorer might wear, possibly by Ernest Hemingway during his safari hunting trips. The hat was everywhere, and everybody seemed to own one: even my father had one. I don't think he had purchased it, as we were always strapped for money during the post-Korean War economy. Where were they from and why in Korea were the questions so bizarre that I still cannot answer. Why French Pith Hamlet of all things? Why not chocolate bars, clothes, school supplies, and other stuff in common-day life?

"Dumping" in economics, especially in international trade is a trade practice in which manufacturers export a product to another country at a price below the sticker price. Of many possible reasons, the primary one is increasing market share by driving out the competition, possibly resulting in a monopoly. Many nations have now installed anti-dumping laws to prevent such a situation. In the context of the above proverb, however, dumping appears to be one way to get out of a stagnant state of the business for rejuvenation.

As explained in Entry #179, "Save a penny, or *pun*, to lose a fortune," *pun* is the coin of the least value circulated in the Joseon Dynasty of Korea (1392-1897), equivalent to American pennies. This proverb says that, even for a business dealing with *pun*, it is a better practice to sell merchants with a loss for the cash flow. Although the proverb seems to target small businesses, there is no reason why it cannot be applied to huge corporations dealing with global markets, like the company that dumped Pith Hamlet in Korea. Here, a temporary loss sounds like a strategic retreat in military affairs. In a broader perspective, it emphasizes the importance of small sacrifices for bigger returns later, or "Good things do come only after many difficulties." One can further extrapolate to, "Easy come, easy go."

Without any willpower to take risks or sacrifice, one may not harvest anything significant later in their life. Take education, as an example. It is one of the most important tools in the struggle for survival in any society. How can fish survive without water, and how can a plant exist without soil? Education needs not to be with an advanced degree like PhD in an esoteric field or engineering certificates. Any technical trade know-how can serve as the tool for secure finance: plumbers and electricians, for instance. A take-home message here is that one needs to prepare for the future, be it simply one's life, anticipated war, ongoing climate change, collapsing market, even pending death.

"Lean and mean" has been a motto of various business models. It entails, for instance, maintaining a minimally required stockpiling. Storing unsold goods in the back storage area is an unforgivable crime, as it represents frozen capital as well as wasting of store space. For a manufacturer, an abundance of parts does not necessarily lead to a product unless all components needed are available, ideally in proportion: if one component allows for only 10 final products while supplies of all other parts afford as many as 1,000 products, they can manufacture only 10 products.

Early in the COVID-19 pandemic, this country suffered from the paucity of personal protective equipment like a simple face mask. Soon, the nation learned that the domestic ventilator manufacturers could not produce it because some components are from other countries and their supplies were hampered by the pandemic. It was a rude awakening for this nation, which is technologically so much advanced to send astronauts to moons as if visiting the next door and to manipulate genes at will for cloning a whole animal. People, including President Biden, start to believe that maintaining a minimal level of stock items or diversifying supply sources just to cut the production cost has its own disadvantages.

Soon, the popular online shopping revealed the supply-chain issues involved also, including the lack of truck drivers for delivery of goods piled up on the port from oceanic shipping from, say, China. We, consumers, began to complain about delivery delays, empty shelves for toilet paper, etc. There was a strong resentment of our nation's dependence on others, especially China, and the Biden administration began to promote "reshoring," or making more things in America. Throughout the painful experience, what clearly emerged was "lean" business management relying on the cheapest source supplies is not always best for all parties involved and can indeed backfire. (10/04/2021)

386. A cantankerous bullock with horns on the hip,

못된 송아지 엉덩이에 뿔난다.

As any Spanish fighting bulls would show, adult bulls weighing 1,000 to 2,000 pounds (roughly 500 to 1,000 kg) can display aggressive behaviors and thus requires careful handling to prevent any harm to others including humans.   But here is a rebellious young bull constantly giving his owner hard times: it's just an unexpected nuisance from a young bull. Sure enough, the bullock is found to have a pair of horns on the hip! No wonder why people sneer at him. We don't know if the horns on the hip cause the bullock cantankerous or his bad temper produces the horns at an unexpected place. The way it was written, the proverb suggests that it is the latter: that is, the ill-natured bullock grows horns on his back.   The English equivalent would be, "The lean weed lifts its head high." It implies that a wicked person tends to display strange, unacceptable behaviors. We can easily find many excellent examples from politicians such as the former president or Roman Catholic priests involved in sexual abuse scandals and Archbishops who tried cover-ups. Here, I offer one example from Korean history.

Yeonsan-gun, 연산군 (1476–1506), was the 10th king of the Joseon Dynasty. He was the eldest son of King Seong-Jong by his second wife and is considered the worst tyrant throughout Korean history. If there was a silver lining, it would be that he lived a rather short life of 30 years and was in reign for only 11 years (1494–1483). It would be difficult to speculate how much more the nation could have suffered, had he lived longer. He purged the scholars and convert what one arguably considers the first Korean university, the Seong-gyun-gwan campus, to a personal pleasure ground full of young women recruited from the provinces. Because of his notoriety involving hedonism and cruelty during his reign, he was not called *Jong* as in Seong-Jong, a traditional posthumous title bestowed upon a king. Instead, his title ends with *gun*. That he was a bad guy is quite an understatement. Perhaps we can equate him to Roman Emperor Nero (37–68 AD).

A contemporary Korean historian, Ham Seok-Hun, pointed out three major flaws in Yeonsan-Gun's character and tried to find the cause of each failing: see *Quintessential Korean History*, 뜻으로 본 한국역사. His cruelty is said to have been inherited from his mother. Although she was a queen, the second wife of King Seong-jong, she was quite wild and crude such that she even scratched King's face, leaving scars. However one may look, it is beyond anyone's comprehension. She was eventually removed from her Empress position and died unceremoniously and unfairly according to then young Yeonsan-gun. Ham seems to believe that his trait of meanness thus originated from his vengeance against "establishment," deeply rooted in this tragic event unfolded when he was a child.

His decadent and corrupt lifestyle, according to Ham, was from what he had observed when he was a prince. Apparently, his father King Seong-Jong was also very fond of debauched parties. So, "What do you expect from his father then?" Finally, his hatred of scholars of Confucianism was the result of his distrust of the ruling class of scholars. In addition, Yeonsan-Gun forced people into involuntarily working for various projects for his personal pleasure. In return, commoners mocked and insulted the King with posters written in hangul. Out of anger and frustration, the King banned the use of hangul as well as Chinese characters. He eventually abolished the Office of Censors and the library of Confucian teachings. His ultimate gag order was having his ministers wear a sign, "A mouth is a door that brings in disaster; a tongue is a sword that cuts off a head. A body will be in peace as long as its mouth is closed and its tongue is deep within."

When a eunuch, who had served three kings, pleaded Yeonsan-gun to change his ways, the King not only killed him but also punished his relatives down to the 7th degree. When Yeonsan-Gun asked his men if such punishment was appropriate, they did not dare to say otherwise. He also exiled a minister of rites for spilling a drink that he had poured. In summary, the current North Korean dictator must be a direct descendant of his.

In 1506, after the 12-year reign of Yeonsan-gun, a group of officials successfully launched a coup, sending him "with horns on his buttocks" into exile on Ganghwa-do, an island in the northwest of Seoul, where he died quickly of some sort of plaque. His consort, or 'femme fatale,' was summarily beheaded. (10/07/2021)

387. A sage follows the aged custom,

성인도 시속을 따른다.

The spontaneity of a given process or phenomenon is a big deal in thermodynamics. When two bodies at two different temperatures come into direct contact, we all know that heat spontaneously flows from the hot body to the cold one. It is as natural as water flowing downward or things unattended becoming disorganized. Much effort will be needed to reverse the natural progression of matters. Would it be worthy of the effort? A holy man, *seong-in* (성인), of profound wisdom not only would raise such question but also may decide to follow the time-tested natural manners and ways, *see-sok* (시속), rather than fight against it. This is the crux of the proverb. In essence, it is analogous to avoiding "a round peg in a square hole." Although "follow the crowd" sounds like a mantra of passive people, there is certainly some sense of comfort and security if you are part of a crowd. On some occasions, however, one has to get out of the comfort zone, standing up for justice and truth. Advocating principles and speaking the truth may require courage, possibly including one's own life as in *hara-kiri*: see Entry #42, "Good medicine is usually bitter."

 The Republicans who have been defending the notion that former President Trump lost the 2020 election in fraudulent voting are deceitful cowards as they know deep in their hearts that Trump lost the election fair and square. Obviously, they never find in their vocabulary a word like integrity, honesty, principle, and truth, not to mention courage. I may not agree with their philosophical approach on how to run a government, I do respect a small number of courageous Republicans such as Liz Cheney, Adam Kinzinger, Peter Meijer, Mitt Romney, and others who are not afraid to speak the truth. So, there appears to exist a finite but significant distinction between becoming an outlier standing up for a principle and hiding in a crowd. The above proverb says that even a saint follows *see-sok* (시속), but the question is when. The third option is "hear no evil, see no evil, and speak no evil," to which I have lately found myself rather often.

 If a mass of refugees is fleeing in one direction on a rural road, you would join the crowd as it is reasonable to assume that their collective wisdom of avoiding invading armies might offer a better judgment than your own. If everybody, following a government's recommendation based on the best medical science available, receives the COVID vaccine, there must be some important benefits for everyone. Even if you can refuse the vaccination based on religious grounds, you may as well accept that it not only saves your own life but also others including your own family.

In a 1996 ruling by the State Supreme Court of Connecticut, the plaintiff, Stamford Hospital, lost the case when they asked the State to force the defendant to receive a blood transfusion: the Court stated that the Hospital violated the "defendant's common law right of bodily self-determination." The defendant was a member of Jehovah's Witness and bled heavily following the birth of a healthy babe. The attending physician from the Hospital argued that the blood transfusion was essential for the survival of the mother and that the baby would have been abandoned had the defendant died. The Court was essentially saying that the hospital's interest in protecting its patients did not extend to the defendant's baby, whose health was not in danger.

One of the most frequently used arguments in the case of refusing the COVID vaccines and mask mandate has been the freedom of choice by individuals. The proponents insist that it is a matter of fundamental right of every citizen to protect their own interest. In many instances, the authorities find that most of the resistance is from misinformation or distrust of the government and science underlying the vaccine. Some Republican politicians seem to take the opportunity of "adding fuel to the fire" for their political advantage: again, using an angry mob in any political arena has been as old as human history.

Standing up for individual freedom is one thing but they seem to have forgotten their responsibilities for the right. As far as I am concerned, these are the most selfish people on earth. Occasionally we hear that some folks who had refused the vaccine died of COVID-19. I am sorry, but I do not share any sympathy for their tragic ending. The professional basketball team, the Brooklyn Nets, have just benched all-star guard Kyrie Irving indefinitely due to his decision not to get the Covid vaccine. Irving repeatedly requested "privacy," calling his decision a personal matter. Wasn't it the same guy who once insisted that the Planet Earth is flat? (10/12/2021)

388. A belly button bigger than the belly.
배보다 배꼽이 더 크다.

The navel, or belly button, is the site on the abdomen where the umbilical cord was once attached and cut off upon birth. The other end of the cord branches out to the placenta just like a tree root, maximizing absorption and transfer of essential items like oxygen and nutrients to the fetus. As such, all placental mammals have a navel. The doctor, or most likely a midwife in the old Korea, cuts the umbilical cord and a tiny stump is left. When this stump falls off after a few weeks, the infant is left with their very own belly button. This proverb offers an outrageous claim that a belly button can be bigger than the belly itself. Would it be really impossible in this world?

Most of the non-profit charity organizations maintain a financially viable program largely from donations either directly from individuals or private foundations. Their administrative costs typically include salaries of staff, building utilities and rent, office supplies, legal services, part of Board of Director expenses, and promotional costs including an annual report. Unless there exists an independent auditing system, this is where our donation can go astray. Various charity watchdogs say that lower than 35% of the total budget for the administrative cost is quite acceptable, but even this number sounds like a big belly button considering the voluntary nature of their enterprise. More importantly, donors have a right to ask what constitutes the 35% of their budget.

The United Way of America (UWA) was one of the programs I used to support: once a year the company I worked for automatically deduct my donation from the salary and sent it to the organization of my choice. In 1992, its president of the previous 22 years resigned amidst allegations that he siphoned money from the UWA through spin-off companies he helped to create. Three years later, he was convicted on 25 felony counts and sentenced to seven years in prison for fraudulently diverting $1.2 million of the charity's money to benefit himself and his friends. Most maddening was the finding that the president had spent a great sum of money to keep a 17-year girl as his lover. He was then 59 years old. His former aide, with whom he also had an affair, testified that they falsified various expense records for several years so that he could afford champagne, flowers, and plane tickets for his young girlfriend. The scandal very much discouraged my good intention for supporting all charity activities.

As I briefly mentioned in Entry #63, "Flying creatures above the running ones," any excessive administrative structures and personnel in an educational institute have always made me feel as if they are a belly button bigger than the belly. In a university, theoretically, there are only two necessary constituents: students and teachers. And yet, there are many positions associated with administration, ranging from administrative assistant to university chancellor and department deans. Often, I had to remind myself that a university exists for students.

Here are a few examples of "a belly button bigger than the belly." I lived in a suburb of a small town in Michigan for more than 15 years during the 1980s. Every year, I attended the July the Fourth parade that consisted of a fire truck, a high school marching band, a whole bunch of kids on a decorated flat truck, and a twirler or two. There were more people on the parade than bystanders. I felt obliged to partake in the celebration just to add one more on the sideline. The National Assembly of Korea has 300 seats, which I think is somewhat excessive for a country significantly smaller than the State of North Carolina. Compare it with a total of 435 members of the US House. The cost of interior decoration, relative to the price of a new home, can be a belly button bigger than belly by the time it includes the costs for a new set of curtains and blinds, light fixtures, hardwood flooring, furniture, etc.

Here are some more: waiting at a doctor's office for a 15-minute checkup, visiting the Department of Motor Vehicle for a non-productive five-minute outcome, the weight of distilled water I buy for humidifiers, one important mail buried in a heap of junk mails, the cost of printer cartridges relative to the price of the printer itself, cost of altering a trouser length, more bosses in a road crew than repairmen, "too many chiefs and not enough Indians," inflation rate higher than pay raise, driving a truck to a corner dime store for a pack of cigarettes, Monday morning quarterbacks at the water fountain, etc.

An indirect interpretation of the proverb would be, "Things that are supposed to be small become bigger, while those to be large become smaller." Why do the seeds germinate so slowly, whereas my fingernails grow so fast? (10/19/2021)

389. Ill comes often on the back of worse.

흉년에 윤달 온다.

In the lunar calendar, one year consists of 354 days, or 11 days shorter than the solar calendar. In 19 years, the difference amounts to 209 (11x19) days. To accommodate the difference, the lunar calendar introduces a new leap month, or *yoon-dal* (윤달), every seven years (209 ÷ 7 = 29.9, or ~30 days). That is, during a 19-year period, the lunar calendar inserts a total of seven leap months, usually in May.

In the old days, a bad year, referred to as *hewng-neon* (흉년), is usually associated with a poor harvest likely due to drought or some sort of natural disaster. Here, people are anxiously looking forward to a new year but, alas, it happens to be a year with a leap month and thus there is another month to "survive." Although the time period people would suffer remains the same, regardless of which calendar year they are in, an additional month means extra agonizing days in the mind of our ancestors. The logic was never their strongest suit.

The above proverb thus implies that a bad thing tends to happen at the heel of a preceding tragedy. In this sense, it is similar to Entry #36, "An unlucky man breaks his nose even when falling backward." Independent of the above interpretation, our ancestors considered a year with a leap month a bad year with a prolonged rainy season and a possibility of a plague. Leap month itself was not necessarily bad though. In fact, a leap month was recommended for moving to a new house, preparing a shroud and burial ground for old men, holding a Buddhist mass, and even wedding. It is the month of "no problem of hanging a dead man upside down."

Going back to the standard interpretation, the succession of bad events must be a matter of probability and yet those who encounter a string of bad lucks may attribute them to a higher calling and simply lament their fate of misfortunes, or *un-myung* (운명). Admittedly, we can avoid some of the disasters had we invested in certain preventive measures. The dire state of affairs we are facing nowadays seems to offer a good example of the proverb.

The year 2021 began with an unprecedented number of new COVID-19 cases, nationwide over 200,000 cases a day. As of today, the total number of infections is 45.1 million with the accumulated death approaching 800,000. The pandemic has caused tremendous pressure on every facet of society including the national economy, health care, unemployment, and education. We can stop the pandemic with currently available vaccines, but many flatly refuse to receive them. Now the total number of fully vaccinated people hovers around 57%.

In the meantime, mass shooting, as defined as more than four deaths in one incident, has taken place in every corner of the country from a small town like Muskogee, Oklahoma to Chicago. The nation has become so numb that such an incident appears to become a norm. Just to name a few, in March, a series of mass shootings occurred in Atlanta at massage parlors killing eight, most of them Asian. Less than a week later, 10 people were killed in a shooting at a grocery store in Boulder, Colorado. Nine people were killed in a shooting outside a FedEx facility near Indianapolis International Airport. As of October 2021, mass shootings have left 482 people dead and 1,927 injured.

The California wildfires have burned a total of 2.5 million acres, also destroying almost 4,000 buildings. The season began a bit earlier than usual with an ongoing drought and historically low rainfall. In January alone, 300 fires burned 1,200 acres which is almost triple the number of fires and more than 20 times the acreage of the five-year average for January. Every part of the Southwest experienced a record-breaking drought and temperature more than 2°F warmer than average. Then we saw historic flooding in the Northeast after the region Hurricane Ida.

Man-made events that I would like to forget about may include: the January 6th riot, ever-widening gap between the rich and the poor, heart-breaking scenes from our southern border per immigration, the pathetic retreat of our military from Afghanistan, fake news wildly spreading through social media, issues involved in the supply chain, labor shortage with ample job openings, collapsing of a Florida condo, attempts to reverse the duly executed 2020 election, and most recently one Democratic senator trying to kidnap the national plan for climate change.

Are these some kind of a biblical omen? Am I the only person on this Planet Earth who is about to lose faith in humanity? Let us pray for help! (10/20/2021)

390. Neither push nor pull is an option.

빼도 박도 못 한다.

As you nervously watch the price of the stock you own sliding downward, a few options occupy your mind. Shall I sell it with some loss right now? After all, the capital loss is tax-deductible, right? Or shall I sit tight to override the storm, hoping it will recover the value? In a long run, the stock market always yields gain, right? You are fidgeting without any good options, neither selling nor keeping is an option. Such a situation is depicted by the above proverb.

Most parts of Indochina including Vietnam had been a French colony from the late 19th century to the mid-20th century. See, for background, *Build Your House Around My Body*, by Violet Kupersmith. Even after World War II ended in 1945, the French tried to maintain control over Vietnam with aid from the US against Hanoi-based North Vietnam supported by China and Russia. In 1954, the French surrendered and negotiated a ceasefire agreement with North Vietnam, also granting independence to Cambodia, Laos, and Vietnam. This was the end of French influence on the territory and the beginning of the US involvement with strategic ambiguity if not outright greed. Unlike the Korean War of three years, the Vietnam War lasted for almost 20 years at a cost of approximately 60,000 lives of American GIs along with social unrest stemming from the anti-war movement. Just like the US took over from the French a quagmire in Vietnam, they also inherited the Afghanistan mess from the Soviet Union after the latter fled from the Soviet-Afghan War (1979–1989). In response to the terrorist attacks on New York and Washington on September 11, 2001, the US invaded Afghanistan in the "war on terror." The War lasted a bit longer than Vietnam War with an embarrassing retreat of the US from Kabul earlier this year.

If the beginning of our involvement was similar in both Wars, the ending was nearly identical: the last helicopter departing the roof of the US embassy with desperate Vietnamese trying to grab the landing gear of the chopper to flee Saigon and the scenes of chaos and violence as the evacuation effort took place in Kabul just last September. Most of all, in both cases, the US did not know what to do: neither continuing our presence in those foreign lands nor fleeing and leaving our collaborators behind was an option. We were completely lost under some ill-defined doctrines.

North Korea has been a hot potato to American policymakers as far back as the time when the communist regime was born in the land during the chaotic period after the Second World War ended. In recent years the US policy toward North Korea has been all of "carrot and stick," oscillating between threatening posture and appeasement. The Biden administration has thus far maintained the same wait-and-see mode, which once again reflects a passive stand at best. In short, the US still does not seem to have any guiding principle, reflecting the crux of the above expression.

From a broader perspective, the American foreign policy in the past has been offering a perfect situation depicted by the above epigram. It is particularly true when global economic and hegemonial issues are at the front and center of given policy development. To name a few, we should look at the situation with Saudi Arabia and the rest of the Muslim world, mainland China not to mention Russia, Pakistan and India, far East Asia covering South Korea and Japan, Mexico with whom we share a border, and even with Australia and France with a nuclear submarine deal. It is of course a very difficult job to develop diplomacy that is fair to all parties involved, but that is why we elect intelligent and compassionate people for the responsibility.

We all have come across in our lives a situation where we got stuck with no simple way to get out. It could have been simply a moment of embarrassment like when I found myself awfully drunken in a women's restroom at a bar: see Entry #44, "Embarrassment lasts longer than poverty." Had I been a bit sober, I could have left the restroom "whistling Dixie," but I was not. What would you do when you find no toilet paper after you finish your job in a men's room, or realize that you forgot to bring your wallet after the cashier completed her job at a grocery store? What would you do when you find yourself accidentally eavesdropping on a conversation of colleagues talking about you? A more tragic scene was people jumping to certain death out of the burning World Trade Center during the 9·11 Attack. What about those passengers on the planes that were about to collide with the Center towers? In these instances, there is no option, neither push nor pull. Life, as superimposed with natural death, is the same, but we do not feel or think in advance as such. (10/21/2021)

391. Fanning a burning house.

불난 집에 부채질한다.

While a house is burning down, a guy is fanning the flames, as in "adding oil to the fire." An evil-minded person, perhaps one of your enemies, would do such a terrible act. It is the same as "rubbing salt into the wound." Here, the word, *boo-chae-jil* (부채질), means stirring the air with a small hand-held fan. It generates little wind in affecting the ongoing fire, but that is not the point. It is the gesture of the person that is irritating you to no end.

If you have never encountered such a person, you are fortunate since hating other people, no matter what the cause might be, is not a good feeling to live your life with. That said, we have either witnessed such a case in real life or read many similar stories in fiction. *Cinderella* introduces two nasty stepsisters. So does the most famous Korean fable, *Heung-bu and Nol-bu*, in which the older brother *Nol-bu* is portrayed as a terrible bully: see Entry #17, "When it rains, it pours."

The Republican-controlled Texas legislature passed a bill that would criminalize performing an abortion, which Texas Governor Abbott signed into law on May 19. It is one of the strictest laws banning abortion in the nation. Pregnancies from rape or incest are no exception in the bill. I do not wish to pour fuel into this controversial topic with my own opinion, but I strongly oppose one aspect of the law that empowers any private citizen to sue abortion providers or anyone who "aids or abets" an abortion. It is mean-spirited.

The person suing would get a minimum of $10,000 for a reward. In September, as soon as the law became effective, a self-described "disbarred and disgraced former Arkansas lawyer," was suing for $100,000 a physician who had performed an abortion. Ironically, the plaintiff confessed that he does not personally oppose abortion. At any rate, the clause in the new law encourages ordinary citizens to become a whistleblower after spying on neighbors, friends, and even siblings. It reminds me of the so-called Cultural Revolution of China unfolded in the late 1960s that ended only when Mao Zedong died in 1976.

Launched by Mao Zedong, the stated goal of the Revolution was to preserve Chinese communism by purging not only capitalist remnants but also traditional elements from Chinese society. In short, they wanted to reinstate Maoism in the nation with renewed vigor. This was Mao's public ploy to divert the national resentment to the Revolution from the failure of the Great Leap Forward and the subsequent Great Chinese Famine during the previous several years. Young Red Guards with Mao's *Little Red Book*, equivalent to Hitler's *Mein Kampf*, waving over their heads grabbed power from local government and Communist Party branches to eventually form the revolutionary committees in 1967.

To those overjealous young Red Guards, the long Chinese history and proud culture of several millennia mean very little to a point they arbitrarily arrested anyone as a traitor and humiliated them in public. Their target could be their teachers, neighbors, friends, grandparents, or siblings. They became blinded and hysteric with ill-directed national ambition, destroying priceless historical relics and artifacts as well as ransacking cultural and religious sites. In terms of the human toll, the estimated number of deaths is as high as 20 million from many massacres throughout the country. Their movement was not with a small hand-held fan but with a biblical windstorm.

During my professional life in both academia and industry, I met many Chinese who were visiting the States. I noticed there was a distinct difference in character and behavior between pre- and post-Revolution Chinese. One night, it happened to be Christmas eve of 1979, I had to go back to the lab at the University of Chicago just to check some ongoing experiments, I heard much laughter from the next door. Several Chinese chemists were having a break from their own experiments. I poked my head to their lab and joined their pleasant night. They were pre-Revolution scholars: all very polite, kind, generous, and most accommodating.

Beginning about a decade later, I began to have a series of Chinese PhD students in my lab. They were invariably smart and studious but generally lacked the gentleness and civility that I had expected from my earlier encounter with their older generation. They were sons and daughters of the Red-Guard generation and simply did not have any opportunity to learn about the traditional Chinese way of life and human interactions. In my mind, those traits I had admired so much were gone forever irreversibly. (10/22/2021)

392. See neither a bottom nor an end.
밑도 끝도 없다.

This proverb says that, in a state of helter-skelter, no one can find the end, *ggeut* (끝), or the bottom, *miet* (밑).

The history of Korea is the account of a country that has been constantly threatened by more powerful nations resolved on domination. They might have been tempted by Korea's strategic location: bordered with Russia and China on the north and with Japan and the US through the Pacific Ocean. The political and social turmoil following the cease of the annexation by Imperial Japan led to the long-lasting, perhaps permanent, division of the Korean Peninsula. The chaotic state of this particular period, from 1945 to 1950, is the topic of this essay. In particular, I would like to dedicate this essay to one particular activist during that period of time, Kim Goo, 김구.

In late December of 1945, foreign ministers from the US, Soviet Union, and the United Kingdom met in Moscow to draw a plan to govern the nationless Korean Peninsula under the trusteeship of the above three plus Republic of China. This scenario was totally unacceptable to Koreans who had just tasted freedom and independence after 35 years of Japanese occupation. The Soviet Union and the US often met in Seoul but deadlocked over the issue of establishing a national government, and finally recommended two "temporarily separated" nations, one backed by the Soviet Union and the other by the US, until a single united government can be established under the trusteeship. It never happened. Instead, both North and South Koreas developed their own governments under separate political ideologies. In 1948, the UN General Assembly recognized the Republic of Korea as the sole legal government of Korea.

During the Japanese occupation, the independence movement by Koreans took place mainly in China and the US. Kim Goo (1876–1949) exiled himself to Shanghai in 1919 to join the Provisional Government of the Republic of Korea, which vowed to liberate Korea from Japan. He served several times as the president of the Provisional Government. Kim returned to Korea when the Japanese surrendered to the Allies in 1945 and fiercely opposed the establishment of separate governments in the Korean Peninsula.

Rhee Syngman (1875–1960) became involved in the anti-Japan movement around 1895 when he graduated from a school established by American Methodists. In 1904, he left Korea for the US and attended George Washington University (BA, 1907), Harvard (MA, 1908), and Princeton (PhD, 1910). During the Second World War, he was actively seeking approval of the Provisional Government of Korea from President Franklin D. Roosevelt. He aligned himself with the anti-Japan sentiment that was prevailing at that time in the US. Note that he was then the head of the foreign relations department of the provisional government in China. Although Rhee had lived in the States and thus not well known to Koreans, that he can speak English rendered him the most trusted and favored politician in the US.

The anti-Japan movement by Koreans was suffering from factionalism and in-fighting among the political activists and their leaders often hated each other as much as they hated the Japanese. There was a palpable tension between Kim's and Rhee's cohorts before the first presidential election by the National Assembly in 1948, in which Rhee outpolled Kim with a significant margin: 92% versus 7%. His lobbying in the States during 1947 through early 1948 for a nation independent of North Korea was fruitful and US President Harry Truman's endorsement was a key to his successful candidacy.

In June 1949, Kim Goo was assassinated at his residence by Army Lieutenant Ahn Doo-hee. Ahn insisted that Kim was an agent of the Soviet Union. Ahn was initially found guilty but later he as well as all of his superiors were rapidly promoted. Moving fast forward, in 1992, Ahn confessed that he just followed the order from his boss Kim Chang-Ryong. The latter is the same person who appeared in Entry #81, "Big trees face more wind," and was also assassinated by a fellow general in 1956. He was a Major General by that time serving as the head of national security under Rhee. Ahn's confession agreed with a claim in 1949 by Kim Il-Sung of North Korea, the grandfather of the current Kim Jeong-un, that Kim Goo was killed by Rhee's people. By 1996, when Ahn himself was murdered by one of Kim's followers, he had been a successful military contractor.

All said and done, it was quite a turbulent era in Korean history that dashed the hope of establishing a united nation. No one was able to see "the end or the bottom." (10/25/2021)

393. Good times pass fast.

신선 놀음에 도낏자루 썩는 줄 모른다.

Elon Musk, one of the wealthiest men on this planet, is said to work on average for 17 hours a day. How is it possible, many ask, and the explanation is that he enjoys what he does. For those, who enjoy every moment of their lives, time flies unconsciously.

A direct translation of the above proverb may read as: one fails to realize that the handle of an ax has all rotted to the core while they indulged in a fun time, forgetting their responsibilities and commitment. The fun time they are having is referred to as *sin-sun nol-uem*, or 신선 놀음, where *sin-sun* and *nol-uem* stand for an imaginary person with super-natural powers and merrymaking play, respectively. Together, *sin-sun nol-uem*, or 신선 놀음, means some serious fun time. Their fun also lasts for a long time, long enough that the handle of an ax has all decayed. Hickory wood is hard, stiff, dense, and shock-resistant, and thus used in ax handles. The wood can last "forever."

Two highly accurate atomic clocks were first synchronized, and one was placed on an airplane flying around the Earth and the other left on the ground. When the airborne clock returned, scientists discovered that the clock was a tiny fraction of a second behind the one that remained on the ground. This was the experimental verification of Einstein's Special Theory of Relativity. It establishes that time is relative depending on the frame of reference.

A person who is moving very fast with a clock in his pocket, say, at a speed approaching that of the light, does not think that his clock is running slow, because everything in his frame of reference will have slowed down as well. Only a stationary observer in space watching us on Earth moving around the Sun would notice our clock running slowly. Once again, time is a relative concept: see also Entry #299, "A moment is three years when waiting," or "일각이 삼 년 같다."

The *sin-sun nol-uem* of fun is supposedly a laidback affair surrounded by peaceful sceneries of high-rising mountains and a winding stream, where the *sin-sun* enjoys every moment without any external pressure from the lowly world of reality. If you feel like a *sin-*

sun in the *sin-sun nol-uem*, pleasure comes from two sources. One is what you see and feel every moment of the party. Indirect though it may be, perhaps a bigger appreciation may well be the fact that there is absolutely nothing that you must do at this very moment. It allows a complete dedication to the *nol-uem*, unaware of time flying.

You cannot fully appreciate the pleasure at hand when there are; a few semester finals to prepare for, a backyard in disarray, trash bins to be placed on the curb, home mortgage and bills to take care of, a planned visit to ailing parents, dirty dishes in the sink, your wife and children all alone at home, and most of all job to fulfill. Even at the peak of the *sin-sun nol-uem*, you acknowledge these inconvenient reminders in some corner of your mind. And you know full well that you will suffer from a guilty conscience, which will remain self-induced mental torture for a while once the fun time is over. The fun party for the *sin-sun* would excuse you from all these!

Would such bottomless self-indulgent pleasure constitute a fun time without any reference of work?

A recent novel by Jonathan Franzen, *Crossroads*, introduces an associate minister of a church in a small town close to Chicago, Reverend Russ Hildebrandt, who is rapidly falling in love with a young and attractive widow, Mrs. Frances Cottrell. He has a family with a rather chubby and joyless wife and four children, the oldest one in college already, while Mrs. Cottrell has two young kids. His inner struggle from the virtue from his Christian faith pitted against his desire to be with Mrs. Cottrell could have been a moot point, had they been in *sin-sun nol-uem*. How can he divorce himself from the family he established himself with solemn vow and duty? But then, without any of this bothersome reality, how would he have been so excited with the prospect to be with Mrs. Cottrell?

Lately, I cannot help, but my life of almost 80 years appears as if it were the blink of an eye. Then, how is it possible that such a long period is so severely condensed to less than a second? Does it mean that my life was like one *sin-sun nol-uem* without any hardship? If it were, I cannot remember. Am I modern-day Rip van Winkle who has just woken up in Las Vegas? Am I just imagining Korean War, the life in the States, and all those events in tucked-away memories? I have had a happy and uneventful life, but I would not have enjoyed it as much as I have, if there had not been any hardship and misfortunes. It has been far from being *sin-sun nol-uem*. (10/28/2021)

394. Having wasabi in tears.

울며 겨자 먹기.

A green paste or dried powder made from Japanese horseradish is a pungent condiment commonly used for sushi and other foods. Taste-wise, it is similar to hot mustard or horseradish rather than chili peppers as it stimulates the nose more than the tongue. Thus, when taken more than one can handle, it always induces tears. When you are forced to take it in a spoonful, as nuanced in the above idiom, the tears you shed reflect resentment rather than enjoyment of, say, sushi. In our lives, we often do things that we wish we don't have to, and yet we do as we are obliged to or inadvertently.

In a classical example of the former, many Korean women and girls were forced into sexual slavery by the Imperial Japanese Army in Japanese-occupied territories during the Second World War. They were called Comfort Women, or *wee-an-boo*, a euphemism for prostitutes. It is difficult to pinpoint how many were involved, but a crude estimate ranges from 50,000 to as high as 200,000 if we include women from other Japanese-occupied territories such as China, Philippine, Burma, Thailand, Vietnam, and Malaya. Japanese women were the first victims to arrive at military brothels, but as their territories expanded local pimps lured them promising work in factories or restaurants.

Today we have only a handful of surviving victims in Korea. Many former Korean comfort women were reluctant to reveal their past, as they were afraid of being disowned or ostracized further. This is in spite of the public condemnation of Japan and concerted effort to compensate the victims. Damage to the vagina caused by rough sex and venereal diseases caused unusually high rates of sterility among the victims. A survey indicated that less than 30% of the interviewed former Korean comfort women produced biological children.

During the Korean War, the US military is said to regulate prostitution services around military camps. I cannot tell how "official" their efforts were, but it was quite common to see American GIs with Korean women on the street of Busan where our family lived for almost a year away from the battlefront. I suppose there would be a significant difference in nuance between these women on the street for survival and bona fide forced "comfort women." Who was Cio-Cio-san to the US naval officer Pinkerton in Puccini's opera *Madama Butterfly*? Was she simply a comfort woman to him?

On October 21, actor Alec Baldwin discharged a prop firearm on the set of the movie "Rust" in Santa Fe, New Mexico, killing a 42-year-old Director of photography and seriously injuring 48-year-old film Director Joel Souza. We all saw the picture of the distraught actor, crouching down facing the ground, in the parking lot outside the sheriff's office after being questioned. Another picture shows the mustached actor with a white beard, talking on the phone, perhaps to his wife, almost crying, while his left hand was holding a facemask.

It was an accident, most likely caused by someone's mistake along with Baldwin's carelessness. The first response that my wife and I had was a shock of disbelief, which was followed by deep empathy as well as sympathy for the actor: we share his agonizing moment and pray for his mental recovery to normalcy without much undue guilty conscience on his part. After all, what could he have done? My reaction must be what most people would display. Then, we thought of a darker and ugly side of the follow-up reality involving legal litigation of sorts and swarming mass media.

Donald Trump, Jr. started to sell T-shirts with a printed statement of "Guns don't kill people, Alec Baldwin kills people." The shirt is priced at $27.99. We all understand that he has a bone to pick with Baldwin, as the latter called his father a sociopath and used to spoof the President on *Saturday Night Live.* But still.....

I would agree with the general sentiment found in social media: the Trump Junior has proven himself to be "the lowest of the low." But he was not alone in speaking ill of Baldwin: this is what Ted Nugent, one-time singer, has to say: "I know Alec Baldwin is just a nasty, nasty man. He would attack the good families of the NRA (National Rifle Association) that did nothing wrong and blame us when there was a school shooting. So we know he's a liar and his brain is fried and he's just a prick..... it's not an accident; that's negligence." I can almost see hatred coming out of his body with no end in sight.

These reactions were simply made in retaliation of Baldwin's political stand against the previous President and the NRA, but no one forced them to do so. It was not like making them eat a spoonful of wasabi so that they have to shed tears. If one cannot stand the pungent taste of wasabi, they should have stayed away. (10/29/2021)

395. Scold in private, praise in public.
책망은 몰래 하고 칭찬을 알게 하랬다.

If one of your subordinates has messed up something, you have to let him or her know of your displeasure. Otherwise, they may assume that they have done an acceptable job. But do it privately. Conversely, if someone has completed an outstanding job, praise him or her profusely while others are watching. This is the crux of the above proverb. Publicly condemning someone for something they have done is one sure way to make a new enemy. Someone who has received your public praise and support will put much more effort into their work from now on. Praise is the best form of incentive.

Everybody knows what is said above. There are two possible exceptions though. At the spur of the moment in anger and frustration, one can lose temper to explode with harsh words of reprimand without realizing that others are also around. I used to belong in this category when I was young with a short fuse. The worse part was that I seldom apologized later for the outburst. I have now become mellowed down very much, but it is not clear if this change was due to maturation or because there is no one around to yell at nowadays.

Deliberately condemning someone in public is, of course, an attempt to humiliate someone as mercilessly as possible. In some instances, the victim may not have done anything wrong. We can find such examples in the behavior of our previous president. See, for instance, how many and how often his cabinet members were dismissed. The departed members did not have anything nice to say: recall what the witnesses in his impeachment hearings testified under oath and the memoirs they wrote.

People remained in his administration gave the impression of yes-men who were afraid of standing up even when he made some nonsense: where were they when he promoted the idea of using common home disinfectants for treating COVID-19? See Entry #292, "A dragon's head with a snake's tail." Occasionally, these people were praised for their blind obedience and loyalty. Perhaps more importantly, they may also deserve public humiliation by him.

In the Parable of the Prodigal Son (Luke [15:11–32]), a father has two sons. The younger one squanders his portion of the inheritance from his father on a life of debauchery in a distant country to become penniless. When he returns home empty-handed and intends to beg his father to accept him back as a servant, his father, instead of scorning him, welcomes him with celebration and a big feast with the "fatted calf" and all. He is now given the best robe, a ring for his finger, and sandals for his feet. It is far from what he has expected.

Envious as well as angry, the older son refuses to participate in the welcoming party. The father tells the older son: "My son, you are here with me always; everything I have is yours. But now we must celebrate and rejoice, because your brother was dead and has come to life again; he was lost and has been found." The older son is looking at the whole episode in terms of "law, merit, and reward," rather than "love and graciousness."

The story seems relevant to the present essay in two aspects. First, the father welcomes the prodigal son in a most public way by throwing a big party, a remarkable development. Had I been the father, I would have yelled at him and asked him to leave the premises immediately in front of everybody, just to make sure that we understand what is right and what is wrong. Secondly, the father brings his elder son to a quiet corner and tries privately to appease him with words of persuasion. On one hand, he assures his son that he will inherit all properties. But to me, the father is teaching the son what is the true meaning of forgiveness. No matter what a standard interpretation of the parable might be, it appears to support the notion that praising and scolding have their own appropriated timing and place.

As with individuals, condemning and humiliating a nation on a global stage may not be the best way to achieve something the instigating nation wishes to achieve. A case of the point is the current relationship between the US and the People's Republic of China. On virtually every subject matter, the two nations stand afar posturing for the best gain possible. The situation was not like this all the time. Once China looms larger to cast its shadow over all continents especially in Africa, the US almost automatically has become quite defensive to the extent that some hawkish politicians started to use the word "enemy" for China. Even in scientific research collaborations between two countries have become a matter of politics. Does the trend reflect the true nature of humanity? (10/29/2021)

396. Get to blow a trumpet thanks to the boss.

원님 덕에 나팔 분다.

A low-ranking officer has finally gotten an opportunity to blast a horn, all thanks to his boss, *won-nim*, or 원님, a local administrative appointee from the central government of the Joseon Dynasty. It is perhaps equivalent to a city mayor, some kind of superintendent, or a magistrate of a county. This man, throughout his tenure of many years as the subordinate of *won-nim*, has followed his order with little authority, but today he gets a moment of catharsis. He is now blaring a trumpet, say, at the head of a palankeen team carrying their big boss. This man is indebted to his *won-nim* for the "15-minute" bragging right.

A certain level of perk always follows powerful or famous people. This proverb goes one step further, describing how the others, who either work for or are simply acquaintances of the powers-that-be, often claim a special recognition and treatment. We see many examples in our daily lives: namedroppers tend to expect and usually receive special services wherever they go. At workplaces, often middle managers well-liked by their bosses are the ones who bully colleagues, ask for sexual favors, ask staff to perform personal errands, and force subordinates even to break the rules.

The boastful and arrogant behaviors of these power-seekers were not unnoticed by our ancestors, resulting in the above proverb. They even thought that animals belonging to the powerful family adopt arrogant attitudes: see Entry #282, "A minister's cow is not afraid of a butcher." In April this year, someone shot a professional dog walker to kidnap Lady Gaga's French bulldogs. Immediately, Los Angeles police hunted down the offenders and charged as many as five men for the crime. Their prompt and flawless action was impressive. Her dogs are, well, after all, Lady Gaga's dogs. Speaking of a dog commanding perks, here is another story about a wealthy hotel heir, Leona Hemsley of New York. When she died in 2007, she left $12 million for her lapdog, while ignoring her family the will.

In contrast to the above stories, there are instances in which an ordinary person receives an unexpected inheritance through a warm heart and plain kindness. I found the following story on the web.

In 1992, a waitress of a restaurant in a small town in Ohio inherited $500,000 from a regular customer. This old man loved hanging out in the restaurant, just making the most out of his remaining days. Every day, he sat at a table in the same section where Cara Wood, a friendly and cheerful teenager, manned. Occasionally, Wood also ran errands for the old man and helped him around his house. Wood was not only his favorite waitress but his best friend. When he passed away at the age of 82, Wood was named the sole beneficiary of his entire estate.

A kid with a big brother usually avoids bullying. Members of known gangster families get favorable seats in a restaurant. Children of a wealthy family, once revealed, receive special attention wherever they go. The First Ladies of the nation enjoy a slew of helpers including their own spokesperson. The overly boastful American tourists backed by the nation's prowess in Europe used to be the butt of a joke. The January 6th rioters on the US Capitol thought themself brave and patriotic because they believed that their actions were in accordance with the thinking of the former President Trump. Two Koreas, one backed by the Soviet Union and the other by the US, fought like cats and dogs since 1950 and still remain enemies.

Because the children of a powerful family often receive special treatment, it is not surprising that many conmen tried to pretend they are sons and daughters of a wealthy family. Earlier I introduced a conman named Marc Hatton who pretended that he was an illegitimate son of one of the rich Rothschild families: see Entry #74, "A leaky dipper at home leaks also in the field." Conversely, a powerful politician can pretend to be an obscure Joe to mingle freely with ordinary citizens, perhaps to directly sample the sentiment of the nation or the "pulse of the street" so to speak.

The Joseon Dynasty (1392-1897) used to have royal secret agents called *amhaeng* and *uhsa* (암행어사), who were appointed by none other than King himself. Everything about them was kept in secret, ranging from appointment itself to travel schedule. They were roving around the country to discover any wrongdoings of local government officials and their cronies. Albeit very powerful, they would disguise themselves in tatter and pretend to be an ordinary traveler, often mistreated by locals but endure till they declared the power of authority. See more in Entry #77, "Hot tea doesn't show steam." *Amhaeng-uhsa* did not need *won-nim*. (11/01/2021)

397. A mute with troubled thoughts.

벙어리 냉가슴 앓듯 한다.

Nobody knows the trouble I've seen
Nobody knows my sorrow
Nobody knows the trouble I've seen
Glory Hallelujah

......

Sometimes I'm up sometimes I'm down
Oh yes Lord
Sometimes I'm almost to the ground,
Oh yes, Lord

The above is the lyrics of a spiritual song of African Americans of the gone era. In particular, the song sung by Marian Anderson (1897–1993) remains one of the well-survived melodies in my precariously preserved memory. If these lines of words fail to convey the sorrow of the African American, none would.

A mute who has accumulated so many troubled thoughts throughout his life wishes to relate them to us but, alas, how can he? Do remember that our ancestors did not have any sign language when the above proverb was spoken. The frustration from such impotence is the crux of the proverb. It presents a desperate situation where a person cannot explain what is "eating" him or her. Earlier we came across a similar proverb but it was about an opposite situation encountered by a mute, who has tasted honey but not being able to express gratitude or appreciation: Entry #271, "A mute with honey, a centipede with acupuncture."

If we cannot say loudly to the whole world what we want to say, it can harm one's wellbeing as in Entry #82, "Say the words; chew the meat." In the fable introduced there, a barber cannot tell anyone what he has just witnessed: the king's ears are donkey's ears. Here, the frustration from the gag order must be similar to what the mute is going through. There is no way for us to understand him when he makes some gurgling guttural noise. In many other instances, however, people may not reveal what they have in mind possibly because of shame to themselves or being hurtful to others. This is actually the nuanced theme of the above idiom. The more one thinks about a given experience, the more they feel they must "confess," but they just cannot. We all have such secrets in our lives. It is a matter of the gravity involved. Even on one's deathbed, the secret may not be revealed. What happens to the truth then?

One's confession on their deathbed is usually considered true as we believe that there is no practical reason for the dying person to lie anymore. It is indeed their last opportunity to "come clean." What is said to the beloved family members can be quite shocking. Just like an opening scene of a B-movie, the dying father could say that the mother of one of his sons is not the one everyone has believed. This would leave a long-lasting quandary among the remaining family. Some may decide not to believe the father's last word insisting that the old man's memory has recently deteriorated quite badly. Others may begin to speculate who the real mother might be.

In the 1941 movie, *Citizen Kane*, we see the elderly Charles Foster Kane, played by Orson Welles, is on his deathbed in his humongous mansion called Xanadu on his palatial estate in Florida. He is holding a snow globe and utters a word, "Rosebud", and dies. This last word remains a mystery forever although the movie viewers understand that it was Kane's last memory of the eight-year-old himself playing on a snowy day that he was taken from their home in Colorado. In the last scene of the film, we see a sled burning revealing its brand name, "Rosebud."

In November 1969, Sister Cathy Cesnik in her late 20s was brutally murdered in Baltimore. She taught English in an all-girl Catholic high school and was very popular among students for her empathy and kind heart. She was almost an older sister of the students. The documentary drama released by Netflix in 2017, *The Keepers*, implies that she was murdered by the hired hand of a priest at the school because she was aware that the priest was sexually abusing students. One of the key witnesses, "Jane Doe," did not come out with the abuse she had suffered until 1994. Everyone naturally raised the question as to why she had waited that long: by the time she came forward with her tragic story, the priest had died. She did not have a satisfactory reply but many scholars attribute it to suppressed memory. Perhaps it was a good thing that she has survived without the terrible memory torturing her every day. (11/03/2021)

398. No news is good news.
무소식이 희소식이다.

So long as we do not receive any bad news, the silence is okay until it arrives. That is, no news remains good news, and the new news is often bad. This is the essence of this old saying. But there is more to it for old people like me. This particular proverb, we find in both Eastern and Western cultures, exactly the same, word for word. Its meaning must have a universal appeal to humanity and have been appreciated for generations. We have already come across a few such cases: Entry #10, "An empty wheelbarrow makes more noise" and #81, "Big trees face more wind."

I belong to a chat group on Kakao Talk of over 160 high school classmates. Most of them live in Korea with 14 hours difference from where I live. I usually read the new posts all at once in the morning. Every day there are, on average, about five posts from Korea and about three from the States. Besides updating our whereabouts, we see pictures of seasonal change, videos recording of piano playing, the cover of the books they authored, the Chinese calligraph they tried, poems we wrote, and lots of re-directed posts especially in the realm of politics and music from YouTube.

Whenever I receive in the morning notification of more than, say, 30 postings, I know instinctively that one of our classmates has passed away. They are invariably words of prayer for the deceased and reminiscence of our time together many years ago. At this advanced age, a prolonged silence from old friends, with whom I used to have frequent correspondences, causes alarm of apprehension. It is certainly not a good feeling and makes me queasy. It is, of course, equally possible that new news can be indeed good news. Just last month, my wife and I learned that a son of a good friend of ours in Korea has been promoted and thus no longer has to travel all the time all over the world. Now he can spend some quality time with the family especially with two young sons.

Last August a friend in Chapel Hill, NC, with whom I tracked Appalachian Trail some years ago, was diagnosed with diffuse large B cell lymphoma. After four rounds of chemotherapy with nasty compounds, he responded quite well so that they think he is in remission. The Mean Corpuscular Volume (MCV) of my red blood cell was found to be slightly bigger than normal and hence my physician suggested I have a lab determine the level of folic acid and Vitamin B12. After several months of hesitance from laziness, I had it done to find that they are all in a good range. It was useless news.

I have always assumed that the English word "news" is from the first letters of North, East, West, and South, but apparently, it was derived as the plural form of "new." Rightly so, as the word presents new information. An old story cannot be news, although an unusual event can be: the famous dictum that "Dog bites man" is not news, but "Man bites dog" is. How fresh a given story is, of course, depends on how fast the information travels.

In 490 BC, a Greek messenger ran 26 miles (42 km) from the battle of Marathon to Athens to inform its citizen that "we have won," before collapsing to death. During the American Revolution, Paul Revere rode his horse all night through villages yelling, "The Redcoats are coming," to alert the people that the British soldiers were coming. It was in April 1775. In between these two historic events, the speed of communication had accelerated exponentially from light signals reflected by metal mirrors, smokes from fire, firing cannon and raising flags, and other primitive means.

We have now mobile phones, having gone through Morse code (1843) and telephone by Alexander Graham Bell and Thomas A. Watson (1876). Sending a text message has become a matter of a few seconds, while the US Postal Service seems to be losing the competition with other private carriers such as FedEx. Indeed, it has been a while since I sent out a personal letter via regular US mail, including an X-mas card. Now the cell phone uses the fifth-generation, 5G technology for additional capacity and higher speed.

The speed with which news travels nowadays is so fast that a printed version of a newspaper does not seem to be a viable option anymore. Gone are the days one can enjoy the thick Sunday edition of a newspaper over a cup of coffee and omelet breakfast. Even a TV outlet that specializes in breaking news appears to lose ground to various apps on the cell phone. I also noticed some subtle but significant changes in *Time* magazine that is geared into depth rather than breaking news. In these changes, what is new is the speed at which those changes are being made. (11/08/2021)

399. A mayfly attacking fire.

하루살이 불 보고 덤비듯 한다.

The lifespan of a mayfly is very short, less than 24 hours. Due to limited experience, they cannot know much about anything except their primary function, reproduction. So, the above proverb describes their challenge to an impossible task; that is, attacking the fire. In this sense, it is the same as Entry #114, "One-day old puppy isn't afraid of the tiger." If we consider their impossible task, it is similar to Entry #317, "Beating the boulder with an egg."

In May 1967, then Egyptian president Nasser announced that the Straits of Tiran would be closed to Israeli vessels and mobilized the Egyptian military along the border with Israel. Using this move as a *casus belli*, the Israeli military began a series of airstrikes against Egyptian airfields. Egyptians were caught by surprise, and nearly the entire Egyptian Air Force was destroyed with few Israeli losses, giving Israel the advantage of air supremacy. In due course, the Israelis inflicted heavy losses on the retreating Egyptian forces and conquered the entire Sinai Peninsula by the sixth day of the war. Egyptians should have known what they were about to deal with before instigating the war. It resulted in an embarrassing situation not only for themselves but also for the neighboring Arab coalition.

The Falklands War began when the Argentine forces invaded the Falkland Islands on April 2, 1982. The Islands had been under the rule of the British government and the sovereignty dispute had preceded the war for almost two decades. The British government, under Prime Minister Margaret Thatcher, reacted swiftly and forcefully. Argentina which occupied the Islands were soon surrounded by the British taskforces comprised of more than 60 warships. The skirmish, primarily on the sea and amphibious landing, lasted for only about two months. In June, the Argentine forces surrendered and control of the islands returned to the UK.

One of many lessons that one can learn from these two wars, one in 1967 and the other in 1982, was the essence of the above proverb. Before you start a war, you should know the enemy. You do not wish to become those mayflies who are not afraid of fire. I cannot stop comparing these two wars, both of which were started by the eventual losers, with the American involvement in the Vietnam War and Afghanistan War. Here, what we underestimated was not so much the physical aspect of war such as the warhead and battle strategy but the willpower of the native.

This writeup has now drifted to two topics: war and ignorance. As to the former, there are numerous theories on what motivates humanity to engage in a war. Some believe that we always have wars because human beings are inherently violent. It is certainly supported by the fact that we have always had war at a given time. Others point out that a war is a manifestation of our competition over resources, commerce, and territory. As a given ethnic cohort, we wish to dominate the world with our own cultural and religious beliefs. Any conflicts are subject to analysis in this context. What is missing in these theories is using war as a tool of controlling population, especially a discontent mass, and ultimately consolidating power: see also Entry #61, "I can't find my sword in somebody else's scabbard."

Hatred, an important fuel of war, is always an essential component in unifying a population against another, and thus "Divide and conquer!" and the political wisdom from Machiavelli: see Entry #290, "Charcoal briquettes burn better together." Last year, in the nick of time, we saved this nation from becoming such an authoritarian ruler, Donald Trump. How we can erase the chasm between the Red and the Blue states is certainly beyond the scope of this essay. The division seems to get larger every day.

A fight against the pandemic COVID-19 is similar to going to war as both cases are a matter of life or death and that much should be prepared in great care for a successful outcome. Here, medical science and epidemiological data are what warfare is in a war. Unlike a war, where clever generals and courageous soldiers may be sufficient for winning the war, such pandemic diseases as COVID-19 would mandate the participation of the whole citizens.

It is thus unfortunate the Green Bay Packer quarterback Aaron Rogers and earlier Brooklyn Net basketball team forward Kyrie Irving publicly questioned the merit of those vaccines available now. Their claims are not only ignoring the science behind the vaccine approach exposing their naïve ignorance but also reflecting their egocentric behaviors. In the case of Rogers, he has outright lied in public. Oh, what a shame! (11/10/2021)

400. Vacillating between the gallbladder and the liver.

간에 붙고 쓸개에 붙는다.

Something is going back and forth between the liver or the gallbladder: here, we do not know what that "something" is, but it is likely referring to a person who lacks principle, loyalty, honesty, integrity, spine, etc. Such people can change their minds whenever there is a change in the wind direction. It depends on their short-sighted interests. First my confession: I don't have any foggiest idea why, of all things, our ancestors used words, "liver" and "gallbladder." The latter sits just beneath the liver and releases bile to the small intestine. Thus, perhaps two organs in close proximity?

One of my favorite spy novels still remains *Tinker Tailor Soldier Spy* by John le Carré. The story develops as aging spymaster George Smiley tries to uncover a Soviet mole in the British Secret Intelligence Service, the current MI6. The fiction carries some significant relevance to the eventual defection of Kim Philby in 1963, a member of the so-called Cambridge Five. They were all highly educated and served the British government. Their espionage activities peaked during the Second World War but were leaked to the public only in the 1950s.

The slow discovery of their espionage shocked the nation and sowed the still lingering mistrust of British security by the US. Although Cambridge Five and other intellectuals betrayed the British government, their actions were based on the firm belief that Marxism offers a better pollical system for social and economic equity and opposes more effectively the fascism of Germany, Italy, and Japan. So, they were traitors of true believers in a certain ideology.

Last week, as many as 13 Republican House members supported the $1.3 trillion infrastructure bill of the Biden administration. This is remarkable considering the current state of the "Divided States of America." This is the first time in my recent memory that Republicans agree on anything that originated from Democrats. To be fair, there were also six dissenting votes from Progressive Democrats such as Alexandria Ocasio-Cortez from New York. To some, these dissidents are bona fide traitors of their party. Sure enough, one caller suggested Republican Representative Adam Kinzinger of Illinois slit his wrists and go for "rot in hell." I do not see how building bridges and repairing old highways is so disagreeable to curse those who cast their vote for the best interest of their constituents.

We have also witnessed two Democratic US senators betraying the party and threatening to kill another ambitious bill from Biden Whitehouse, named "Build Back Better." It is essentially a social safety net and climate bill. Since the current US Senate is split into exactly 50 to 50 members from each party, it is imperative for Democrats to have all members agree, followed by the vote from Vice President Kamala Harris to break the tie. Under this circumstance, every Democrat member is the "president" according to Biden.

There are two Democratic Senators who have expressed some reservations about the massive spending bill: Joe Manchin from West Virginia and Kyrsten Sinema from Arizona. In recent weeks, we saw Manchin almost every day on national news with his argument for his standing in spite of the tremendous pressure from the party. I can understand and appreciate some of the statements he has made: after all, he speaks for his constituents as in slowing down the ban on coal mining, which is one of the major industries of his State. Still, many people think his publicity stunt is just for a "15-minute fame."

Sinema is different. She was a social worker and worked as a criminal defense lawyer. Her political career began with the Green Party and progressive stand such as supporting LGBT (lesbian-gay-bisexual-transgender) rights. Sinema is the first openly bisexual US Congresswoman. As a Congresswoman, she has slowly changed to a moderate to conservative Democrat: for instance, she voted against an increase of the federal minimum wage to $15 an hour, a proposal from a progressive wing of the party as part of the COVID-19 American Rescue Plan Act of 2021.

Her seemingly sudden progressive-to-conservative change on several highly controversial issues has puzzled many political analysts in the news media. The bottom line is that we, including those pundits in the field, do not know much about her in terms of her policy guideline, not to mention the philosophical backdrop of her political inclination. This is not so much because she avoids the limelight but often comes across that she does not have concrete ideas on issues. It is a further possibility that she has been just sitting on the fence contemplating the next move. Time will tell us one way or another. (11/12/2021)

INDEX (in essay number)

Abortion law (in Texas), 391
ACE 2, 375
acetic acid, 315
active ignorance, 338, 360
Afghan(istan), 352, 354, 361, 378, 381, 389, 390, 399
Ahn, Doo-hee, 392
al-Qaeda, 352, 368, 382
Alzheimer's Disease, 355, 381
American Cancer Society, the, 307
amhaeng uhsa (암행어사), 396
Amorphous, 334
amygdalin, 307
Anderson, Marian, 397
antonymous proverbs, 372
Armstrong, Lance, 316
Atwater, Lee, 371
Austin, Lloyd, 352

baeg-je (백제), 325
bbong (뽕), 370
Baldwin, Alec, 394
Barrack, Tom, 374
Bell, Alexander Graham, 398
Bezos, Jeff and MacKenzie, 343, 356
Biden, Joe, 311, 316, 329, 332, 346, 352, 361, 363, 373, 385, 390, 400
Big Bang Theory, 360
Blinken, Antony, 352
blood transfusion, 387
Blue Screen Loops, 309
Brady, Tom, 313

Brawley, Tawana, 357, 358
British East India Company, 304, 354
British Empire and Commonwealth, 343
Bronfman kidnap, 379
Brooks, David, 380
BTS, 338, 367, 374
Buffett, Warren, 362
Build Back Better, 400
Build Your House Around My Body, 390
Busan, 308, 348, 394
Bush, G.H.W., 371
Bush, G.W., 306, 337

Cambridge Five, 400
Capitol Riot, 316, 319, 322, 326, 340, 360, 373, 382, 389, 396
Capone, Al, 368, 371
Carolina Panthers, 313
Carr, C.M., 311
Cavalleria rusticana, 376
Cesnik, Sister Cathy, 397
Chamberlain, N., 307
Chaplin, Charles, 356
charity organizations, 388
Cheney, Liz, 336, 337, 373, 387
chi (치), 357
Chinese zodiac, 324
Cho, June, 317, 358
Choe, Chang-Sik, Colonel, 348
Choi-Soonsil-gate, 335, 338

Christie, Chris, 352
Christmas Carol, 304
Chun, Doo-Hwan, 335, 337, 347
Cinderella, 391
Citizen Kane, 331, 397
Clark County, 332
Clinton, Bill, 336, 345
Clyde, Andrew S., 340
Coats, Dan, 374
Cohen, Michael, 374
collapse (of a condominium building), 356, 364
Comey, James, 320, 374
Confucius, 319, 323, 357, 386
Conservative Political Action Conference, 316
cooperative pulling paradigm, 363
COVID-19, 310, 314, 322, 330, 332, 340, 343, 353, 363, 375, 376, 377, 380, 385, 387, 389, 399, 400
Crossroads, 393
Cruz, Ted, 316
Cultural Revolution (of China), 391
Current Contents, 350

Daley, Bill, 374
dams (in the States), 349
David facing Goliath, 317
De Niro, Robert, 376
Diamond, Betty, 321
distrust, 380
doe, 312
Dukakis, Michael, 371
dumping (in trade), 385
Duncan, G., 311

Dust Bowl, 346
Dyson vacuum cleaners, 369

Education of Little Tree, 382
Edward VIII, King, 342
eForensics analysis, 353
Einstein, Albert, 318, 319, 359, 360, 393
Emanuel, Rahm, 374
Epstein, Jeffrey, 336
Escher, M.C., 375

Falklands War, 399
fight or flight, 376
Flynn, Michael, 374
folic acid, 398
folk medicine, 368
Forrest Gump, 384
Franklin, Rosalind, 318
freedom of choice, 387
French influence (in Indochina), 390
French Pith Hamlet, 350, 385

gaat, 322
gamcho (감초), 368
ga-moon (가문), 367
Ganghwa-do, 386
Garfield, Eugene, 350
Gates, Bill and Melinda, 336, 341, 343
Gide, André, 350
Gipp, George, 314
Giuliani, Rudy, 313, 357
Gobi Desert, 330
Gödel, Kurt, 359
gom-tang (곰탕), 347
good (굿), 326

goong-hap (궁합), 324
Gordon Research Conference, 302
Goryeo Dynasty, 342
Grapes of Wrath, The, 346
Gresham's Law, 365
gui-shin (귀신), 324
gwa-go (과거), 328
Gwangju Massacre, 335

Ham, Seok-Hun, 386
Harris, Kamala, 400
Hatton, Marc, 396
hedonism, 327, 386
Heisman Trophy, 314
Hemingway, Ernest, 350, 385
Henry, Patrick, 325
hewng-neon (흉년), 389
hickory wood, 393
Higuchi, Takeru, 302
Hinduism versus Buddhism, 382
Hitler, Adolf, 319, 391
humpback whale, 351
Hung-bu and Nol-bu, 304, 320, 391
hydrogen bonding, 324
hyung-sik (형식), 342, 355

I care a lot, 355
IgM and IgG, 375
illegal immigrants, 346
imjin-oeran, 328
incarceration of Japanese-American, 345
Indian Removal Act, 345
Industrial Revolution, 325
Institutional Review Board, 317

Into the Wild, 323
IPO (initial public offer), 381
Irons, Jeremy, 376
Irving, Kyrie, 387, 399
Isaiah [40:15], 377
Israeli–Palestinian conflict, 379

ja (자), 357
James [4:14], 323
jangnal, 312
Japanese Imperial Army, 343
Japan–Korea Annexation Treaty, 325, 329
jeong, 333
jeo-seung (저승), 323
jesa (제사), 355
John [11:1-44], 315
Johnson, Ron, 340, 360
Jones, Jim, 319
jook (죽), 314
Journal of Irreproducible Results, 359
Journey to the Edge of Reason, 359

Kakao-Talk, 333, 365, 366, 398
Keepers, the, 397
Kelly, John, 374
Kennedy, John F., 383, 384
Kim, Chang-Ryong, 392
Kim, Dae-Gun, 325
Kim, Dae-Jung, 307, 335, 337
Kim, Goo (김구). 392
Kim, Hoon, 358
Kim, Il-Sung, 392
Kim, Jong-Un, 362, 365
Kim, Saat-Gat, 323

Kim, Won-Bong, 340
Kim, Young-Sam, 335
King, Rodney, 354, 376
Kinzinger, Adam, 387, 400
Knievel, Evel, 369
Korean
    alphabets, 370, 372
    athletes, 377
    comfort women, 394
    Constitutional Court, 319
    Empire, 325
    expatriates, 310, 333
    folk medicine, 310
    Peninsula, 308, 325, 329, 330, 336, 348, 392
    poets, 323, 347
    War, 308, 329, 344, 348, 362, 367, 381, 385, 390, 393, 394
Kushner, 352

Lady Gaga, 396
Lake Mead, 346, 349, 380
Lander, Ann, 343
Larson, Erik, 331
Lazarus, 315
Le Chatelier's principle, 315
leadership, 383
Lee, Jae-Yong, 338
Lee, Myung-Bak, 335, 340
Lennard-Jones Potential, 366
Lennon, John, 384
Let Justice Be Done, 379
Lewinsky, Monica, 345
LGBTQ, 366, 400
Limbaugh, Rush, 326
Lincoln, Abraham, 314
liposome, 334
Little Red Book, 391

Luke [15:29–30], 341
Lynch, Mel, 379
Lysol, 340

Ma, Jack, 338
MacArthur, Douglas, 348
Machiavelli, 357
Madama Butterfly, 394
mag-geol-li, 310
Make America Great Again (MAGA), 373, 382
Malcolm X, 303
man in a yellow shirt, 384
Manchin, Joe, 400
Mandela, Nelson, 308, 337
Mang-gun (망건), 322
Marathon, 398
mass shooting, 389
Matthew [6:1-4], 316
Mattis, James, 374
McCandless, Christopher, 322
McCarthy, Kevin, 311
McDonough, Denis, 374
McMaster, H.R., 374
McNamara, Robert, 371
Meadows, Mark, 374
Mean Corpuscular Volume, 398
microgram, 373
Middle Nation (중국), 343
Mission, The, 376
moo-dang, 326
mool (물), 374
Moon, J.I., 307, 314, 335, 338, 340, 370
Mother Teresa, 314, 363
Mount Charleston, 349
Mount Jiri, 348
Multitasking, 370

Mulvaney, Mick, 374
Musk, Elon. 393
Myanmar, 320, 354

nak-hwa-ahm (낙화암), 325
Nasser, President, 399
National Assembly of Korea, 388
National Soccer Team, 329
Nero, Roman Emperor, 360, 386
Nixon, Richard, 345, 348
Norte Dame University, 314
North Korea(n), 307, 308, 314, 329, 335, 337, 338, 340, 344, 348, 354, 361, 362, 366, 370, 386, 390, 392
Nugent, Ted, 394
Nuremberg Trials, 369

Obama, President, 374
Ocasio-Cortez, Alexandria, 400
Occupy Wall Street, 317
ock (옥), 347
oh-jang (오장), 325
On Golden Pond, 302
Opium War, 325, 354
Orphan Master's Son, 362
Ostwald Ripening, 317, 354

paat-jook (팥죽), 336
Paik, Kun-Woo, 355
Parable of the Prodigal Son, 395
Park, Chung-Hee, 335, 337, 368
Park, Geun-Hye, 319, 335, 338
Park, Won-Soon, 345, 353

Pauling, Linus, 318
Pavlov experiment, 305
Paxton, Ken, 311
PCR (polymerase chain reaction), 375
Pearl Harbor Attack, 345
Philby, Kim, 400
Platelets, 377
Pollock, Jackson, 375
polymorphonuclear neutrophil, 334
Poong-do, 357
Pope John Paul II, 337
portal vein, 341
Presley, Elvis, 384
Price, Tom, 374
pride, 367, 377
Priebus, Reince, 374
Proust, Marcel, 367
public humiliation, 345, 395
pun (푼), 303, 364, 385

Queens Public Library, 321

Raffensperger, Brad, 311
Raiders, 332
Reagan, Ronald, 314, 332, 345
Real Estate Investment Trusts, 322
receptor-mediated endocytosis, 375
Red Guards, 391
regional conflicts, world, 354
Research Triangle Park, 332
reshoring, 385
Revere, Paul, 398
Rhee, Syngman, 335, 347, 392
Rockne, Knute, 314
Rockwell, Norman, 375

Rogers, Aaron, 399
Roh, Tae-Woo, 335
Roh, Moo-Hyun, 335
Roman Empire, 343
Romeo and Juliet, 342
Rooney, Mickey, 355
Roosevelt, Franklin D., 345, 392
Rothko, Mark, 375
Ryan, Paul, 322

Sabre, F-86H, 344
sa-gong (사공), 361
Salem Witchcraft, 319
Sampoong Department Store, 303, 364
Sanford, James Terry, 332
Scaramucci, Anthony, 374
Schrödinger, Erwin, 318
Schweitzer, Albert, 363
Science Citation Index, 350
Sea of Poppies, 304
see-sok (시속), 387
Se-Jeong, King, 314, 372
Seo, Jeong-Ju (서정주), 347
Seogye-dong (서계동), 344
seo-min (서민), 372
Seong-jong, King, 386
Sessions, Jeff, 374
seu-seung (스승), 383
Sewol, 335
Shannon Entropy, 334
Sharpton, Al, 357
Sinema, Kyrsten, 400
Sino-Japanese War, 325, 329
Smith, Anna Nicole, 327
smog, 330
Spears, Britney, 355

Special Theory of Relativity. 393
Spicer, Sean, 374
spitting, 382
stargazing, 359
Stocking, Michael Cloise, 330
Stone, Roger, 374
subarachnoid hemorrhage, 315
sun-sori (선소리), 340
Super Flower Blood Moon, 343
syntax, Korean, 337

taichi, 310
Taliban, 352, 354, 378
tax collector, 262
Teresa, Mother, 314
Thatcher, Margaret, 399
thermodynamics, 346, 359, 387
Thoreau, Henry David, 323
Tillerson, Rex, 374
Tinker Tailor Soldier Spy, 400
torpedo attack, 340
Tortoise and the Hare, 378
traditional Chinese medicine, 310
Trail of Tears, 345
Treaty of Nanking, 304
Truman, Harry, 383, 392
Trump, D.J., 310, 311, 313, 316, 320, 322, 323, 326, 330, 336, 346, 352, 354, 357, 362, 365, 370, 373, 374, 376, 387, 394, 396, 399
Tulsa Massacre, 345

Unidentified Flying Object, 361
United Way of America, 388

un-myung (운명), 310, 343, 389
Uyghur, 315, 354

Vitamin B12, 398

Waikiki Beach, 380
Watson and Crick, 318
Watson, Thomas A., 398
Weisselberg, Allen, 362
Welles, Orson, 331
Western horoscope, 324
Whitmer, Gretchen, 382
Wilkins, Maurice, 318
Winkle, Rip van, 393
won-nim (원님), 396
Wood, Cara, 396
Wuhan Institute of Virology,
    330

Wyeth, Andrew, 375

Xi, Jinping, 320, 338, 354

yang-ban (양반), 328
Yankee Stadium, 376
Yeonsan-gun(연산군), 386
Yi, Baik (이백), 323
Yi, Seong-gye, 342
yi-seung (이승), 323
Yi, Soon-Sin, Admiral, 328
yoon-dal (윤달), 389
Yoon, Jeong-Hee, 355

Zeno's paradoxes, 315